ILHAM

Portrait of a President

ILHAM
Portrait of a President

GRAEME H. WILSON

AuthorHouse™
1663 Liberty Drive
Bloomington, IN 47403
www.authorhouse.com
Phone: 1-800-839-8640

Published by AuthorHouse 04/04/2013

ISBN: 978-1-4772-3769-4 (sc)
ISBN: 978-1-4772-3770-0 (e)

This book is printed on acid-free paper.

Contents

Acknowledgements

Many people made this book possible. You can take a view of Ilham Aliyev, Heydar Aliyev, Azerbaijan or Nagorno-Karabakh, but far too many foreign 'observers' do this from a distance, influenced to some degree by the propaganda machine of Caucasus' great interloper.

It was Churchill who called the Soviet Union "a riddle, wrapped in a mystery, inside an enigma" in 1939. The U.S.S.R. may be consigned to history, but two decades after the Soviet Union's collapse many parts of that failed entity remain just as unknown and misunderstood as in Soviet days, even one as mainstream as Azerbaijan.

Discovering some of this untold story required support and I was grateful for the access granted by the Presidential Administration in Baku. My thanks to the various Heads of Department and officials there, many of whom went out of their way to nurture the project. I highlight and offer personal thanks to the venerable Ramiz Mehdiyev, Head of the Presidential Administration, for a very fruitful interview and his ongoing support.

From the inception of the biography project I had the valuable support of Faik Bagirov and Rahman Hajiyev, who tolerated my steep learning curve on Azerbaijani history with patience. I value that this project gave me two new friends.

In Azerbaijan, among others, I met with Ali Hasanov (Deputy Prime Minister, Chairman of State Committee for Refugees and IDPs), Natig Aliyev (Minister for Industry and Energy), Elmar Mammadyarov (Minister of Foreign Affairs), Ali Abbasov (Minister of Communications and Information Technology) and Shahmar Movsumov (Executive Director of the State Oil Fund).

Also generous with their time were Sheikh Ul Islam Allahshukur Pashazadeh (Head of Caucasian Muslims), Khoshbakht Yusifzade (Vice-President of SOCAR), Hafiz Pashayev (Deputy Foreign Minister of Azerbaijan, former Ambassador of Azerbaijan to the United States), Rasim Musabayov (Political Analyst, member of Milli Majlis), Sardar Jalaloglu (Chairman of the Democratic Party of Azerbaijan) and Etibar Mammadov (leader of the National Independence Party of Azerbaijan).

Elsewhere in the region, in Armenia we were grateful to former President Levon Ter-Petrossian, former Foreign Minister Vartan Oskanian and others. We also had time and support from Lord Raymond Hylton, Dr Mana Saeed Al Otaiba and Malcolm Corrigan.

In Moscow, I met with the articulate and outstanding Polad Byul-Byul Ogly (Azerbaijan's Ambassador to the Russian Federation), Mikhail Gusman (First Deputy of General Director of ITAR-TASS), journalists Aleksandr Gurnov, Sergey Brilev and former teacher of President Ilham Aliyev at MGIMO Natalya Kapitonova.

Publishers Media Prima contributed a great deal to this enterprise, not least Grace Magnaye, Joanne Evans, Natasha Vallen, Arlene Dulay, Leslie Cox, Jemima Matullano, Mohammad Mosleh and Paul Wilkin. Media Prima's Editor-At-Large Mike Simon contributed a lot, as did Lisa Becks-Hampton, Frank Mendez and Declan Heinz at Media Prima in London.

Contributions were gratefully received from Barbara Saunders, Dave Waters, Chris Fernando, Jason Ford and the amaranthine Susan Wilson.

Of the many images carried herein, we received cooperation from AzerTAC, Chris Harrison, Rosanna Mascarenhas, Gracelene Morales and photographic master Wouter Kingma.

Organisations such as the North Atlantic Treaty Organisation, Human Rights Watch, Organisation for Security and Cooperation in Europe, Parliamentary Assembly of the Council of Europe, Guinness Book of Records, Christian Science Monitor, Library of Congress, Wall Street Journal Asia, Boston Globe and Washington Post all contributed.

Author's Preface

Abraham Lincoln served as the 16th President of the United States. He led his country through its greatest period of crisis, a bloody and divisive Civil War. He saved the union and ended slavery, both beyond expectation, and showing a political savvy that continues to see him recognised as one of that nation's greatest leaders. By modern standards, Lincoln was handicapped. He had no polling data, no Gallup, no Zogby, no CNN to tell him what would be popular to say and do. Instead, Lincoln did what he thought was right. He gained a reputation through his own moral compass.

Lincoln's political *nous* has gradually been replaced in the modern political lexicon. Political evolution has seen decision making, all too often, removed from the head and heart of a leader and replaced by short-termism, driven by pollsters. Winning power, and retaining it, is now the dominant aim. Just as evolution put paid to the Neanderthal and outflanked by Homosapiens, the political evolution of the 20th century saw leaders replaced by poll driven drones. As Tony Blair commented: "The art of leadership is saying no, not yes. It is very easy to say yes."

'Yes' is not a luxury that the President of a former Soviet-state, which is located on the crossroads of East and West, and has influential neighbours such as Iran, Russia and Turkey, can afford. Popularity cannot be the abiding concern of a leader facing down foreign aggression, occupation and dealing with the effects of an eighth of his population made Internally Displaced Persons.

Ilham Aliyev is not a popularist. He is a fighter. He comes across as unassuming and soft spoken, yet Azerbaijan's

Presidency is pure political pugilism, requiring from its incumbent a metronome ability to take on a myriad of struggles. There has to be a physical and mental toll. Which is why the biography of Ilham Aliyev is so fascinating. Never before related in an English language biography, this is the story of a man forged in the dying years of the Soviet Era. An intellectual, teacher and businessman, the strange narrative of his life eventually led him to high office.

In Azerbaijan the Presidency is not a position that comes with inherent popularity. And, indeed, nor do the difficult decisions that face him each day. Since 2003, Aliyev has stoically led his nation during a remarkable era. On top of an economic boom, Azerbaijan has won international plaudits for reforms in governance and transparency and moved forward with democratic liberalisations, while dramatically improving the living standards of its people. These have come at a price. Aliyev has made the hard choices, and continues to do so. Because of this, at home, his popularity remains. It is perhaps a lesson in hard-nosed politics. Do what is right, not what is popular, and maybe the people will follow.

Graeme H. Wilson
2011

Chapter One

The Search for Peace

Great spirits have always found violent opposition from mediocrities. The latter cannot understand it when a man does not thoughtlessly submit to hereditary prejudices but honestly and courageously uses his intelligence.
— Albert Einstein, German theoretical physicist

Nobel Peace Prize winner Barack Obama stated that: "...War, in one form or another, appeared with the first man. At the dawn of history, its morality was not questioned; it was simply a fact, like drought or disease, the manner in which tribes and then civilisations sought power and settled their differences." From before recorded beginnings war has been a feature of the human condition. According to Lawrence Keeley's groundbreaking *War Before Civilisation*, half of the people found in a Nubian cemetery, dating back to as early as 12,000 years ago, had died of violence. Since the rise of nations and states, around 5,000 years ago, armed conflict has occurred in every part of the globe.

The invention of gunpowder and more recent technological advances led to modern warfare and increased the death toll. According to authors Ziad Obermeyer, E. Gakidou and Christopher Murray, in *Fifty years of violent war deaths from Vietnam to Bosnia*, it is estimated that 378,000 people died each year due to war just between 1985 and 1994.

It is a ghastly figure, though dwarfed by other dark points in history. Up to 56 million people died in World War Two, 36 million in the An Shi Rebellion of China and perhaps 40 million during the Mongol Conquests. In more contemporary times — and closer to Azerbaijan — over one million died during the Soviet invasion of Afghanistan, a million during the Iran-Iraq War, and as many as a million during the current travails in Iraq.

Less of a headliner, but equally spurious, the Nagorno-Karabakh War claimed some 25,000 lives between 1988 and 1994. Armenia engaged Azerbaijan in an undeclared war in the mountainous heights of Nagorno-Karabakh. During the turmoil of the demise of the Soviet Union, a deeply divided and weak political elite in Baku contributed to chaos as Azerbaijan lost Nagorno-Karabakh and swathes of surrounding territory.

By the time advancing Armenians were stopped, Azerbaijan had lost nearly one fifth of its territory to occupiers.

Worse was the human cost. According to a major United Nations Department of Public Information report on Internally Displaced Persons (IDPs), published on June 18, 2009:

> *The situation of such people in Azerbaijan is as heart-shattering as elsewhere around the globe. With 800,000 refugees and IDPs, Azerbaijan has the largest internally displaced population in the region, and, as of 2006, had the highest per capita IDP population in the world.*

Ilham Aliyev ascended to the Presidency of Azerbaijan in 2003, some nine years after his father had forged a difficult ceasefire with Armenia. Ahead lay difficult years.

The younger Aliyev faced the same occupation and IDP crisis. Yet before him lay a nation that was desperate for social change, economic growth and democratic transformation.

Also he is a 'War President'. A stalemate of 'no war, no peace' exists. If Azerbaijan has resources but not the military victory, Armenia has the victory but lacks resources. Both states suffer, yet there remains an abiding feeling that Aliyev has to free his lands, while in Yerevan a succession of leaders have fed their people a staple diet of rhetoric in order to explain away economic failure.

In Baku, a reluctant 'War President' has quietly restrained himself, and pursued a diplomatic agenda while his armed forces have been built with an eye on a liberation conflict.

Sun Tzu was an ancient Chinese general and strategist who authored *The Art of War*, an influential ancient Chinese book on military strategy. It is a tome that remains in evidence today, some two and a half millennia on, a reference point that military strategists the world over have invariably read. According to Sun Tzu's long-relevant doctrine, the art of war is of vital importance to the state. It is a matter of life and death. The path to safety or ruin.

It is a subject that has occupied the time of military men and some political leaders for the thousands of years since Sun Tsu put pen to paper. The doctrines of Sun Tzu, to some degree, shaped modern military thinking worldwide, and will have shaped Azerbaijani military strategy in this regard. Certainly to the President of a country one-fifth under occupation, "vital importance to the state" is a sentiment he knows well.

The human cost of the occupation is well known to the President of Azerbaijan.

"I talk about this issue every day, every single day," he says. "One ninth of the people of my country are Internally Displaced Persons. That issue dominates my life."

During his Presidency, Ilham Aliyev has been responsible for providing accommodation for hundreds of thousands of people in temporary homes, as well as ensuring schools for children, healthcare and other norms of civil society. They want to go home, but at least while they wait they can live — relatively — normal lives.

Ilham Aliyev reels off the statistics. They are well practiced. In the 2,863 days between his assumption of the Presidency on October 31, 2003, to September 1, 2011, not a day has gone by without recourse to the awful truths they represent. According to the Internal Displacement Monitoring Centre, established by the Norwegian Refugee Council and the leading international body monitoring conflict-induced internal displacement worldwide, Azerbaijan has one million IDPs as a result of the Nagorno-Karabakh War.

It's grim, especially considering that on January 15, 2010, Azerbaijan's nine millionth citizen was born in the Babek District in the Nakhchivan Autonomous Republic. More than 11 per cent of Azerbaijanis are IDPs, a frightening statistic.

Aliyev is impassioned and energetic as he spits out this figure. That 11 per cent equates to 34 million Americans being displaced, seven million French, 16 million Russians or 14 million Japanese.

Yet outside of Azerbaijan these are a forgotten million. Afghanistan's estimated 200,000 IDPs are far more visible on our television screens, as are Sri Lanka's 300,000 IDPs or Burma's (Myanmar) 500,000 IDPs. That is not to lessen the burden of those suffering in these countries, but to highlight that the suffering of Azerbaijan's IDPs is far less conspicuous...

One million people forgotten, in international media terms. Forgotten too in terms of international law. Unlike the case of refugees, there is no international treaty which applies specifically to IDPs. Bahame Tom Nyanduga, Special Rapporteur on Refugees, IDPs and Asylum Seekers in Africa for the African Commission on Human and Peoples' Rights states that: "The absence of a binding international legal regime on internal displacement is a grave lacuna in international law."

While battling on this front, Aliyev has had enviable success elsewhere. Achieving tangible economic growth is another form of war, where many nations fail. Boosted by oil revenues, Aliyev's Azerbaijan has seen a transformation since 2003...

Official statistics show a drastically decreasing level of poverty over the last five years, from 49 per cent to nine per cent, an increase of the state budget from $1 billion up to $20 billion in 2011, 1,200 new schools built, hundreds of new private sector businesses, vast water and electricity projects, a new 'National Strategy for Transparency and Combating Corruption'... the list goes on.

In 2004, during the first 12 months of his Presidency, Aliyev stepped up to the plate on employment, particularly youth employment. He decreed that government and the private sector needed to create 600,000 new jobs in five years. By 2009, this figure had been bettered, reaching 800,000.

In the last six years the economy grew approximately three fold and remained as one of the fastest expanding economies in the world. Even during the global downturn and crisis of recent years Azerbaijan's economy was robust, in 2009 GDP growing by 9.3 per cent.

Azerbaijan leads the world in regulatory reforms to make doing business easier, according to *Doing Business 2009* — the sixth report in an annual series published by the World Bank and International Finance Corporation. Azerbaijan reformed in seven of the 10 regulatory areas studied by the report. Its overall rank on the ease of doing business rose to 33 from 97 — the biggest jump in one year ever recorded by *Doing Business.*

The Ilham Aliyev years have seen the emergence of a stable foundation of economic development, highly visible economic growth, development of a welfare state for lower income families and evolution of a civil society within a country that had previously been part of a totalitarian system. Add to this the completion, or initiation, of a series of global transportation and energy projects, and the eight years of Ilham Aliyev can be viewed as a success — except on one front. Like his father before him, Ilham Aliyev faces the gravest of tasks that will ever burden a Head of State.

It was Martin Luther King Jr who commented: "I refuse to accept the idea that man is mere flotsam and jetsam in the river of life, unable to influence the unfolding events which surround him. I refuse to accept the view that mankind is so tragically bound to the starless midnight of racism and war that the bright daybreak of peace and brotherhood can never become a reality."

Like many other leaders before and after him, on Aliyev's command, tens of thousands of young men may go to war. In order to liberate the swathes of occupied Azerbaijan, it is likely that some will not return. It is something that any right thinking leader does his best to avoid.

Yet as a 'War President', on his shoulders alone sits responsibility for balancing years of fruitless diplomacy and the intransigence of his counterpart in Yerevan, along with military readiness, battlefield balance of power and time.

Does he believe that Nagorno-Karabakh will return to Azerbaijan during his lifetime?

"In my Presidency," he fires back.

The message is clear. If international diplomacy fails to back up international law, and see the country whole again, Azerbaijan will seek its legitimate rights another way. The 'War President' would be forced to restore his nation's territorial integrity.

It is a somewhat odd position for a man whose career took him from academia during the last years of the Soviet Union to private business in its aftermath. A quiet life learning from his father, a giant of the Communist Era and then saviour of post-independence Azerbaijan, which served to mould a man, and a President. Aliyev has arguably been the most successful Caucasus leader of the post-Soviet era, balancing civil society and democracy, with stability and an economic miracle. Many others have failed.

This is a legacy that he will bequeath to the nation: A progressive endowment that kick-started Azerbaijan's rise from post-Soviet ruins. To achieve this in a nation effectively on a war footing adds to the lustre of this achievement.

But how will history and future generations remember Azerbaijan's 'War President'?

Quiet spoken and modest, Aliyev is no Winston Churchill. But he is just as stoic in the face of a threat. "In my Presidency" is his conviction — and his promise to an expectant nation.

In his seminal book, Sun Tzu opined that 'For to win one hundred victories in one hundred battles is not the acme of skill. To subdue the enemy without fighting is the acme of skill.'

Aliyev's commitment has thus far been pursued by diplomatic means, a skill as the Chinese general observes. But, if indeed Sun Tzu was correct about war being of 'vital importance' and a matter of 'life and death', then the ultimate legacy of Aliyev is perhaps not in his own hands.
It's time for the international community to get serious.

Chapter Two

Origins of a Nation

A civilisation is a heritage of beliefs, customs and knowledge slowly accumulated in the course of centuries, elements difficult at times to justify by logic, but justifying themselves as paths when they lead somewhere, since they open up for man his inner distance.

— Antoine de Saint-Exupery, French author

It was 1939 as the storm clouds of war gathered over Europe and a 50-year-old Austrian-born politician, as Führer and Chancellor of Germany's Third Reich, threatened the downfall of great European cultures, that a centuries-old lost culture was being unearthed in a largely forgotten part of Eurasia.

As Adolf Hitler planned his invasion of Poland and the great Soviet dictator, Josef Stalin, imposed the Cyrillic alphabet on a Muslim-populated Transcaucasian nation, a determined archaeologist in the Caspian seaport of Baku was readying to explore an accidental find just 54 kilometres away amid the unlikely setting of a stone quarry.

Isaak Jafarzade mounted the first archaeological investigation of the rock paintings and etchings of Gobustan — a quarry town set amidst 100 square kilometres of volcanic mud, semi-desert. This turned out to be a huge collection of rock art, with many scenes dating back to the Stone Age, which had long been hidden in caves secreted by huge boulders, and which had been uncovered, by accident, by a quarry worker. The worker's name has been lost to history — but he had unearthed a magnificent record of his country's ancestry — a highly complex past which spoke of an ancient 'cradle of civilisation' forged by invasions, by incursions of cultures, assimilation and nationalistic passion perhaps incomparable in any other nation's history.

Over the next 25 years archaeologists were to discover no less than 3,500 individual rock paintings on 750 rocks across the 'ravine land' of Gobustan. It was to become one of the world's largest open-air museums paying tribute to the history, culture, economy, customs and traditions of ancient Azerbaijan. These archaeological findings were further enhanced by the discovery in 1968, by Mammadali Huseynov, of the Azykh six-cave complex in Azerbaijan's Fizuli district. This housed a Neanderthal-style jaw bone, thought to be 300,000 years old, which is now on show in Baku's Academy of Sciences. This Azykh cave system was evidence of man's earliest habitation. Azerbaijan's history was older than even its most enthusiastic proponent could have promulgated.

Dating back between 5,000 and 20,000 years, the awe-inspiring collection of rock paintings delivered up a fascinating picture of prehistoric life in the Caucasus.

They told of men who would hunt deer and antelope, of a rural people who would reap harvests, of ritual sacrifices and battles, even of people with their hands and arms linking shoulders in a dance which could easily be a precursor to the *Yalla* (food) dance still performed in Azerbaijan today.

The artistic hoard also told of people who would travel in reed boats strangely similar to the longboats which carried Vikings on their terrorising raids throughout Northern Europe — a similarity not lost on famed Norwegian adventurer Thor Heyerdahl. The man who mounted the 1949 Kon-Tiki raft expedition across the Pacific Ocean studied Gobustan in the late 1980s and early 1990s. He quickly became convinced that ancient Azerbaijanis emigrated to Scandinavia around 100 AD taking their boat-building skills with them and there evolved the dramatic Viking longboats.

The drawings, said Heyerdahl, "testify to the fact that boats were of extreme importance to early man, as they provided security and transportation millennia before there were roads cut through the wilderness."

And a wilderness is what archaeologists began to believe ancient Gobustan was — a land with a damp climate, close to sub-tropical where flowing rivers helped feed rich, fertile soil — all in stark contrast to the area which hosted the excavations of Isaak Jafarzade.

The paintings and etchings charted the history of Azerbaijan. Depictions of camel caravans provide testimony to Gobustan's ancient 'silk route' status as a vital crossroad between Asia and Europe. Persian inscriptions talk of the area's importance to trade in the 7th century. There is Latin graffiti carved by a centurion of the 12th (Lightning) Roman Legion, present in the region during the 84-96 AD reign of Emperor Titus Flavius Domitianus, the last Emperor of Rome's Flavian Dynasty and the longest serving since the enigmatic Tiberus. These were evidence of a place much sought after by foreign powers, of a cultural crossroad — a mantle Azerbaijan was to retain for centuries to come.

The origins of the name Azerbaijan are still being debated. Some argue its name derives from Atropates, a satrap of the Achaemenid Empire, others that the meaning has evolved from the term 'Land of Fire' — a moniker which epitomised the natural gas and oil wells which erupted from the earth around Baku. These natural resources were famed across continents from as early as the beginning of the first millennium BC. Ancient Azerbaijanis believed these rich natural gas and oil deposits were the elixir of life — and so they have proved to be.

But gas and oil were not the land's only God-given blessings. This country, which spans 87,000 square kilometres, encompasses one of the world's most diverse landscapes and soil structures. Azerbaijan boasts no less than eight mountain ranges and 1,250 rivers. Its rich and ancient landscape was a treasure trove of iron, copper, silver, coal, salt and precious stone.

The diversity of landscape — from salt lands to desert, marshlands to mountain ranges and humid forests — was matched by an equally great range of climatic conditions. Indeed the mountains of the country's extreme south-east are noted for their own distinct micro-climate where a fragile balance of air pressure, humidity and temperatures are legendary for promoting long life. The mountain village of Lerik is in fact famed for its centenarians and has been the centre of much international medical research into the secret of long-life — all of which has proved inconclusive and which has given rise to a mantra of simple diet, hard work and karma-like acceptance of one's lot in life. Here it was that Shirali Muslimov, who was born in 1805, sprang to unexpected fame when he was entered into the *Guinness Book of Records* as the world's oldest surviving male. He is thought to have died aged 168.

The Azerbaijan of rich natural deposits, of diverse landscape and climates drew ancient peoples and civilisations to its shores — each infusing proudly held cultures with distinct Middle Eastern/Turkish characteristics which, in many cases, still form the collective Azerbaijani personality.

The earliest records, around 2300 BC, speak of a land inhabited by tribes — the warlike Gutis, Lulubis, Kasis and Hurris — the latter forming a union which gave birth to a great eastern civilisation which pursued active foreign policies and successfully defended their territory from foreign invaders. Likewise the aggressive Gutis went on to conquer Mesopotamia (large parts of modern-day Iraq) and rule it for a century through a relatively sophisticated political system which saw their leaders democratically elected. During this time their culture emerged as one with advanced medical practices. Having absorbed the traits of Sumerian and Acadian medicine, Gutis cured their ills with lavender, myrrh, dates, saffron and garlic accompanied by oils from Egypt, Syria and Palestine.

The societies established by these tribes gave rise to states and kingdoms the names of which echoed with reverence around the East — Manna, the Scythian Kingdom, Atropatena and Albania.

Manna, established in the first millennium BC and ruled by a Czar whose powers were absolute and hereditary, proved to be a prosperous and highly cultural kingdom, where sovereigns ruled with the help of a council of seniors. It was the birthplace of Zoroastrianism, which it took as its official religion. Zoroastrianism — the oldest of the creedal religions — evolved from the teachings of the Prophet Zoroaster who exalted the worship of Ahura Mazda as the supreme divine authority. The religion's preference for ritual purity by fire is thought to have stemmed from Zoroaster's stay around Baku where the presence of flames from the gas and oil fields influenced all.

It fell to Manna to play a decisive role in the historic development of Azerbaijan. Wealthy, sophisticated Manna attracted the envy of its neighbours though attempts to occupy its lands by Ashshur and Urartu came to naught. Instead Manna annexed all other small states in the Urmia basin and expanded its territory from the Araz river in the north, which today forms a border between Azerbaijan and Iran, to the Caspian Sea in the north-east. Manna survived as the prevailing state for 300 years.

As Manna progressed, other tribes — the most ancient peoples of Eurasia — began to make their influence felt in the late 8th century BC. Kimmers, Scythians, Saks and Massagets became known for their military and political prowess across a vast territory which took in the major Caucasus foothills of North Azerbaijan and eastern Anatolia, now present-day Turkey.

The Scythians, originally a semi-nomadic pastoral people, expanded their kingdom throughout Azerbaijan, north of Manna, driven by the need for grazing land for their herds. They worshipped the God of the Sun and sacrificed what they believed to be the quickest animal on Earth — the horse — to him. The Massagets were similar people and the Rulers of these two tribes successfully defended their lands from foreign invaders. Indeed the Massagets inflicted a severe defeat on the then powerful Achaemenid Empire which had ambitions on the Massaget Kingdom. The Empire's Ruler — Cyrus II, known as Cyrus The Great — had created the world's largest state through expansionist policies that saw him conquer vast tracts of land from Egypt in the West to the Indus River in the East. Cyrus, though, did not fare well against the Massagets and Scythians. A wily attempt to gain control of the Massaget Kingdom through a marriage alliance with the widow of Massaget Ruler, Tomiris, failed and the Azerbaijani Kingdom led a successful drive to smash the Persian army, despite being outnumbered. The battle is renowned as one of the greatest in Azerbaijan's history with Cyrus being fatally wounded.

The Scythian and Massaget Kingdoms brought prosperity to Azerbaijan and laid the foundations for its rich culture — music for instance was heavily promoted — and the culture went on to survive not only the colonisation attempts of the Achaemenid Empire, but also the expansionist strategy of the extraordinary Alexander The Great.

Azerbaijan came into its own thanks largely to an army general — Atropat. This notorious warlord joined forces with the Achaemenid Empire's King Darius II in a bid to halt Alexander The Great's advance through the region. Darius was defeated but Atropat's reputation reached Alexander's ears and the Macedonian legend then appointed Atropat governor of a southern state. Atropat then shrewdly married into Alexander's family and was rewarded with independence for his state — Atropatena — the first independence granted from Macedonia.

Independence brought renewed vigour to the south of Azerbaijan which underwent something of a geopolitical, economic and cultural renaissance. Strong Atropatena brought international recognition to the region while trade flourished with the Caucasus, the Volga region, Central Asia, India, Asia Minor, Mesopotamia as well as the Black Sea and Mediterranean Sea basins. Atropatena's own currency dominated the local market while relations with Greek state organisations strengthened, spreading the use of Greek as a language and prompting huge improvements in the state's legal infrastructure.

Atropatena's star was in the ascendancy and shone ever brighter when the state fought off occupation attempts by neighbouring states and later mounted a force of 40,000 infantry and 10,000 cavalry to defeat Roman troops which entered the region. Atropatena's name resonated throughout the Near and Middle East and the Roman Empire to the extent that Emperor Octavian August met with its leaders and entrusted them to govern the neighbouring Armenian Kingdom. The Armenian Tsars sought a diplomatic solution to the dilemma thrust upon them by marrying the daughter of Tsar Tigran to Atropatena Ruler Mitridat — Armenia now fell under Atropatena.

In the north of Azerbaijan territory lay Caucasian Albania. With a history dating back to the first millennium BC, this state stretched from the Caucasus Mountains to the mighty River Araz in the south, from the Goycha lake basin in the West to the shores of the Caspian Sea in the East. Albania's capital was Gabala — a large city set amid mountain forests — and one of 30 cities within the state which all served as important commercial and cultural centres where the Albania alphabet held sway.

Albania was home to a number of Caucasian tribes and ethnic Turkish communities which created a multi-cultural society.

Azerbaijan's fortunes rose in Albania's heyday. This was the seat of Christian stirrings in the country following the conversion of Albania's King Urnayr who helped found the independent Albanian church reporting directly to the Pope in the Vatican. Albanian Rulers were paramount — they were the secular and religious leaders of the country. They issued laws and commanded an army of over 80,000 infantry and cavalry. Here too, the Azerbaijani tradition of advisory councils, even for omnipotent Rulers, was evident.

The Albanian advisory council was housed in the Ruler's palace and the state minted its own currency and, as with its southern state counterpart Atropatena, Albania was successful in resisting the Persian and Roman Empires which threatened its independence. Once again, Rome used its diplomatic skills to forge links with Albanian envoys also negotiating with Emperor Octavius.

The Azerbaijani state's fortunes, though, were to change and the country was about to enter one of its darkest periods.

Chapter Three

A Fight for Independence

An empire founded by war has to maintain itself by war.
— Charles de Montesquieu, French Philosopher

Persia had seen the formation of the Sassanid Empire. The Empire pursued an aggressive expansionist strategy — and successfully occupied parts of Azerbaijan and began settling its people there. These immigrants, who benefited from privileged affirmative policies, settled on the country's most fertile land and in the most strategic of regions.

Despite fierce attempts to assimilate indigenous people into Persian culture, the Azerbaijani states resisted and moved further towards the formation of one nation in the face of continuous persecution. The Azerbaijani states forged robust ethnic-political and cultural links and despite 400 years of Persian occupation, their ancient traditions of statehood survived and were reinforced as the emerging state headed towards another watershed.

Over the centuries ethnic communities of Turks had settled throughout Azerbaijani territories — most assimilated in the large native Caucasian populations with the exception of the Oghuz Turks, from what is modern-day Turkmenistan, who arrived in significantly larger numbers and began to convert the Caucasian Albanians to Islam and their own language. The Turkish tribes began to dominate both the north and south of the country using Turkish as their language and bridging both ends of the Azerbaijani landscape. These

Turks adopted a leading role in preserving independent traditions of Azerbaijani territory.
Arab historian Ubeid ibn Shariyya Al-Jurhumi refers to Azerbaijan as having, through consistent immigration, "long been a land of Turks." Indeed the Arab name for Azerbaijan — Bilad Al Qybchaq — translates as 'The Land of Kupchaks,' who made up a Turkish tribe.
But it was the Oghuz Turks who made a real difference. Their language, culture and religion was assimilated into Azerbaijan's identity to form the character of the nation. The adoption of Islam in the 7th century was a turning point in Azerbaijan's history for it brought unity of nation and language, commonality of religion, forged cross-ethnic boundaries, expanded ties and deepened integration.
Albania, however, remained the exception, steadfastly retaining its Christian identity, taking advantage of the commitment to tolerance of its Islamic neighbours. Christians, however, were now a national minority, later becoming assimilation targets for Armenia and Georgia.
And then came another turning point for the emerging nation which put all the territory's previous incursions, numerous though they were, in the shade — the invasion of Muslim Arabs. This was devastating in its force with thousands upon thousands of Muslim infantry and horsemen, fresh from their triumphs in the Near East, overrunning the countryside.
This profound watershed came in the reign of the Caliph Omar around 639. Domination of Albania did not come easily however. The Christian Albanians mounted resistance under their last Prince, Javanshir Mikhrani and they became embroiled in the Arab-Khazar wars.
The legendary Javanshir — or Young Lion — was of Parthian ancestry. After several attempts to resist the Arab

invasion alone, he surrendered. Javanshir's decision had been prompted by a need to turn his attention to the Khazars, who ended up in battle with the Arabs and suffered a major defeat near the historic city of Ardabil in present-day north-western Iran.

Javanshir's capitulation, though, had not gone down well with his people, particularly the nobles, who now found themselves at odds with Arabs from Basra and Kufa who arrived and seized land abandoned by indigenous people, setting themselves up as a land-owning aristocracy. Tempers and intrigue boiled over and Javanshir was assassinated by opposition nobles whose powers he had tried to restrict. Albania was no longer independent but a vassal state of the Caliphate.

But the underlying resistance to Arab domination rumbled on and over a hundred years later, in the 9th century, large parts of southern Azerbaijan came under the leadership of the fervent nationalist Babek Huremdin. Babek began a movement which was to go head-to-head with the Arabs for decades, causing the occupying force untold stress and anguish. Babek's forces resisted Arab rule in a revolt which became known as the Hurramid Movement and which lasted for 20 years despite Arab moves to encircle them with garrisons in strategic towns.

In 835 Babek, now a national hero and whose name had become synonymous with freedom of religious and cultural traditions and identity, was captured, along with his brother Abdulla, in a trap laid for the Arabs by the Persian aristocrat Afhsin, in cahoots with the Armenian, Sahl Ibn Sunbat. Both captives were, brutally and publicly, tortured to death but their names have gone down in the annals of Azerbaijan history as symbols of national freedom.

With the problematic Prince Javanshir and the frustratingly popular Hurramid Movement now well and truly crushed, the Arabs completed their domination. Islam spread throughout the country as the population used conversion to avoid paying the head tax *(jizaya)*, which applied only to non-Muslims. The aristocracy opted for Islam as a means of strengthening their power base. Some were more sincere and spiritual in their adoption of the Islamic faith, having been swayed by Sufis and their more philosophical and congenial interpretation of the Muslim religion. Sufis, sometimes known as dervishes, followed the mystic dimension of Islam with the aim of purifying the heart and ensuring it focuses only on God.

With an acceptance of Islam serving to unify the masses, Arab domination brought stability and subsequent prosperity to the country for over two generations — that is until the Caliphate weakened and crumbled. The Caliphate's downfall came as the Arabs concentrated on trade, leaving the Caliph to depend on Turkish mercenaries for defence, along with the Mamelukes, who had previously ruled Egypt. The Mamelukes, however, soon grew in influence in various states throughout the country and sparked a political revival in many of the ancient states which were strongly supported by powerful dynasties.

Suddenly there was an eruption of independent states — Sadjis, Shirvanshahs and Salaris to name a few — and Turkish once again became the main language of communication. What all had in common was their language and Islam as their predominant religion.

But the downfall of the Caliphate brought opportunity to a Christian coalition of feudal lords of the Byzantium Empire, Armenia and Georgia who began to look with interest at these independent states.

As Christian eyes turned on the fractured political scenario of Azerbaijan, waves of Oghuz Turkic tribes from Central Asia rode into the area seizing swathes of territory as they passed. One of these tribes — the Seljuqs — stood head and shoulders above the rest and they were to have a defining impact on Azerbaijan's history.

Led by Tugrul Beg, the second Ruler of the Seljuq Dynasty, the Seljuqs advanced across Persia and the Caucasus and parts of Anatolia, even Baghdad, conquering states and uniting them into a confederacy of tribes which made up a vast Great Seljuq Empire. Yet Tugrul did not have it all his way. He first faced a revolt led by forces loyal to his foster brother Ibrahim Yinal. But Tugrul crushed this revolt, captured Ibrahim and personally strangled him.

During the rule of the Great Seljuq Empire in the 12th century, Azerbaijan emerged as an important cultural centre for the Turks. Palaces built by the vassal 'Atabeg' governors Eldanizid and Shirvanshah hosted the intelligentsia and glitterati of the day including outstanding Muslim artisans and scientists.

A Christian coalition on the doorstep was consistently causing trouble, until it attempted to occupy Azerbaijan and the Empire gained a definitive victory in the famed Battle of Malazgird.

The Azerbaijani nation was now unified though it comprised of a heady mix of tribes, and ethnicities. Assimilation led to the creation of the Azerbaijani-Turkish language which fast took hold and became the main language of communication throughout the southern Caucasus. Azerbaijani-Turkish culture also gained significant ground with the emergence of folk poets and singers and later recorded literature in the Azerbaijani-Turkish language.

The Great Seljuq Empire, though, was in decline and was to be succeeded by vassal 'Atabeg' governors who had served the Sultan. The era of the Atabegs came in 1136 when Sultan Mas'ud appointed the academic Shamseddin Eldaniz to be a tutor to his young successor and transferred the territory of Arran to him. Shamseddin quickly set up a virtual court in his residence in Arran's most important trade and cultural city — Barda. In his 'seat' of provincial government, amid an agricultural territory renowned for its cotton, silk, poultry and dairy production, Shamseddin quickly attracted local 'emirs' to his 'court' where, through continuous intrigue, he built a substantial power base.

In time, Shamseddin became Ruler of the parts of northern Iran and the southern Caucasus left over from the Seljuq Empire with important governors paying homage to him.

Shamseddin, though, was quick to discover that power also brought enemies and his nemesis was to be Georgia, with its army strengthened by the inclusion of 40,000 Kipchak Turkish warriors.

Shamseddin's downfall began on December 1, 1138, when Demetre I, the Czar of Georgia, still smarting from previous Seljuq Empire occupation of the Georgian-held Armenia city of Ani, decided to wreak his revenge.

Ganja, the second most important city in Atabeg territory and a main centre on the caravan route, was in disarray after being hit by an earthquake. Demetre I saw his chance. He attacked Ganja, ransacked the city and, on leaving, took away with him the cherished landmark iron gate of the city as his trophy, later donating it to a Georgian monastery. Emboldened by his success, Demetre's forces undertook successive raids on numerous cities held by the Atabeg.

Shamseddin's response was to form a union with other Seljuq leaders to fight the Georgians. Over 13 years the pendulum swung with minor victories, but overall seeing Georgian expansion until 1173. That year Shamseddin led a 'last stand' campaign against Georgia. He was defeated and died a year later.

Muhammed Djakhamn Pekhlevan, Shamseddin's son, came to power and began a 12-year rule considered by many historians to be the most peaceful in the territory's history. Muhammed made his younger brother, Qyzil Arslan, Ruler of Azerbaijan. The young Qyzil Arslan went on to capture Tabriz, the capital of Eastern Azerbaijan and declared it the capital of the Atabeg State.

Though Muhammed's reign is recorded as peaceful, it began with bloodshed. He suppressed all the rebellious Emirs in the area and replaced them with Mamelukes — Turkish mercenaries who were loyal to him. The Mamelukes were rewarded well for their faithfulness — each became a feudal lord of a region or town.

Such was the reputation of the Mamelukes that peace then descended on Atabeg territory and it remained free of foreign incursions. Indeed during Muhammed Djakhamn's reign friendly relations were forged with the Khorezmshakhs, Rulers of a Central Asian Empire renowned for its rich agricultural industry, the regime having mastered techniques of ploughing, irrigation and cattle breeding.

The Khorezmshakhs were also prodigious producers of handicrafts and astute traders and their influence brought a spurt of new scientific, artistic and trading developments to Muhammed's Kingdom.

On Muhammed's death in 1186, his younger brother Qyzil Arslan ascended the throne, but he failed to retain the loyalty of the Mamelukes. The now powerful Mamelukes refused to follow Qyzil Arslan's lead and the strongest among them, Shirvanshakh Akhsitan, attempted to seize territories, judging his influence to be on the wane. But Shirvanshakh misread the situation and Qyzil Arslan inflicted a crushing defeat and pursued the rebel troops all the way to Baku, retaking the Mameluke's territories as he went.

Qyzil Arslan's rule, though, was beset by intrigue and the self-proclaimed sultan was assassinated in 1191.

On Qyzil Arslan's death power was handed over to his three sons — Abu Bakr who governed Azerbaijan and Arran and his brothers Qutluq Inandj and Amir Amiran who ruled the mountainous and desert province of Khorasan and several neighbouring regions.

Given the political intrigues of the day it came as no surprise to anyone that brotherly love failed to stop the three siblings competing for overall power. Abu Bakr emerged the victor but with his forces in tatters and with the country's erstwhile allies, the Khorezmshakhs and Georgians, mounting almost continuous forays into his territory which began its gradual disintegration.

On Abu Bakr's death, when he was succeeded by Atabek Uzbek, the situation worsened and the legendary Czarina, Tamara the Great of Georgia, seized the moment and invaded. Numerous Azerbaijani towns fell to Georgian invaders — who followed their renowned military style of occupation and then speedy withdrawal.

The damage to the Atabeg state though was complete and it disintegrated in 1225 when it fell to the 'Scourge of God'.

Chapter Four

The Scourge of God

The greatest happiness is to scatter your enemy, to drive him before you, to see his cities reduced to ashes, to see those who love him shrouded in tears, and to gather into your bosom his wives and daughters.

— Genghis Khan, Mongol warrior

The 'Scourge of God', as Genghis Khan became known, gathered, trained and incentivised the most relentless and unconventional of armies that the world would ever see. His army was terrifying and waged ruthless campaigns fed by its leader's desire of revenge for past family insults and tragedies.

The Mongols were an illiterate, religiously shamanistic and sparsely populated people. Historians agree that they numbered perhaps no more than around 70,000, but they would emerge to become the world's most dominant force. From his late teens to age 38 in 1200, a Mongol named Temujin rose as Khan over various families. He was a good manager, collecting people of talent. In 1206, at the age of 44, Temujin took the title Genghis Khan, which translates to Universal Ruler.

Khan forged within his people a belief that they were the centre of the universe, the greatest of people and favoured by the gods. They justified his success in warfare by claiming that he was the rightful master of the world, not only over the 'peoples of the felt tent'. He created order in his realm that strengthened it — and had ability to expand.

But he did more than just invade and conquer. He established a code of laws for the Empire, a standard written language for his people and he set up a kind of postal system to help different parts of the Empire communicate with each other. His greatest skill, though, was as a military leader. In 1211 the Mongols began a full assault on China by invading the entire region north of the Great Wall. In the summer of 1215 Peking was captured. Success in China helped people acquire the impression that Khan had the 'Mandate of Heaven' and that fighting against him was fighting heaven itself.

Khan now wanted trade and goods, including new weapons, for his nation. Leaving one of his generals in charge of further operations in North China, Khan returned to Mongolia to devote his attention to events in central Asia.

Küchlüg the Naiman, who had taken refuge among the Kara-Khitai, had overthrown the Ruler of that people and taken over his Kingdom. An army sent by Khan chased him into Afghanistan, where he was captured and put to death. The takeover of his territory gave the Mongols a common frontier with Sultan Muhammad, the Ruler of Khiva, who after recent conquests had claimed all of central Asia as well as Afghanistan and the greater part of Persia. Khan and his army pushed into Afghanistan and then Persia, boasting 100,000 to 125,000 horsemen with his Uyghur and Turkic allies, engineers and Chinese doctors, resulting in a total army strength of 150,000 to 200,000 men.

It was only a matter of time before the two Empires went to war. Khan set out in the spring of 1219. By April 1220 he had captured Otrar and the cities of Bukhara and Samarkand. Khan sent his two best generals in pursuit of

Sultan Muhammad, who fled across Persia and was killed on an island in the Caspian Sea.

Khan, in the meantime, had attacked and captured Termez in the autumn of 1220 and spent the winter in what is now Tajikistan. Early in 1221 Khan destroyed the city of Balkh, in the Persian province of Khurasan.

He advanced through Afghanistan to attack Sultan Jalal al-Din, the son of Sultan Muhammad. Jalal al-Din's defeat concluded the campaign in the west and Khan returned to Mongolia.

While Khan was consolidating his conquests in Persia and Afghanistan, a force of 40,000 Mongol horsemen pushed through Azerbaijan and Armenia. They defeated Georgian crusaders, captured a Genoese trade-fortress in the Crimea and spent the winter along the coast of the Black Sea.

In 1225, Khan returned to Mongolia. He now ruled everything between the Caspian Sea and Beijing. In 1227, around the age of 65, while leading the fighting against the Tangut, it is said that he fell off his horse and died.

In terms of square miles conquered, Khan had been the greatest conqueror of all time — his empire four times larger than the empire of Alexander the Great.

Khan had moved into the Caucasus enriched by victories and the Azerbaijani territories never stood a chance. His incursions were merciless and the Atabeg state was no match for the sheer might and muscle of the Mongol army and the alternative military and psychological strategies that Khan used. He conquered all in his wake. His reputation spread terror well before his arrival with the Mongol warrior working hard on a well-earned reputation as a bloodthirsty barbarian so that many rolled over and submitted in advance of his coming.

Yet Khan was not the ignorant barbarian his propaganda machine professed. He destroyed cities for punishment and propaganda but also in the interests of trade. With singular tenacity he was clearing the trade routes to his Empire giving them greater access and infusing increased efficiency.

Eldanizes turned into one of the most powerful countries of the Near and Middle East and played a significant role in Azerbaijan's ethnic-political history.

It was from Eldanizes that something of a cultural revival occurred. Art, trade, science and culture flourished, religious schools *(madrasas)* were opened, magnificent mosques and iconic architectural monuments were built. This was an era when the great Azerbaijani poet and thinker Khagani Shirvani came to fame. A master of the highly stylised 'qasida' poetic form, Khagani wrote satires, epigrams and a ballad inspired by a period spent in prison after falling foul of his patron, the Prince of Baku. It was also a time when the great romantic poet Nizami Ganjavi won a huge following with his colloquial and realistic style and the architect Adjami was in much demand for his monumental mausoleum designs.

A brilliant intellectual and artistic cadre dominated the landscape. Names such as scientist and philosopher Bakhmanyar, scholar/writer Khatib Tabrizi and poets Ganjavi and Shirvani took medieval literature to new heights.

The region was also experiencing a construction boom with unique architecture producing a legacy of awe-inspiring fortress walls, stunning mosques, impressive schools, monumental mausoleums and spectacular bridges in Baku and Ganja.

In this Golden Age a Turkish-Islam Empire progressed throughout the whole Caucasus spreading its influence also to the Near and Middle East.

The 15th to the 18th centuries saw the re-emergence of Azerbaijan's statehood culture when the vast Gara Goyunlu *(Black Sheep)*, Agh Goyunlu *(White Sheep)*, Safavid and Afshar Empires of the East, were directly ruled by Azerbaijani dynasties. This brought huge benefits to the nation — its military and political influence spread as did the use of the Azerbaijani Turkic language. Azerbaijan soon found itself playing an active role in East European military and political relations and the international relations of the Near and Middle East.

The establishment of the Azerbaijan state of Safavids in 1501 was marked with the beginning of the centralisation of all Azerbaijan lands. One of the four provinces established by the Safavids was named the Karabakh or Ganja province. After the death of Nadir Shah, who had put an end to the existence of the Safavid state, new independent and semi-independent entities, khanates and sultanates, emerged in Azerbaijan. One of them was the Karabakh khanate.

It was from the Agh Goyunlu state that one of Azerbaijan's greatest statesmen emerged. The tall, lean, affable Uzun Hasan built up a strong, centralised state and drew up a special 'code of law'. This far-sighted leader eased the burden of taxpayers, developed the economy and brought to an end the military-political independence of tribal leaders.

A far-sighted man, Uzun Hasan believed divergence of religious and tribal loyalties would create further unrest in the country — he saw marriage as the answer to statehood dramas. He married his sister off to Shekykh Djuneyd, Ruler of the Safavids, and his daughter to another Safavid leader, Sheykh Heydar. At the same time, he believed a strong armed force was the best deterrent against invasion. Closely watching developments in military science, he built a strong regular army, increased his mercenary forces and began production of firearms and artillery under the directorship of Italian specialists.

Science and education also came under the watchful eye and progressive guardianship of Uzun Hasan. He gathered around him an impressive faculty of the region's scientists-60 alone worked in his private library. The Koran was translated into Azerbaijani Turkic language and diplomatic relations were launched with European and Eastern states alike. Azerbaijani envoys were familiar sights in the palaces of Venice, Naples, Caucasian Albania, Hungary, Poland, Germany, Burgundy, Cyprus, Rhodes, Moscow and even the Vatican.

Uzun Hasan's mother — Sara Khatun — became the only female diplomat in the East and one of the first in the world, while the Venetian Republic opened an embassy in the Azerbaijani leader's Tabriz palace. Azerbaijan was now a power-broker between East and West.

Over in the north of the country, the Shirvanshah state was aiding national development, its Rulers having retained a high degree of autonomy from 861 to1539, providing continuity which outlived that of any other dynasty in the Islamic world. Shirvan, which was formed by a Persianised dynasty of Arab origin founded by the Yazidid family, had a history which fell into two distinct periods — that of the 12th century and another in the 15th century.

It was under the 12th century dynasty, noted for its strong commitment to cultural advancement, that Baku came into its own as a state capital.

The dynasty was still plagued by frequent Mongol incursions which it counteracted by building a series of impregnable fortresses around the state leaving a fascinating legacy of mediaeval military architecture. On Sultan Manuchehr's instructions, defensive walls had already been built to surround and fortify Baku and its narrow, winding streets.

Then, following a devastating earthquake of 1191 which virtually destroyed the ancient Shirvan capital and the mountainous stronghold of Shamakha, Manuchehr moved the capital to Baku and began work on the Shirvanshah complex including its stone Maiden Tower fortress near the waterfront. Constructed on the highest point of the city, the complex became a striking monument to mediaeval Azerbaijani architecture.

Manuchehr was noted for his strong patronage of poetry and literature and his court was frequented by celebrated literati of the age including Khagani and Nizami who both paid tribute to the state, and the Shah, in their work. Shirvan's fortunes dipped however in 1235 when it was devastated by a massive Mongol invasion from which it took over a century to fully recover.

It fell to Shirvanshah Ibrahim The First to revive the country's fortunes.

Equipped with a highly attuned sense of political cunning, this ruler, who rose from the ranks of an impoverished noble to be selected Shah by his peers, played a successful game of opportunist alliance with Emir Timur. Timur was founder of the Timurid Empire and Timurid Dynasty who had conquered much of west and central Asia and had made the fabled Samarkand as his capital.

Ibrahim managed to resist foreign invasions by the Turko-Mongol army of Timur, often referred to as Tamerlane, and of his erstwhile ally turned foe, Tukhtamysh, the last Khan of the White Horde. Both would-be invaders were descendants of Genghis Khan and both were individually determined to emulate their ancestor's great successes. Despite an earlier accord to divide territory, ambition got the better of both and led them to clash repeatedly.

Ibrahim first allied himself with Timur in skirmishes against Tukhtamysh, who, buoyed with confidence after having reunified Mongol lands from the Crimea to Lake Balkash, started a wave of punishing reprisals against the Shirvanshah by ravaging the countryside of Shirvan on his way to Tabriz in 1386.

However, Timur, a controversial and contrary man who was a military genius, playing chess as a hobby to hone his strategic skills, rallied Ibrahim once more and just a year later they launched a joint force against Tukhtamysh, defeating him in a major battle along the shores of the Kura River.

Timur, whose mercurial character caused him at one time to be a patron of the arts and at another the destroyer of major centres of learning, then used his influence over Ibrahim to utilise Shirvan as a base to move his armies to attack Georgia and Dagestan. In 1399 the two allies launched a devastating three-year expedition against Georgia which involved seven incursions. Timur, whose name was a Sanskrit derivative for the word 'iron' and who personally led the invasions, sacked the Georgian capital Tbilisi and captured its monarch, yet Bagrat V. Bagrat's successor bravely fought back and Timur failed to occupy the country. The two settled a peace treaty which saw Georgia pay tribute to the Emir. Some 36 months of fierce and relentless battle left the young King with a country crippled by gutted towns, ravaged countryside and a monarchy teetering on the brink.

Timur then turned his attention to the ruling Chinese Ming Dynasty and in an uncharacteristic move began a campaign in one of the most bitter winters on record — it was to prove a fatal mistake with the 'iron man' succumbing to illness brought on by the cold.

Shirvan, though, had benefited greatly from the alliance with Timur. Encouraged by his acquired power base, Ibrahim tried to conquer Tabriz but failed due to the emergence of the Gara Goyunlu state — the Black Sheep Turkomans — a new Turkish Dynasty in Azerbaijan.

Ibrahim, Ruler of Shirvan, then became gamekeeper turned poacher striking an alliance with his previous Georgian enemies, joining forces with Constantine I of Georgia to try and halt the Gara Goyunlu advance into the Caucasus. The new alliance failed to make headway and was roundly defeated in a titanic struggle at the Battle of Chalagan in 1412. Constantine, his brother David and Ibrahim were taken prisoner. The Georgian king was executed but Ibrahim managed to escape the executioner by paying a heavy bribe and he returned to Shirvan in the Spring of 1413 to live out his days.

Ibrahim was succeeded by his son Khalilullah I, who in turn was succeeded by his son Farrukh Yasser. These men presided over the most successful period in Shirvan's history — building the Palace of the Shirvanshahs — the largest monument of Azerbaijan architecture — which doubled as a burial site for the dynasty.

The peaceful, successful reigns came to an end as a result of religious strife.

The Shirvanshah rulers belonged to Islam's orthodox Sunni sector and opposed the Shi'a brand of Islam promulgated by the Safavid dynasty of Persia. The two clashed. In 1462, the Safavid leader — Sheikh Junayd — was killed in battle against the Shirvanshahs — an event which was branded into collective Safavid memory. The Safavids bided their time, built their strength and influence throughout southern Azerbaijan and, by 1500, seized the moment. Emboldened by a vengeful thirst, Shah Ismail I led the

Safavids and sacked Baku. Shah Ismail wrought vengeful humiliation on the Shirvans by exhuming the bodies of the Shirvanshahs and burning them. Thereafter the majority of Baku's population was forcibly converted to Shi'ism.

The vassal Shirvan staggered on until when, weakened by internal conflict and an uprising by wandering Sufi dervishes — known as Qalandari — the state became easy prey to Shah Ismail's son, Tahmasp I, who installed his brother, Alqas Mirza, as provincial Ruler.

The convoluted history of Azerbaijan entered another evolutionary era in the late 15th and early 16th centuries when Shah Ismail Khatayi, Uzun Hasan's grandson, took over leadership of the Agh Goyunlu — and continued his grandfather's work of building a Safavid state.

The Safavids were descended from a Sufi religious order which had openly converted to the Twelver denomination — one of three denominations — of Shi'ism and named for their adherence to the 12 Imams. Religion was an overriding influence of the Safavids. Many of them, most notably the Qizilbash Turks, believed in the mystical and esoteric nature of their Rulers and their relationship to the house of Ali, the fourth Caliph and husband of Fatima, the Prophet Mohammed's daughter. Their belief that their Rulers were direct descendants of Ali left them strongly disposed to fight for them. So it was that in 1501, the young Safavid prince, Ismail I, rallied his forces, unified all Azerbaijan lands in the north and south under his rule and created the united, centralised Safavid state with Tabriz as its capital and with Azerbaijani Turkic as its official language. Ismail was a complex character — a prolific Sufi poet writing, in Azerbaijani Turkic, under the pseudonym Khatayi and devoting many of his compositions to love, yet who also displayed a streak of bizarre cruelty. He soon proved a force to be reckoned with. Ismail's expansionist ambitions led him to invade the country's northwest where he sacked Baku and persecuted the Shirvanshahs. He went on to seize key commercial and political strongholds including Shiraz, Baghdad and Herat. In 1510 he moved against the Sunni Uzbeg tribe. In a battle near Merv, which two centuries earlier was reputed to be the largest city in the world, Ismail's forces ambushed some 17,000 Uzbeg warriors. The ruler, Muhammed Sheibani, was caught and killed when trying to escape and Ismail had his skull made into a jewelled drinking goblet.

But 13 proved to be unlucky for the expansionist Shah — and 13 years into his reign, the Ottomans determined to take him on headlong in order to halt the spread of Shi'ism. Ismail suffered a crushing defeat at the hands of the Ottomans at the 1514 Battle of Chaldiran, fought close to the modern-day Turkish city of Van. Ismail's 40,000 strong force was heavily outnumbered by the mammoth, 100,000 strong army of the Ottoman Sultan Selim I. The young Shah also made the mistake of relying on traditional weapons in his artillery whereas the Ottomans made headway with heavy artillery, complete with weapons utilising gunpowder. Ismail was wounded and almost captured — an incident which left him a shattered, broken man.

Selim I entered Tabriz, though a mutiny among his troops quickly forced him to withdraw — a fortunate occurrence which saved Ismail. Selim also took Ismail's favourite wife hostage, demanding huge concessions for her release. Ismail refused, retired to his palace and withdrew from active participation in the affairs of the state, leaving this to his minister, Mirza Shah-Hussayn. He is said to have died of a broken heart on May 23, 1524, at the early age of 36, never having seen his beloved wife again.

He was succeeded by his 10-year-old son Tahmasp I who was initially faced with uprisings among the ruling class Qizilbash tribesmen but was able to reassert his power on attaining adulthood.

Tahmasp's reign was marked by foreign threats, primarily from the Ottomans and the Uzbegs. Indeed so strong was the Ottoman threat that Tahmasp was forced to abandon Tabriz as his capital and decamp, instead, to the city of Qazvin deep in the Persian interior. It was during this period of Safavid history that the area today known as Iraq became part of the Ottoman Empire. In 1555, however, Tahmasp regularised relations with the Ottoman Empire through the Peace of Amasya which lasted for 30 years.

One of Tahmasp's more lasting achievements was his promotion of the Persian rug industry on a national scale — a move which went some way to countering the economic effects of the interruption of the Silk Road trade during the Ottoman wars.

The next major cultural milestone in the region's history came in the 1587 to 1630 reign of Shah Abbas I — perhaps the most prominent of the Safavid dynasty Rulers — who took over a substantially weakened Safavid Empire from his semi-blind father, Mohammed, who had allowed inner feuds to fracture his army.

It was under Abbas that the monarchy took on a distinctly Persian identity. Abbas attained the throne in 1588 by mounting a coup d'etat against his father whom he imprisoned. Determined to revive the fallen fortunes of his country, he signed a separate peace with the Ottomans, including the cessation of large areas of west and northwest Persia and then directed his efforts against the predatory Uzbegs. Within a decade Abbas launched a decisive offensive with an army made up of a cavalry of Christian Armenians,

Georgians and descendants of former Circassian prisoners of war, while Persian peasantry made up the infantry. Abbas won strong support among commoners with whom he spent a great deal of time in bazaars and other public places.

After a long and severe struggle, Abbas regained Mashhad and defeated the Uzbegs in a great battle near Herat in 1597. In the meantime, taking advantage of Tsar Ivan The Terrible's death in 1584, he gained the homage of the southern Caspian provinces which were previously dependent on Russia.

In 1592 Abbas moved his capital from Qazvin to the more central and more Persian Isfahan. Embellished by a magnificent series of new mosques, baths, colleges and caravansaries, Isfahan became one of the world's most beautiful cities.

Abbas launched a major overhaul of the armed forces with the help of the English gentleman of fortune, Robert Shirley, and his favourite chancellor Allahverdi Khan. Muskets and artillery were introduced and with his new army Abbas launched a campaign against the Ottomans in 1603, winning back previously seized territory. In 1605, following a victory at Basra, he extended his empire beyond the Euphrates. The Ottomans were compelled to cede Shirvan and Kurdistan in 1611. Hostilities ceased momentarily in 1614 with the Persian army at its peak.

The united armies of the Turks and Tatars were completely defeated in 1618 and Abbas made peace on very favourable terms. A few years later, in 1621, with the support of British ships, Abbas captured Hormuz from the Portuguese. Determined to control the Gulf trade routes, much commerce was diverted to the coastal town of Bandar Abbas which he had previously seized from the Portuguese in 1615 and had named after himself. The Gulf now opened to flourishing trade with Portuguese, Dutch, French, Spanish and British merchants, which were granted privileges.

In 1623, Abbas launched another attack on the Ottomans, who were preoccupied by wars with the European Hapsburgs, capturing Baghdad and much of Iraq. In 1638 however, the Ottomans retook Baghdad and the Persian-Ottoman border was settled.

Abbas' reign, with its military successes and efficient administrative system, raised Persia to the status of a great power. Abbas was a skilled diplomat, tolerant of his Christian subjects in Armenia and Georgia. He sent Robery Shirley to Italy, Spain and England to create a pact against the Ottomans.

Under Abbas, Isfahan became a centre of major architectural and artistic achievement. Great mosques and palaces were built and the artists of the Isfahan school which he patronised created some of the finest art in the region's history, including work by some of the most illustrious painters of the era — such as Reza Abbassi and Mohammed Qasim.

By the time Abbas died in 1629, his dominions extended from the Tigris to the Indus and he became a legendary historic figure, his reputation being tarnished only by deeds of tyranny and cruelty against his own family. Afraid of a family coup he imprisoned many of its members — a policy which resulted in a weakened succession. He killed his eldest son, Safi Mirza, leaving his throne to his grandson Safi which marked the beginning of the end of the Safavid Dynasty.

The dynastic collapse left a void filled by the pre-eminent Azerbaijan military leader Nadir Shah — 'The Second Alexander' — who founded the short-lived Turkish Afsharid Dynasty. Nadir was a former slave who rose to military leadership within the Afshar Turkoman tribe of a Safavid vassal state. He went on to have military control under Shah Tahmasp II. Nadir ruled as Regent of the infant Abbas III until 1736 when he had himself crowned Shah. In an ambitious military spree, he expanded the Safavid Empire taking control of Iran from the Afghans in 1729 and going on to conquer lands as far east as Delhi.

Nadir idolised the legendary Central Asian conquerors Genghis Khan and Emir Timur and imitated their military prowess and — especially later in his reign — their cruelty. Nadir's victories briefly made him the Middle East's most powerful sovereign, but his military spending had a ruinous effect on the economy. This last great Asian military conqueror built a huge empire — stretching from the Indus in what is now Pakistan to the Caucasus mountains in the north, to India in the east — but his reign was marked by remarkable cruelty.

The financial demands of his military ambition led him to extort excessive taxes which sparked revolts that he ruthlessly put down, building towers from his victims' skulls. In 1747, Nadir set off for Khorasan to wreak revenge on Kurdish rebels but already some of his weary officers were plotting. The mighty military leader's career ended when he was surprised in his sleep by a captain of the guards, and stabbed — but not before, according to legend, he had killed two of his assassins. Nadir was succeeded by his nephew — Adil Shah — the 'Righteous King' who was widely believed to have been involved in the assassination plot. Adil Shah was deposed within a year. A family feud broke out which led to provincial governors declaring independence and establishing their own states — Nadir Shah's vast empire fell into anarchy.

It was now the turn of an Azerbaijani Turkic Dynasty to take control of southern Azerbaijan and Iran and reassert sovereignty over territories in Georgia and the Caucasus. In 1796 Agha Mohammad Khan was formally crowned Shah. The Qajar's quickly came up against the mighty Russian Empire as both determined to occupy the southern Caucasus. Azerbaijan was now a bloody battleground for the two superpowers.

The political map was changing. Azerbaijan was split in half — a pawn in the ambitions of two opposing empires. The north of the country fell under Russian control and the south under Iranian jurisdiction. Russia began its regime with a policy of ousting the Muslim population from the Caucasus, preparing the ground for a popular expansionist move on the south. Russia sought its popular base among the Christians of the Caucasus — Armenians and Georgians — and it began to forcibly convert the local Muslim population.

The Tsarist government strengthened its Christian-domination by resettling Russians in its Azerbaijan territories. Armenians settled in the mountain regions of Karabakh, Iravan and Nakhchivan. Imperial Russia created an 'Armenian' province in the west of Azerbaijan, bordering Turkey — establishing a 'Christian' buffer from the Ottoman Empire. The independent Albanian church was then quickly sub ordinated to the Armenian-Gregorian church and Armenians were armed against the Turkish-Muslim population.

Georgian feudal lords quickly seized the advantage and began to convert the Muslim population to Christian orthodoxy. The Tsarist regime met with some local resistance which it solved by the distribution of confiscated Muslim land to Christian converts and the granting of special privileges.

Ancient Albanian churches were turned into orthodox places of worship while the Russian Caucasian governor ordered the building of new orthodox cathedrals.
In the south, the situation was directly the reverse under the reactionary leadership of the Shah. Here Christians were forced to become Muslims and so Azerbaijan suddenly found its former enemies allying in a bid to crush the liberation movements which worked underground throughout the country.
But nationalistic fervour was not easy to dispel and rebellions regularly broke out in both north and south.

Chapter Five

23 Months of Freedom

Nationality is the miracle of political independence; race is the principle of physical analogy.
— Benjamin Disraeli, British statesman

By the end of the 19th century the Russian Empire spread across some 22,400,000 square kilometres, or almost one sixth of the Earth's landmass. Its only rival in size at the time was the British Empire. Azerbaijan was a mostly unwilling constituent of a Russian Empire described in the *Almanach de Gotha* for 1910 as "a constitutional monarchy under an autocratic Tsar."

Tsar Nicholas II and his nation entered World War One with enthusiasm and patriotism, but this would prove the undoing of the Russian Empire, placing strain on an entity that was already in turmoil. On March 3, 1917, a strike was organised in a factory in the capital, Saint Petersburg. Within a week nearly all workers in Saint Petersburg were striking and riots had broken out. When Nicholas II dismissed the Duma, and ordered strikers to return to work, his orders triggered the February Revolution.

In 1917, the Russian Caucasus Front collapsed following the abdication of the Tsar and in March 1917, the Special Transcaucasian Committee was established to fill an administrative gap. But this stop-gap measure failed and led to terrible bloodshed. This and the instability caused by civil war within the Russian Empire would instigate a period of hell in Azerbaijan. This culminated with the so-called March Days of March 1918, inter-ethnic genocide that resulted in the massacre of between 2,000 and 12,000 Azerbaijanis and other Muslims in Baku and other locations within Baku governorate.

Armenian and Muslim militia engaged in armed confrontation, with the Bolsheviks on the Armenian side and non-Azerbaijani groups following the Bolsheviks. In addition to the thousands of deaths, thousands more Muslims were expelled from Baku, while the rest went underground.

The Armenians may have wanted revenge for events in Turkey, but the Bolsheviks had their own agenda. In his book, *Year One of the Russian Revolution*, author Victor Serge presented a Bolshevik version of events when he stated: "The Soviet at Baku, led by Shaumyan, was meanwhile making itself the Ruler of the area, discreetly, but unmistakably."

On May 26, 1918, the shortlived Transcaucasian Democratic Federative Republic also collapsed and its bodies were dissolved. The Azerbaijani division of this was renamed the Azerbaijani National Council (ANC). The Azerbaijani National Council immediately proclaimed the Azerbaijani Democratic Republic on May 28, 1918, and began forging national institutions. The Council was eventually abolished with the opening of a national Parliament on December 7, 1918.

The Azerbaijani Democratic Republic would exist for 23 months — between May 28, 1918 and April 28, 1920 and attempted to steer the fledgling nation during a period of grim regional turmoil, events such as the post-World War period, continuous strife with Armenia and repercussions from the collapse of the Russian Empire. These events, and others would lead to the arrival of the Soviet Army as the newly constituted Soviet Union was forged.

The fathers of the Azerbaijan Democratic Republic were an extraordinary bunch. Figures like Mammad Hasan Hajinski, Mammed Amin Rasulzade, Alimardan Topchubashov and Fatali-khan Khoyski were determined to forge a true democracy. The model they chose was the first secular state in the Orient, with the first Western style Parliament and a formal Cabinet of Ministers. Such institutions and powers were unheralded in the Muslim world. The capital of the state was in Ganja, as Baku was still, at that time, under the Bolsheviks.

Khoyski became Azerbaijan's first Prime Minister. Born in Shaki, he studied at the Law Faculty of the Moscow University, from which he graduated in 1901, and would serve the Republic well. Khoyski was later murdered in Tbilisi in 1920 by Aram Yerganian, part of an Armenian assassination programme.

The Khoyski government moved quickly to establish the nation. On June 4 a Peace and Friendship Agreement was signed with Turkey, and Turkey agreed to help defend the Azerbaijani Democratic Republic. Over ensuing months, Turkish support was fundamental to preventing Communist troops from Baku overrunning Azerbaijan, particularly during a June 16 offensive on Ganja and the Geokchay Battle, when Azerbaijani and Turkish troops defeated the Red Army and their Armenian allies.

On July 31, Azerbaijan's integrity was almost completed when Soviet power was ended in Baku. Yet conflict continued, as skirmishing rumbled on between Azerbaijani and Armenian forces in Nakhchivan, Zangezur and Karabakh. One of the biggest Azerbaijani military failures was in Zangezur, a strip of land that connected Azerbaijan to Nakhchivan, which was lost to Armenian troops. There were ethnic tensions in Karabakh, resulting in riots, although a November 23, 1919 ceasefire agreement, hammered out between Azerbaijan and Armenia, held reasonably well.

On September 9, nationhood was enshrined through the unveiling of a flag comprising of three stripes: blue, representing Turkic ethnicity, red, both for the sacrifices made to achieve statehood and modernisation of society and development of democracy, and green, the colour of Islam, along with a crescent and eight-pointed star. Six days later, Azerbaijani troops entered Baku and the state's capital was officially moved from Ganja to Baku.

Weeks later, the Azerbaijan Democratic Republic enshrined its democracy when, on December 7, Parliament established a provisional legislative body. Parliament would consist of 120 members and was inclusive to all sections of society as it was then. While the majority, Azerbaijanis, had 80 seats, there were guarantees of representation for Armenians (21) and Russians (10), along with a statutory seat for one Jew, one German, one Pole and one Georgian, while five seats were assigned to representatives of professional groups.

On December 7, 1918, the opening session of this body represented a first of its kind in the Islamic world. During its brief life, this body would realise some unique achievements for the era. Members decided on suffrage for women, the first Muslim nation to grant women equal political rights with men, a decision that also preceded Britain and the United States. Members also voted to establish Baku State University.

The first significant foray of the fledgling nation was to France. The Paris Peace Conference was convened in January 1919, in Versailles, to establish terms for peace after World

War One. Nearly 30 nations participated, although Great Britain, France, the United States and Italy dominated.

They would forge the Treaty of Versailles, which included a plan to form the League of Nations, forerunner of the United Nations. Also on the table were a series of controversial agreements on post-war redistribution of territories. Italian demands on the Adriatic were particularly difficult, while negotiations were also weakened by the absence of other important nations. Russia had fought as one of the Allies until December 1917, when its new Bolshevik government withdrew. The Allies got their revenge by excluding the Bolshevik government, citing a Bolshevik decision to repudiate Russia's financial debts to the Allies and to publish the texts of secret agreements. Also excluded from Paris were Germany, Austria-Hungary, Turkey and Bulgaria.

Yet despite the controversies it was clear that the pre-war world map required drastic revision. Azerbaijan's delegation comprised of Abbas Atamalibeyov, Mammad Maharramov, Alimardan Topchubashov, Akbar Agha Sheikhulislamov, Jeyhun Hajibeyli and Miryagub Mirmehdiyev. Among others, the group had a meeting with U.S. President Woodrow Wilson.

On January 11, 1920, the Paris Peace Conference, with the Treaty of Versailles, accorded *de facto* recognition of the independence of the Azerbaijan Democratic Republic, with Baku as its capital.

But the emotional boost that Versailles provided was brief. By 1920, the whole situation transformed, the fledgling country finding itself caught up in an increasingly volatile situation between Russia and Persia, both eyeing Baku's important oil fields as well as a geopolitical desire to extend their influence. Sandwiched between these two giants, the Azerbaijan Democratic Republic (ADR) was a minnow.

Russia and Persia both had vast armed forces, while ADR boasted only a small national army and an unarmed police force.

Between January and March 1920 the Red Army was on the move and reaching the northern borders of Azerbaijan, while in Baku the Communist Party of Azerbaijan was formed on February 1 with a minority Armenian, Anastas Mikoian, one of its leading players, setting the scene for a Moscow-led government once the inevitable happened.

Azerbaijan's last stand came in March and early April when an Azerbaijan Democratic Republic volunteer army was routed by the 11th Red Army. On April 1 the Cabinet resigned and three weeks later the Red Army entered Baku. Soviet power was declared in Baku and by May 20 the remainder of Azerbaijan was occupied. A fleeting uprising in Ganja was suppressed with up to 40,000 Azerbaijanis massacred.

Soviet historians positioned Moscow as the saviour of Azerbaijan, pointing out that 18th century Azerbaijan was devastated by Persians and appealed to the Tsar asking for help. The Soviet-era tome *'History of Azerbaijan'*, published in 1960, stated in its second volume that: "The joining of Azerbaijan to Russia rescued the Azerbaijani people from the danger of enslavement by the backward Iran. Turkey joined Russia to promote the political, economic and cultural development of Azerbaijan". The Communist government in Baku would weed out anyone who did not toe that line and accept that 'the eternal happiness of Azerbaijan is associated with Russia'.

The Azerbaijan Democratic Republic, a first successful attempt to establish a democratic and secular republic in the Muslim world, had flowered all too briefly. Over 23 months two million Azerbaijanis had tasted freedom. During the decades of foreign dominance that followed, the belief in an independent future did not die.

The shortlived nation's motto was *'Bir kere yükselen bayraq, bir daha enmez!'* The flag once raised will never fall! This would not be entirely true. But those who believed in a free, independent Azerbaijan folded up their Azerbaijan Democratic Republic flags, hid them away from the prying eyes of the Soviets, and waited.

It would be 1991 before the Azerbaijan flag would reappear in history.

Chapter Six

'Brotherly Love'

Anyone who doesn't regret the passing of the Soviet Union has no heart. Anyone who wants it restored has no brains.
— Vladimir Putin, Russian statesman

Russian history denotes its influence as akin to 'brotherly love' and so it was that the cable from Azrevkom, the supreme state body charged with running Azerbaijan on April 26, 1920, requesting "fraternal assistance", was met with a resounding affirmative. Indeed the Red Army was just around the corner.

The 11th Red Army, a distinctly Russian division, arrived in Baku on April 28. At its head was Politburo member and friend of Joseph Stalin, Grigori 'Sergo' Ordzhonikidze and the administration supremo Sergey Kirov. Both men were bent on Sovietisation.

Russia claimed the setting up of the Independent Soviet Republic of Azerbaijan was a 'voluntary' affair only made possible by solid Azerbaijani support. It cited the backing of the Azrevkom Chairman, Dr Nariman Narimanov, and other prominent Communists. Most were not even in Baku when Azrevkom was formed, with Narimanov only arriving in the capital on May 16 to assume his Presidency.

Azrevkom quickly evolved into the Sovnarkom, yet power was really in the hands of the army's Revolutionary Military Soviet and most importantly, the Russian Communist Party

Bolshevik — the Kavbiuro — led by Ordzhonikidze who carried out Lenin's and Stalin's dictates.

The Kavbiuro, in which Azerbaijanis were a minority, took a hard-line totalitarian stance.

"Whatever form Soviet power assumes in the Caucasus, we cannot tolerate here the creation of any isolated or independent communist parties," proclaimed the largely Russian and Armenian-led Kavbiuro. But much of the population disagreed.

It was when, having secured Baku, the Red Army moved out of the capital to spread Sovietisation, that it encountered strong opposition — which Moscow quickly dubbed 'counter revolutionary uprisings'. The Battle for Azerbaijan had begun.

Drama unfolded in Ganja, the second largest city in North Azerbaijan during May and June 1920. Greatly outnumbered loyalists led by Colonel Jihangir Kazimbekov attempted to defend the city against a Red Army siege. Much of the loyalists' undoing came about because of their misguided mercy. A Red Army unit it had captured and imprisoned inside the city, escaped to mount a significant internal rear attack. Over 1,000 loyalists died as the Red Army held sway.

But Ganja was only the start of armed resistance to Bolshevik takeover. Uprisings broke out in Karabakh and Zakatala, which resulted in hundreds facing firing squads or being exiled to Siberia. Revolts broke out up and down the country and continued for another four years.

To bed down the Soviet system, the Bolsheviks dispatched experienced party workers to establish local revkoms and kombeds (Committees of the Poor) in towns and villages. One of the most notorious of the Bolshevik faithful was Sultan Mejid Efendiyev, an Azerbaijani Turk, who moved to stamp Soviet authority in the Ganja region. He quickly seized land, nationalised industry, set up state farms and nationalised grain distribution to counter, what the Soviets saw as attempts by local landowners and loyalists to destroy the economy and undermine Bolshevik rule. This policy was an overwhelming success for the Soviets. Within two months there were revkoms and kombedi in 16 towns, 46 districts and 435 villages throughout the country, all strictly enforcing a grain requisitioning policy. Any opposition was dealt with by summary execution with the local populace threatened with huge fines for sheltering any loyalist sympathisers.

Meanwhile, the Azrevkom was nationalising the economy. Industry, agriculture, commerce, communications, the media and transport fell under state control. Oil was requisitioned for use in Russia, Armenia and Georgia. An economic recovery which had commenced during independence quickly evaporated. Even small pockets of success, such as increased cotton production in the Ganja region, failed to benefit the populace as central government acquired the 'harvest,' at fixed prices, as with grain.

While some news of these happenings filtered through to the outside world — the human tragedy brought on by a mammoth exodus of refugees and isolation of nomads went largely unnoticed.

The refugee problem began as Armenians from Julfa looked for territory in Zangezur from where thousands of Azerbaijanis had uprooted to Karabakh, all exacerbating already critical regional food shortages. The nomads' animal herds began to die off as they were prevented from summer pasturing in Dagestan and their owners also began to succumb to famine.

Politically, Azerbaijan's main challenge was endeavouring to be recognised as an independent Soviet republic. However, all attempts were being stifled by emissaries sent from Moscow. The degree of 'independence' that Soviet Azerbaijan possessed at the time can be illustrated with the speech of Joseph Stalin at a meeting of the Transcaucasia Bureau on November 8, 1920, during which he stated: "You are surrounded by bourgeois states, which agitate that 'Russians came here and took everything'. Now it is of benefit for us to demonstrate Azerbaijan's independence. But a communist can never be truly independent from a communist."

This was a task complicated by the Bolshevik conquest of neighbouring Armenia and Georgia, which relied heavily on food supplies from Russia and oil from Azerbaijan. A telegraph from Lenin to Ordzhonikidze dealt another blow to Azerbaijani ambitions.

"I demand urgently the creation of a regional economic organ for all Transcaucasia," it read.

Ordzhonikidze moved quickly to meet his master's demand. Regionalisation of the rail network and trade began. Each republic was forbidden to use free Azerbaijani oil as foreign currency — but Azerbaijan and Georgia were ordered to supply Armenia free-of-charge — this when around a fifth of Azerbaijan's own population were on the point of starvation. Narimanov's opposition to regionalisation fell on deaf ears.

More reforms followed. The Georgian State Bank became a bank for all Transcaucasia as regional unification took hold. Tense territorial border issues were also dealt with as the Turks became occupied with their own battle for independence. The thorny issue of the mountainous region of Karabakh became the centre of political intrigue which rolled on as moves were afoot to create the Transcaucasian Soviet Federated Socialist Republic (TSFSR). Using the opportunity during the ongoing disorder, Armenians, with the participation of Stalin, raised the issue of Nagorno-Karabakh at the Caucasian Bureau of the Communist Party on July 4, 1921. After long debates, the Caucasian Bureau passed Karabakh on to the Armenian S.S.R. But after Narimanov's strong objections, a day later Nagorno-Karabakh was returned to Azerbaijan S.S.R. with broad regional autonomy.

Opposition to the swift establishment of the TSFSR came expectedly, from Narimanov and unexpectedly from Lenin, who told Stalin that it was "premature." Nevertheless, the TSFSR campaign began in earnest in December 1921 with a four-month target deadline for creation.

Federalist supporters, led by Kirov, used allegations of "ultra-nationalism" to shut down opponents and said proof of communism in Azerbaijan was contingent upon the acceptance of the federation.

Not surprisingly, federalists won the day and the process of establishing the TSFSR began on March 12, 1922. While Narimanov ranked among the federation's Soviet, his constant opposition had not gone unnoticed — and by one of the most powerful men of the day — Lenin.

Narimanov was actually in Moscow, sent there by Lenin, preparing for a Western-inspired economic summit in Genoa, when the TSFSR was inaugurated.

Once in Genoa, he remained in the Northern Italian seaport city until the end of May, well out of the way in the critical formative months of the federation.

The establishment process rolled on. The federation's jurisdiction, it was determined, would cover military, finance, foreign affairs, trade, communications and transportation. In December, the entity officially came into being just as the U.S.S.R. constitution was drafted — the independent republics were no more.

With the U.S.S.R. constitution in full swing, all-encompassing central planning became the order of the day with economic and budget decisions emanating from Moscow. Few Azerbaijanis held posts in federal government. Narimanov was on the Presidium though he was moved to Moscow in 1923. Instead Georgians dominated and often held the Presidency, though a small group of young Azerbaijani communists who made their careers under the emergence of the wider state.

The federation was the organ responsible for distribution of regional resources for the benefit of the entire U.S.S.R.. Oil was Azerbaijan's wealth and its distribution relied heavily on the railroad. So, in 1926 a major overhaul of the rail network was given the go-ahead — though this slowed significantly in just three years. Nevertheless an improved rail network carried Azerbaijani oil through the Soviet republics and Russian troops into Azerbaijan.

As central hold deepened, Narimanov, now under watchful eyes in Moscow, continued to be a thorn in the side of the Soviets. He penned a memorandum to Stalin accusing Ordzhonikidze of getting him out of the way so that discussion on Azerbaijan's interests would cease. Azerbaijanis, said Narimanov, would never respond to foreign forces and would never forget the lack of regard for their interests. A year later, Narimanov died in suspicious circumstances with his death attributed to 'heart failure,' his body conveniently cremated and his ashes interred in the Kremlin Wall as an 'honour' to Azerbaijan.

Dissatisfied with the nationalistic activities of Narimanov, Moscow lost confidence in local personnel. Non-nationals were brought to the leadership of Azerbaijan S.S.R. in 1921. The Azerbaijan Communist Party was ruled by Russians. From 1921 to 1926, leadership of the party was granted to Moscow-appointed Sergei Mironovich Kirov.

After Kirov's promotion, the Azerbaijan Communist Party was run by three secretaries. Despite the Azerbaijani nationality of two of the secretaries, the trio were led by an Armenian.

The year 1929 and the early-1930s marked the culmination of Moscow's intrusion, a succession of 'foreign' Azerbaijan Communist Party heads, most of whom trampled over local norms and sensibilities. The result was a lack of leadership and increasing frictions, which led to problems in forging coherent leadership. Finally, in December 1933, Azerbaijani legislator Mirjafar Bagirov was appointed to the post of the leader of Azerbaijan Communist Party.

With the structure for organisational control complete, Moscow turned its attention to 'softer' control methods. Language, literature and education came under the microscope as the Soviets established a 'cultural policy' aimed at shaping future communists. In a move dubbed "progressive", use of the Latin alphabet was banned in favour of the Russian-advanced Cyrillic script. The change of alphabet use had a knock-on effect on language use. An official vocabulary was introduced with Russian words replacing Turkish, Persian or Arabic equivalents. Use of the names of the individual nations was outlawed with mention of being a 'Turk' viewed as dangerous nationalism. Russian "proletarian" literature was promoted as the only literature suitable for the new federal order.

A new "cultural" policy reached out into schools where communist ideology, class struggle and proletarian leadership were the focal point of learning and curriculum texts followed Moscow's templates.

And while Moscow-influenced measures were being put into place throughout the federation, the people of the Karabakh mountains found themselves at the centre of an autonomous administration. Land and water was to belong to existing residents — which robbed the area's traditional nomadic population of their heritage and legacy rights.

By 1936 the federation had outlived its usefulness and with nationalistic tendencies all routed, each republic became part of the U.S.S.R. under Stalin's constitution. A new Azerbaijan constitution was quickly put into place which, while proclaiming the power of the republic over its own territory, reiterated Moscow's overall control, sweetened by guarantees of freedom and autonomy.

So, in 1937, the new Azerbaijan S.S.R. constitution declared the republic as a socialist state of workers and peasants with its nationals now full U.S.S.R. citizens. The new state was to be quickly caught up in the 'Great Purge.'

Azerbaijanis had become used to 'terror' as the Soviets had continued their hunt for, and extermination of, "nationalists", but nothing compared to the 'Great Purge' in Azerbaijan which broke out in 1937-with many of the victims being loyal Soviet supporters.

Azerbaijan Red Army units were at the heart of the purge, which spread throughout political and intellectual circles. Within a year, almost all former and current members of the Azerbaijan S.S.R. Sovnarkom, old and young alike, had been executed.

From summer 1936 to 1939, over 20,000 people were arrested in Azerbaijan S.S.R. Because the decision of courts applied not only to the prisoners, but also to their families, the overall number of victims of the 1937 to 1939 repression was over 80,000. Poets, writers and intellectuals all became victims of Stalin's paranoia which had now spread throughout the U.S.S.R.. Some were tried and executed, others simply disappeared and yet others died in the slave conditions of Siberian prison camps or were exiled with their families to that notorious Northern Asian region, their names now blackened in the history of their homeland — a bitter legacy which would take decades to revert. Noted playwright Huseyn Javid and poet Mikail Mushvig of Azerbaijan were also among those arrested during this period.

The onset of World War Two brought respite from Stalin's purges. Azerbaijan was dragged into the war when Russia entered the fray on June 22, 1941, to fend off German ambitions of 'acquiring' Baku oil through occupation. Azerbaijan rallied to the cause supplying men, machines — and vital energy resources. Its contribution, though, failed to be recognised in U.S.S.R. accounts.

From 1941 Baku was a major Soviet centre for the production of fuel and weaponry, providing, during the war, over 70 per cent of Soviet oil used by the Soviets and around 85 per cent of its aviation fuel and lubricating oils. Aside from this 300,000 Azerbaijanis fought within the Soviet armed forces. Half of them — some 150,000 Azerbaijanis — died in the conflict. The highest national award — Hero of Soviet Union — was conferred upon 126 Azerbaijanis.

Perhaps best remembered today is Major General Hazi Aslanov, who was in charge of Soviet armoured brigades, and was twice awarded Hero of Soviet Union. Today, the monument symbolising World War Two and the Great Patriotic War for Azerbaijan is a monument of Aslanov, erected in the Martyr's Alley of Baku.

The country also became something of a war-time bread basket with an additional 140,000 hectares of land given over to agriculture, women and children put to work in the fields and refineries while their menfolk fought the Nazi threat.

Moscow used its extensive propaganda experience to rally people to its cause. Traditional — nationalistic style — folklore songs were reintroduced and the entire theme of the campaign took on a 'defend your homeland' tone. All sections of the community were mobilised to the war effort. The atheist Soviet leadership used religion in their propaganda and co-opted religious leaders into this. Patriotic wartime stories became the stuff of school lessons.

The Germans used the inherent anti-Russian feelings of their Caucasian prisoners to create special army units which were then given the task of trying to rout their occupier in defence of 'The Fatherland.' Following the war men from these units, who were returned to their homeland, were executed, while others made their way to Europe and America to form significant immigrant communities.

With the war won, Russia's task was to reassert its control over its republics. In what must have been a bewildering about-face, the fight against religion was restored. It should be noted that because of the temporary freedom of religious policy, it was impossible to directly quash it. In order to systematise religious activity, the Caucasian Muslims Ecclesiastical Office was set up in 1947.

At the end of the war, Azerbaijan faced another territorial crisis. On November 28, 1945, the First Secretary of Armenian S.S.R. wrote to Stalin insisting on the annexation of Nagorno-Karabakh to Armenia. His argument centred on the unavailability of good quality education for Armenians and strength of economic ties with Armenia.

On December 10, 1945, the First Secretary of Azerbaijani S.S.R., Mirjafar Baghirov, recalled the history of the Karabakh region and stated that if Karabakh was to be annexed by Armenia, then he would seek the Armenian regions of Azizbayov, Vedi and Qarabaglar — each with a majority Azerbaijani population and bordering Azerbaijan S.S.R. (which was not the case with Karabakh and Armenia) — as well as the Borchali region of Georgia and Darband city in the Dagestan Republic of RSFSR.

The implications of the Armenian demands were clear; the borders of the entire South Caucasus region would have to be redrawn. Moscow backed down at this very dangerous suggestion.

Stalin's death in 1953 brought another roller-coaster ride to Azerbaijan. The Chairman of the Azerbaijan Council of Ministers and First Secretary of the country's Communist Party, Baghirov, was sacked from all his posts and arrested. The former Chairman and his so-called "accomplices" were denounced and tried on a variety of charges resulting from the previous purges. Baghirov and five accomplices were found guilty. He and three of his erstwhile colleagues were executed by firing squad while the remaining two received lengthy jail sentences with hard labour.

Azerbaijan — with a potential leadership stock decimated by purges and war — now turned to academic Imam Dashdemiroglu Mustafayev, a little known plant geneticist, as First Secretary. He inherited a somewhat different scenario than that of his predecessor.

In 1955 the U.S.S.R. government granted the republics greater autonomy in labour, wages, agriculture, income and expenditure. A measure of judicial independence, as well as responsibility for natural resources, was devolved from Moscow. The Soviets also moved to demonstrate their support of Islam sending Soviet-trained Muslim leaders on the Hajj pilgrimage to Mecca — a move which coincided with a campaign to sell Soviet-made weaponry to Arab nations. Jailed or exiled academics, even those who had been executed having fallen victim to Stalin's purges, were exonerated.

Mustafayev, though, embarked on policies that led to his downfall. He backed the migration of Azerbaijanis into Baku, altering the city's demographics. The academic-turned-leader fought a head-on battle with liberal reforming Soviet leader Nikita Kruschev to retain the autonomy of the Azerbaijan Oil Ministry.

Mustafayev met with limited success, but battling with Moscow was eventually his undoing. He succeeded in having the Republic's constitution amended so that Azerbaijani was proclaimed the official language. It was agreed in Baku that Azerbaijan was right to do this, especially when the Georgian and Armenian S.S.R.s pronounced their own languages as official in their 1937 Constitutions. Azerbaijan had not been given the same. Consequently, and without the official consent of Moscow, this historical decision was made.

Mustafayev and his supporters may have got away with this. But emboldened by any lack of admonishment from Moscow, Soviet enforcement of Russian as the language of education was challenged. Kruschev could not allow such a declaration of independence and Mustafayev's days as First Secretary were over.

His immediate successor, Veli Akhundov, was a medical doctor and slavishly followed Moscow's line. Akhundov was very cautious. For a decade, his weakness led to Azerbaijan's diminishing stature in the Soviet pyramid.

Armenia capitalised on this. In May 1969, the Presidium of the Supreme Soviet of Azerbaijan S.S.R., adopted a decision to carve 2,000 hectares of land off Azerbaijan and give this to Armenia.

Before this could actually happen, in July 1969 Akhundov was deposed on charges of corruption — a hallmark of the Kruschev era. In his decade-long reign, he had made little headway on crucial issues such as Baku's serious shortage of fresh water.

Membership of the Communist Party had increased among Azerbaijanis — largely because professional promotion was dependent upon a party card. But during Akhundov's tenure, serious social problems emerged — youth violence and extensive drug abuse.

The General Secretariat post then fell to a different type of man altogether. Heydar Aliyev was promoted to power in July of 1969. He worked to annul the decision on the 2,000 hectares and brought a different style of leadership to Azerbaijan S.S.R..

Much would change under a fresh, strong style of leadership.

Chapter Seven

Heydar Aliyev…

Wealth and children are the adornment of life.
— Holy Koran

Nakhchivan is a landlocked exclave of Azerbaijan covering some 5,300 square kilometres and sharing borders with Turkey, Iran and Armenia. It is a land of Biblical reference. Johann Heinrich Hübschmann, an eminent 19th century German philologist, believed that Nakhchivan meant "the place of descent", a Biblical reference to the descent of Noah's Ark on Mount Agridag, the tallest peak in Turkey, 32 kilometres from the Armenian border.

Claudius Ptolemaeus, the great Roman intellectual and geographer, known in English as Ptolemy, referred to the region as Naxuana. Medieval Arab chronicles referred to "Nashava", while opinion in Nakhchivan contends that the name is derived from the Persian word Naghsh-e Jahan, meaning 'Image of the World,' a reference to the beauty of the region.

Artifacts discovered in Nakhchivan show that man has existed there since the Neolithic Age. This is also called the New Stone Age and was a period of fast development in human technology. The Neolithic Age is generally considered to have begun around 9500 BC in and around Jericho, in the West Bank, Palestine. Neolithic culture is defined by its farming, when men pioneered the use of wild cereals, techniques that evolved into proper farming and the use of domesticated animals.

In pre-Islamic, pre-Azerbaijan times, Nakhchivan fell under control of a variety of empires. Nakhchivan was considered Mannaean territory, an ancient people who lived in the lands of present-day Iran, between the 10th to 7th centuries BC. Around the mid 9th century BC it was part of the Urartu Empire, an Iron Age Kingdom, while later Nakhchivan fell under the Medes, an ancient Iranian people who were part of the first wave of Persian tribes, in the late second millennium BC, as the Bronze Age collapsed.

In 333 BC Alexander the Great crossed the Cilician Gates, met and defeated the main Persian army under the command of Darius III and then swept across the region to become self-proclaimed 'King of Asia'. In a separate three-year campaign, Alexander swept through Media, Parthia, the lands of modern Afghanistan (Aria, Drangiana, Arachosia and Bactria) and Scythia.

In 323 BC Alexander passed away, his empire quickly breaking up. Macedonia had a brief interest in Nakhchivan and the Orontid Dynasty sought control, but the area quickly fell to Antiochus III the Great and his Seleucid Empire.

The instability of the times meant that this did not remain the case. The Sassanid Empire, the last pre-Islamic Iranian Empire, took power. Shapur II the Great, ninth King of the Empire, from 309 to 379, deported 16,000 Jewish families and thousands of others between 360 and 370.

The Roman Empire took Nakhchivan briefly, between 623 and 640, before the Arabs arrived. They took firm hold of Nakhchivan, creating its Islamic roots. For the next millennium, Nakhchivan would be fought over and settled as the balance of power between empires ebbed and flowed. The one constant, or emerging trend, seems to be that Nakhchivan increasingly became wedded to Islam and the political pull of Baku grew strong. Nakhchivan was an important part of ancient Azerbaijani lands like the Atabeg Eldanizes state and Agh Goyunlu. Nakhchivan became Azerbaijani, within the scope of Azerbaijan's own position as part of more contemporary empires. The final Russo-Persian War and the Treaty of Turkmenchay saw Nakhchivan become a Russian possession in 1828. In July 1920, the Red Army invaded and occupied, declaring the creation of a Nakhchivan Autonomous Soviet Socialist Republic with "close ties" to the Azerbaijan S.S.R..

Two citizens of the newly created Nakhchivan Autonomous Soviet Socialist Republic were Alirza and Izzet Aliyev. The family were not well-to-do. Indeed they were very working class.

Alirza, the man of the house, through the first half of his adult life had worked in Baku, a labourer in the oil fields in a variety of seasonal jobs. The late 1900s was an era before mechanisation — and safety. It was back-breaking work, with poor health conditions, long hours and poor pay. But Alirza knew he was well off.

Many men did not come back. Deaths were a common occurrence during that period. For many men in Nakhchivan, the lure of regular work and regular pay would separate them from their families for long stretches, sometimes for many months at a time.

The loss of the man of the house for an extended period, chasing the lure of petro-rubles, was a hard blow to any household. But the technology of the day meant that men working in the oil fields were, literally, at the well head. Many did not return at all.

There was a tradition in Nakhchivan that during a 40-day mourning period, a household kept a black 'X' painted on its door, to signify a family in mourning. The scar of an 'X', each one representing a family thrown into financial destitution through their loss, also represented a generation of one-parent families scraping to get by in an era where there was no social system. The oil companies, who were making fortunes, did nothing other than send due salary. Under the Soviet system there was no discernible difference.

Communities rallied round to help the families of those claimed by the oil fields, but even in the tight knit communities of those days there was not much that could be done. Instead it was the kin of those who died that suffered.

For Izzet, Alirza's wife, the time that her husband was in Baku must have been like that of a military wife during a conflict. A knock on the door could well signify the arrival of news that a well-head had blown, effectively also blowing apart a family with it. She was, understandably, fearful.

"She did not have any choice, neither did my grandfather because the family was very poor," says Ilham. "When my grandfather died he was still young. She was not in a terrible situation, because of his hard work, but she did encounter difficulty because of the social situation…"

Alirza did not die in an accident however. By the time of his death he had left the oilfields permanently. The first railway in the territory of Nakhchivan was the "Armenia-Nakhchivan-Julfa" route, which was opened in 1906. In 1924 another railway was built between the stations of Mingevan and Julfa, which linked the Baku-Armenia main line.

Nakhchivan did not have many economic advantages, but one of the area's best employers was the railway system.

Rail had begun to dominate trade and transportation modes. Thousands of citizens discovered new employment, labouring long hours by clearing the land, laying the road tracks, building bridges, tunnels, train cars and the locomotive engines required for its successful completion. Others were required as factory workers, engineers, conductors, depot builders, morse code operators and hundreds of other related and interrelated jobs.

Alirza initially found a full time job on the construction side. Conditions were hard and the work back-breaking and very dangerous. This included clearing the land of trees, hand drilling rock with short and long metal drills and then blasting the rock with the unstable black gunpowder, to the hauling of this dirt and blasted fill. Tasks also included laying of bed grade and rock for the road, cutting wood for the rail ties and setting the steel rails in place and driving the spikes and securing the steel rails that carried locomotives. At every stage there were inherent dangers.

Later he moved on to a post actually within railway operations, working as a baggage handler and later on as a fireman on board the locomotives themselves. Firemen in the steam era were responsible for the mechanical care of the boiler and its appliances and they fuelled and watered the engine outside of terminals.

Alirza was working on the railways when, in 1923, the couple were blessed with a son. In May 1923 Lithuania seized and annexed Memel, troops from France and Belgium occupied the Ruhr area in order to force Germany to pay its reparation payments and *Time* magazine was published for the first time. Elsewhere during that year, in Mexico, Pancho Villa was assassinated, Gustav Stresemann was made Chancellor of Germany, Miguel Primo de Rivera took over Spain while, in Japan, the Great Kant earthquake devastated Tokyo and Yokohama, killing an estimated 142,800 people.

Just four years after the end of the devastating World War One, Germany began to show signs of its slide towards a second global conflict. Munich witnessed the Beer Hall Putsch, led by Adolf Hitler and his Nazis. It was unsuccessful, but Hitler's popularist touch was already evident.

Closer to Nakhchivan, in Moscow, Vladimir Lenin suffered his third stroke, which rendered him bedridden and unable to speak. As a result, he retired as Chairman of the Soviet government. In July, the storming of Ayan in Siberia ended the Yakut Revolt and brought to an end the Russian Civil War.

On another border, in April, the Turkish Council was founded by Mustafa Kemal Atatürk while, in July, the Treaty of Lausanne set the boundaries of modern Turkey, an agreement signed in Switzerland by Greece, Bulgaria and other countries that fought in World War One. In October Ankara replaced Istanbul as the capital of Turkey and the nation became a republic as the Ottoman Empire was dissolved.

In the corridors of power around the world that year, Grigory Petrovsky, a revolutionary of Ukrainian origin, was serving in Moscow as Chairman of the Central Executive Committee of the U.S.S.R.. Andrew Bonar Law resided in Downing Street. In Washington, Warren G. Harding, 29th President of the United States, passed away in office and was succeeded by Calvin Coolidge.

Other notable birthdays in the year include Norman Mailer, American writer and journalist, Patrick Hillery, former President of Ireland, Henry Kissinger, influential United States Secretary of State, Shimon Peres, former Prime Minister of Israel, Lee Kuan Yew, former Prime Minister of

Singapore, considered the father of that nation, and the late Prince Rainier of Monaco.
The child shared a birthday with Emperor Fushimi of Japan (1265), French composer Claude Joseph Rouget de Lisle (1760), Ukrainian statesman Symon Petlura (1879), Austrian composer Max Steiner (1888), black and white film icon Fred Astaire (1889) and, in more contemporary times, Irish music icon Bono (1960) and Canadian supermodel Linda Evangelista (1965).
Heydar Alirza oglu Aliyev was born at the family home on May 10, 1923. Life in Nakhchivan was largely uneventful. While his father was away at work and mother taking care of the family, he played around the Aliyev home with other children from the neighbourhood. Today there are few residents still alive from this era, but reports from this period, produced in the 1970s, state that he was a gregarious child, always surrounded by other children. The other thing recalled about Heydar Aliyev is that he drove his mother to distraction with his inquisitiveness. She often lost him, as he would wander off in order to investigate things that were going on, or exploring the nearby countryside with other children. Heydar's was a simple childhood of games, music and play. The family was relatively poor and, although it may sound like a cliche, they were happy. Others were in a far worse situation.
Nakhchivan's education system was primitive, but Alirza was keen for his son not follow him into a life of hard, dangerous labour. Paper and pencils were not in evidence. For his primary education Heydar Aliyev learned spelling, rudimentary mathematics and to write properly with a small board, writing with chalk.
"He never forgot the rudimentary early education that he received," says Ali Hasanov, who later served as Deputy

Prime Minister, Chairman of State Committee for Refugees and IDPs. “He had an exceptional intellect and would have emerged even if he had not received any education. That was who he was, but he understood that poor education leads to a lack of opportunity.

“His own rudimentary education inspired him later. When he was leader of the Azerbaijan S.S.R. he put a lot of effort into education. Later again, when he became President of Azerbaijan, education was always high on his agenda. He learned from his own experiences. They stayed with him.”

Indeed, the young Heydar Aliyev also gained a view of the classroom from the other side of the desk. Aged 15, he joined the Nakhchivan Pedagogical School, a teacher training facility. He was the youngest student there, having skipped several years because of advanced grades. Among his peers he stood out, enjoying reading Ekmouladdin Nakhchivani, Hindushah Nakhchivani and Abdurrakhman en-Neshevi, three of the region’s great writers.

Pedagogy is the correct use of teaching strategies. Paulo Freire referred to his method of teaching adults as “critical pedagogy”. The school was heavy on theories and light on actual work. Heydar had his eyes on moving on to fresh pastures. In the event he completed two years at Nakhchivan Pedagogical School before moving on.

In 1939, as the storm clouds of war gathered over Europe, the new high school graduate had building, not destruction on his mind.

He enrolled at the Azerbaijan Industrial Institute, choosing to major in architecture. Studying was his focus, but the war would end any thoughts of architecture. After the war, he continued his education at a special academy in Leningrad as an official of the KGB. Later, in 1957, he graduated from the history faculty of Azerbaijan State University.

Heydar Aliyev, like most of his counterparts in 1943, when he turned 20, became a member of the Communist Party and as World War Two grew grizzly he was called into service. From 1941, he served the People's Commissariat of Internal Affairs of the Autonomous Soviet Socialist Republic of Nakhchivan.

The Battle of Stalingrad, which lasted from late 1942 to early 1943 became a major turning point of the war. After Stalingrad, Soviet forces advanced through Eastern Europe to Berlin before Germany surrendered in 1945. Although ravaged by the war, the Soviet Union emerged victorious from the conflict and became an acknowledged Superpower.

During the immediate post-war period, the Soviet Union first rebuilt and then expanded its economy, while maintaining its strictly centralised control. Heydar's sharp intellect had been spotted long before that. Several officials, within the party and the government, suggested that he pursue other interests. In 1941 responsibility for state security was transferred to the People's Commissariat for State Security. Both agencies became ministries — the Ministry of Internal Affairs (MVD) and the Committee of State Security (KGB) — in 1946.

In 1949, 26-year-old Heydar Aliyev walked through the gates of the KGB Officer Corps Qualifications School. Stalin was in the last few years of his life and the KGB was almost at the zenith of its powers. Officers of the KGB were held in some respect, and not a little fear.

Either way he had won considerable interest from those in a position to prod the career of a promising young KGB stalwart. Heydar's career was now clearly on the up-and-up.

Chapter Eight

Christmas Eve in Baku

Birth is the sudden opening of a window, through which you look out upon a stupendous prospect. For what has happened? A miracle. You have exchanged nothing for the possibility of everything.

— *William McNeile Dixon, British scholar*

Thirteen days before Heydar Aliyev's arrival in the world, Zarifa Aliyeva was born on April 28, 1923, in Shahtakhty in Nakhchivan, a historic small town noted for its old monuments, the ruins of the ancient town of Anabad and artifacts dating to the Bronze Age and Middle Paleolithic Age that had been found near Shahtakhty.

Her parents were Aziz Aliyev and Leyla Abbasova. They, like many, were victims of political mismanagement and ethnic strife. At the beginning of the 19th century, after conclusion of the treaties of Gulustan in 1813 and Turkmenchay in 1828, regional powers sought to create a formal Armenian state. Some 300,000 Armenians in Iran and Turkey were resettled in the regions of Iravan (today's Yerevan), Nagorno-Karabakh, Nakhchivan, Zengezur, Daralayaz, Ordubad, Vedibasar and others. This was to sow the seeds for terrible strife over ensuing centuries and, of course, lead directly to the Nagorno-Karabakh tragedy of present times.

Aziz and Leyla were both born in Iravan. But the constant ethic strife meant that many were leaving, even then. In fact, by the middle of the 1990s the Azerbaijani population would mostly be gone.

Aziz was receiving his higher education in Saint Petersburg from 1919. He hailed from a poor family that had little prospect of supporting him through higher studies. After graduating with a high-school diploma from Iravan Gymnasium, he was determined to pursue a medical career and wrote to a well known philanthropist in Baku, seeking sponsorship.

"My grandfather asked him to support his education and he responded. He gave him the money," says Ilham Aliyev. "It was an act of philanthropy that he extended to many youths and changed a great many lives for the better. My grandfather used this kindness wisely, studied hard and became a famous professor and doctor."

In May 1923 Aziz moved back to Azerbaijan, working his way up to eventually being appointed Deputy Minister in the Azerbaijan Ministry of Health, some seven years later. While working in a high-level position in Azerbaijan, Aziz was also actively involved in frontline activities during the war years.

Sent by the Soviet leadership to Iran, in 1942, Aziz helped prevent an alliance between the Iranians and fascist Germany. After returning from Iran, he was appointed as the First Secretary of the Dagestan region, neighbouring Azerbaijan. Today Aziz Aliyev is honoured in Dagestan. The central street in Makhachkala, the Darband State University and the Caspian Medical Centre carry his name.

In 1948, Aziz was invited to Moscow. He worked in a number of high-level posts, first at the Ministry of Health and then the Council of Ministries, but his success attracted the attention of Mirjafar Bagirov, First Secretary of the Communist Party of Azerbaijan S.S.R., who was made nervous of an Azerbaijani doing well within Moscow's corridors of power. Aziz was then ordered to Baku, to serve as Deputy Chairman of Council of Ministers, a position in which Bagirov could keep an eye on him. It was a top position, but did not last. One year after this appointment he was a victim of political infighting, dismissed for "hiding his parents social status."

Aziz went back to life as a private citizen, working as a doctor and in 1953, after the death of Stalin, appointed as the Director of the Orthopaedic and Rehabilitation Surgery Institute. In later years he returned to state service, working as secretary of the Presidium of the Azerbaijan S.S.R.'s Supreme Soviet.

Zarifa Aliyeva grew up in a household linked with some of that era's major Azerbaijani cultural, musical and scientific figures. Opting for the latter field, in 1942, she entered the Azerbaijan State Medical Institute, graduating five years later. She went on to study at the Moscow-based All-Union Central Doctor Improvement Institute, becoming a specialist in ophthalmology. Eye diseases would become a cause that she pursued throughout her life. In 1963 the U.S.S.R. High Attestation Commission would grant her the academic degree of the Candidate of Medical Sciences.

Of all the stories of Zarifa and Heydar's courtship, the one that stands out is that concerning her father. Having lost all his positions in 1951 as a result of Bagirov's continued actions, the dark shadow of Aziz fell on all his family. Heydar Aliyev, by now a young officer and party stalwart, was taken aside by his superiors and warned that it was unseemly for him to be seen courting a daughter of Aziz Aliyev.

"He ignored this and stated openly that they would continue seeing each other," says Ilham. "It was a risk, as this could have led to his career being stalled by this association. But he was in love with my mother, and that mattered more to him."

In the event, although Aziz remained black-balled, the Communist Party learned to live with Zarifa, evidenced by Heydar's continued rise through the ranks. The couple married in 1948 and remained inseparable for the next 37 years.

On December 24, 1961, the *New York Herald Tribune* ran a story with the headline 'The Code of Life Finally Cracked.' Reporter Earl Ubell was perhaps the first journalist to write a story in a national newspaper on a happening in Moscow some four months earlier. That August, Marshall Warren Nirenberg, an American biochemist and geneticist, was a speaker at the Moscow International Biochemical Congress. In the Russian capital he had announced the beginning of an achievement that would claim him a shared Nobel Prize in Physiology or Medicine in 1968.

He had, he claimed, deciphered the first word of the human genetic code. By December, Ubell reported that a group of researchers at New York University had "taken Dr Nirenberg's code-breaking procedure several steps further". They had, they said, "deciphered fourteen out of twenty words of the code of life, and had thus effectively broken it".

For more than a century, scientists had debated the method by which organisms inherit and pass along certain traits. The genetic code is the set of rules by which information encoded in genetic material, such as DNA sequences, is translated into proteins by living cells.

Dr Nirenberg understood the far-reaching implications of his work, which provided the foundation for genetic research ranging from gene therapies, to Dolly the cloned sheep, to the Human Genome Project, which in the future will provide vast advances in medicine and biotechnology. Once scientists could read the code, the possibilities for genetic research opened.

Although carried on the inside pages of the *New York Herald Tribune* on December 24, 1961, Ubell's article essentially represented an announcement that science would one day be able to provide genetic tests to show a predisposition for malaises such as breast cancer, cystic fibrosis, liver diseases, Alzheimer's disease and many others. Ultimately genetic level cures could follow.

Thousands of kilometres from New York City, in Baku, a family gathered. Life was also on their agenda. There was a baby on the way.

The latter part of 1961 had seen other seminal events. In September UN Secretary General Dag Hammarskjöld died in an air crash en route to Congo. The same month a military coup in Damascus effectively ended the United Arab Republic. Neil Armstrong recorded a world record speed in a rocket plane of 6,587 kph. In October, the Arab League took over protecting Kuwait as the last British troops left. Kuwait, like Azerbaijan oil rich, was beginning a long journey to independence that ended some three decades before Azerbaijan.

December had been notable for events on a tiny island in the Caribbean. In a nationally broadcast speech, Cuban leader Fidel Castro declared that Cuba would adopt Communism. In the east, a few days later, the Vietnam War officially began as the first American helicopters arrived in Saigon under President Kennedy's instructions. In Europe, a major moment was imminent. On Sunday 31, the Marshall Plan expired having distributed more than $12 billion in aid to rebuild Europe from the ashes of World War Two.

Such events were forgotten by the Aliyev family on December 24. In their eyes, a far bigger event was on the horizon. In 1961, Heydar Aliyev was a Major General in the KGB. Major General was the lowest General Officer rank, a two star rank, but Heydar, in his late 30s, was by far the youngest officer serving within Azerbaijan S.S.R.'s KGB. Ali Tagi-zade, Chairman and the Presidium of the Supreme Council, was said to be fond of the young officer and nurturing his career, if not mentoring him. Indeed, it would be only eight years, between 1961 and 1969, until Moscow would appoint Heydar as the First Secretary of the Communist Party of Azerbaijan.

As an officer, he was considered something of a rising star by senior officials in Azerbaijan. Those whose opinions mattered if one was to progress. Yet the party dictated that the Aliyevs were the same as everyone else, the proletariat, and the child was born in the same hospital as the sons and daughters of road sweepers, taxi drivers, metal workers and party faithful.

During late afternoon, Zarifa, wife of the ascendant KGB officer, gave birth to her second child, Ilham Heydar oglu Aliyev. Oglu is Azerbaijani-Turkic for 'son of' when used as part of a male name, in the same way that *bin* or *Ibn* is used in Arabia. Ilham means 'inspiration' in Azerbaijani.

Ilham's birthday coincided with all manner of historical events through history. In 1777 Captain James Cook discovered Christmas Island, in 1906 it was the day that Reginald Fessenden transmitted the first radio broadcast. Eight years later, December 24 was the day of the famed World War One 'Christmas Truce' when, on the Western front, German troops began singing spontaneously. A decade later, in 1924, it was the day that Albania became a republic, while in 1946 France's Fourth Republic was founded and, in 1951, Libya became independent from Italy.

On December 24, 1968, far away from Earth the crew of Apollo 8 entered orbit around the Moon, becoming the first humans to do so. They performed 10 lunar orbits and broadcast live TV pictures that became the famous Christmas Eve broadcast, one of the most watched programmes in history. Ilham Aliyev, then aged seven, recalls watching flickering black and white images on the television set in his home, of the Apollo mission.

The famed photograph *Earthrise,* taken by Bill Anders on board Apollo 8, became about as famous as any image in history. Late adventure photographer Galen Rowell called it "the most influential environmental photograph ever taken" and it inspired contemplation of our fragile existence and our place in the cosmos.

The baby shared his birthday with Howard Hughes, the eccentric American film producer and inventor, Evgeniya Rudneva, the Russian World War Two heroine, and George Patton, the distinguished American general. December 24 is also a day that has thrown up its share of political leaders, including King John of England (1166) and Grand Duchess Elena Pavlovna of Russia (1784).

On December 31, 1961, New Year's Eve, eight day old Ilham Heydar oglu Aliyev was discharged from hospital. He returned home with his parents and sister Sevil, who was six years older.

It was the beginning of an extraordinary life.

Azerbaijan is a place where East meets West, for centuries a country where various religions lived in peace. The Maiden Tower in Baku is one of the most famous symbols of Azerbaijan. (above) The prophet Zoroaster. His name means 'He of the golden light'.

Discoveries made in Gobustan show this to be the cradle of modern mankind and of early civilisation.

Parts of the fortress of Babek Huremdin remain visible today.

Today parts of the Shirvanshah complex are a tourist attraction in Baku. (above) Babek Huremdin remains a hero of the Azerbaijani people.

The grim scene of a collection of dead bodies from the streets of Baku during the infamous March Days.

A generation of Azerbaijani men, including Alirza Aliyev, earned a dangerous living undertaking back-breaking work in Baku's oilfields.

Alirza and Izzet Aliyev with their children.

Nakhchivan, where Heydar Aliyev was born, is a land of antiquity, dotted with monuments and ancient structures.

Chapter Nine

School Number 6

I cannot think of any need in childhood as strong as the need for a father's protection.
— Sigmund Freud, Austrian founder of psychoanalysis

Heydar Aliyev was getting noticed — in Baku and Moscow. Having defied warnings not to marry his eventual wife, amid suggestions that his rise through party apparatus would be stifled, he had emerged as one of the rising stars of Azerbaijan politico circles. Heydar rose quickly within the Committee for State Security — the KGB — to achieve the rank of Major General at the time of Ilham's birth.

The KGB needs no introduction, considered by experts to have been the world's most effective intelligence agency of its era.

The rise and rise of Heydar Aliyev came to the backdrop of Vladimir Semichastny's tenure as head of the KGB in Moscow. The Semichastny era was characterised by mixed results. He was the architect of the disastrous arrest of Professor Frederick Barghoorn of Yale University when visiting Moscow, in October 1963. This attracted the personal and very public ire of President John F. Kennedy.

But despite such problems, Semichastny was also image conscious. He cooperated with an unprecedented article in the newspaper *Izvestia* that quoted 'a senior KGB officer', well known to be the organisation's head, as stating "many young Communist Party and Communist Youth League workers have joined the KGB and none of the people who, during the time of the personality cult of Joseph Stalin took part in the repressions against innocent Soviet people, is now in the Service."

The KGB was slowly distancing itself from its questionable past. And Semichastny was engaged in bringing fresh blood into senior positions. Throughout the Soviet Union there was something of a sea change. New faces were coming through the ranks within KGB hierarchy, throughout the empire.

In 1964, young Ilham was just three years old when his father was promoted to deputy head of the Azerbaijani KGB. It was to prove a short term appointment during an era when Moscow was eagerly looking to bring in new faces. Heydar had been noted and was on a firmly upward curve.

Heydar would be just 44 years old when appointed Chairman of the Azerbaijan Committee for State Security in 1967. His son was six years old.

Ilham recalls a happy, carefree childhood. He was close to his mother, forging with her a strong bond that would remain tight until her death in 1985. But there was also a closeness to his father that belied Heydar's public image as a strongman.

Decades before he became a political mentor to his son, in independent Azerbaijan, Heydar's personality and intellect began to rub off on his offspring.

The KGB boss kept his family firmly out of public view, but his job and position invariably impacted upon family life. Heydar worked long hours. He was away a great deal. But to Zarifa and her brood this was not unusual, this was just how it always was, and would be until the 1980s.

While Heydar and Zarifa forged a settled home, the demands of state and a high position within the Communist Party and state apparatus would inevitably impact on Ilham. The family home was relatively well appointed, for although the system preached egalitarianism, in reality the elite rose above the proletariat quite markedly. Perks of the job, a figment of the human condition, transcended Eastern and Western systems.

Yet where Ilham would share the same experiences of children of the masses was through his state-led childhood. As the son of a rising star of the Azerbaijan S.S.R., one who had won the trust of Moscow, Ilham was exposed to the same influences that were shared by millions across the state, and its satellites in the Eastern Bloc.

"My upbringing was not greatly different in nature to that of others in Azerbaijan," he says. "My father did not like to see great distinctions between us and others. My upbringing was normal. I had friends from school, drawn from families at every level of society and there was no special treatment."

By the 1970's Moscow had succeeded in its desire to begin indoctrination and cement Soviet involvement and intrusion into the life of children as early as possible. Soviet high command had imposed across the empire its own brand of children's culture including musical and language traditions, art, theatre, cinema, powerful graphic symbols, elaborate ceremonies and literature. All were designed as insidiously as Joseph Goebbels' Nazi propaganda, a progressive Sovietisation of life that attempted to stifle free thought and overwhelm indigenous culture in non-Russian regions.

The Soviet childhood was a carefully controlled commodity. Children took part in demonstrations with their parents and listened to often relentless political information on their school radio and at home on television and radio. The stream of unquestioning propaganda came from all sides. Children's books and magazines were seen by Moscow as an excellent way to heist the young mind.

Ilham recalls the demonstrations and the marches. When he began school he was fed a daily diet of state-sponsored pejorative towards the imperialist West and learned by heart why the Party's way was best. This was the accepted reality — and few people possessed another perception. Even Heydar, from his lofty position, only got to grips with the moral bankruptcy of the system and its inherent deficiencies decades later.

Life in the Aliyev household was quiet. If Heydar was absorbed in official business, his wife ran a tight ship at home. Zarifa doted on her children, but was not prepared to see them spoilt. Bedtimes were respected. The children were expected to pull their weight with chores and domestic duties.

As befitted the Aliyev family's position, in 1968 seven year old Ilham joined the Communist-led youth system that was in place. Little Octobrists was a youth organisation for children aged between seven and nine years. Groups represented one school grade level, subdivided into groups called Little Stars, each containing five children. Each group of Little Octobrists was led by an older youth drawn from the Young Pioneers (an organisation for older children).

Each Little Octobrist wore a red five-pointed star badge bearing the portrait of Lenin as a child. It was indicative of the aims of the organisation.

Ilham had joined School Number 6 in Baku city. It was 1971, the same year as the Aswan High Dam was officially opened in Egypt, Idi Amin seized power in Uganda, a new stock market index called the Nasdaq debuted, Hafez Al Assad became President of Syria, the United Arab Emirates was created and the Soviet Union launched the Salyut 1 satellite.

By now, Heydar had been appointed by Leonid Brezhnev to the post of First Secretary of the Central Committee of Azerbaijan Communist Party. He was effectively Head of State, although under Moscow's command. But even the effective head of Azerbaijan sent his son to 'normal' school. This was the done thing and it would have been unseemly otherwise. Some used their positions. He did not.

School Number 6 was typical for Baku in the late-1960s and early-1970s. There was little joy about the somewhat foreboding buildings in themselves. Grey and uniform, they could have done with a brighter colour scheme. There was a competent teaching staff, some of them lively and eager educators. Yet even the most dynamic teachers were stifled by a centralist system, one primed to foster Soviet-ideals and dampen down free thought.

There were roughly three phases to schooling: Primary grades: grades one to three. Intermediate: grades four to eight. Upper secondary: grades nine and ten.

The primary curriculum centred on reading, writing and arithmetic. Children spent from 10 to 12 periods a week learning to read and write in Russian or the native language, and six periods a week on mathematics. The curriculum was rounded out with art and music, physical education and vocational training, interspersed with regular intrusions from the Party and its never-ending rhetoric.

The overwhelming Russian component of pupils' learning was always a bugbear for many in non-Russian parts of the Soviet Union. Local languages were never a priority in Moscow and many Azerbaijanis, even those enthusiastic proponents of the system, worried that Azerbaijani, the indigenous language, was being slowly eroded at the expense of Russian.

This, of course, also placed a burden on non-Russian pupils, resulting in an even heavier academic workload for those to whom Russian was a second language. This enshrined a second class system for non-Russians, even from childhood.

As children grew older, the education system widened to include science. The curriculum also took on an increasingly politicised view, with history and literature biased through selection and interpretation. Communist values and ideology were spun through education, entering fertile, innocent minds as the truth. Only later, during the de-Stalinisation effort of the early *glasnost* years, was education weaned off indoctrination, leading official Soviet press to denounce elementary and secondary school history books as "lies".

Today, Ilham remembers his time at School Number 6 with the fondness of anyone with great weight on their shoulders in later life. School represents more simple times, the innocence of youth, an absence of burden.

"It was a good school, the teachers were very kind, and indeed there were some superb educators there," he says. "I recall the Sovietisation, but my abiding memory, which I carry with me until the present day, is the difference that an inspired teacher can make. At my school there were several inspirational teachers.

"It is our job, today, to make sure our teachers are given the best chance to inspire a new generation of school children."

The future President of the country remains in touch with several of his school friends until the present day. Several remained in touch as distant friends since they left School Number 6. Others resurfaced in more contemporary times.

Ilham progressed well over the course of his school years. Family members recall a fastidious boy who took pride in his work. This was his nature, yet even if it had not been, it was something that was demanded of him. Heydar was a difficult taskmaster, a reputation that he never lost. A well known stickler for results in his political life, he also had high expectations of his son. He followed his son's studies and results with the same keen interest he showed in government reports and records.

"He was always trying to achieve perfect results from himself and demanded that from those around him," says Ilham. "It was the same for me. He really wanted me to achieve perfect results and paid big attention to that."

From accounts of those familiar with the family during that era, entering his teens Ilham had a broadening academic capacity. Perhaps either due to genetic inheritance, or his background, he was a serious young man, a child who read a lot and one given to spending time in adult company rather than among his peers. He was the sort of kid who was full of questions, tormenting elders with an inquisitive mind and plenty of avenues of enquiry.

That sponge-like effect helped at school — and in his personal life. By now he had passed through the Soviet plan for childhood relatively unscathed, graduating between youth movements to the Pioneers. As one author recalled: "Pioneers were the members of the Young Pioneer organisation of the Soviet Union, which was a second step in the official Soviet brainwashing pyramid. After general but unorganised brainwashing from ages 0 to 7, a child entered the first stage of the pyramid by becoming a Little

Octobrist. By age 9 being a Little Octobrist wasn't cool and exciting anymore and kids were looking forward to joining the Young Pioneers. Pioneers wore red ties. They went to summer camps. They had meetings. They were cool. Or so it seemed…"

Via the Pioneer organisation, each child's life met with a series of 'rules for the behaviour of pioneers' and 'pioneer laws'. For most, time, space, everyday life and holidays were strictly regulated. Ilham graduated through the pyramid uncomplainingly, although even then he questioned some of the system's validity.

As a child of a senior figure in Baku, there were both burdens and bonuses. The downside was that his presence was expected at many events and that eyes were always upon him. Ilham was a child-surrogate for Heydar. His performances at camps and at Pioneer events were viewed through the prism of his father, as if the son was an extension of the father.

It was a task he understood early. And carried with him throughout. Heydar never stated the fact, but Ilham quickly grasped that his father's position effectively propelled him onto centre stage. As a youngster he was not the gregarious character of his father, but fought to live up to the Aliyev moniker.

There was a big upside however. A very big bonus was that life was able to throw up greater opportunities other than the camps and the events organised by the Pioneers. As a party stalwart and leader of Azerbaijan, Heydar had a well appointed dacha (summer house) on the coast. He regularly travelled to Moscow and other parts of the Soviet Union on official business, often with family in tow. Ilham got to see the better sides of life in the Soviet Union: Hotels for party leaders, what amounted to first class travel, good cars and shops that were reserved for those in the higher echelons of the supposedly egalitarian society. The perks were never on a scale of Heads of State and their families in many Western countries, but nevertheless they made life more comfortable in Soviet times. The monolithic Communist system was not in the tattered state that it was in the 1980s, but the wheels were just beginning to slow and the Soviet Union had passed its zenith.

By the time of his final exams at School Number 6, Ilham was a card-carrying member of the Komsomol, the youth wing of the Communist Party of the Soviet Union (CPSU). Komsomol played an important role as a mechanism for teaching the values of the CPSU in the young, and as an organ for introducing the young to the political domain, especially political activism. One of the strong attractions of the organisation for many was that active members received privileges and would receive preferences in promotion.

By the 1970s, Komsomol had millions of members, so many in fact that it is believed that up to two-thirds of the present adult population of Russia were members. In Azerbaijan much the same applied. If you wished to get on in life, rise up the promotional ladder and escape the existence of a modest member of the proletariat, you were wise to be active and a vociferous player within the Komsomol. Ilham dutifully played his part.

Decades on, in his role as President, he enjoys the nuts and bolts of the job, but only tolerates the pomp that comes with the position, something which has to be done. His interest is to get things done.

He may have believed in the message, but the maze of mechanisms that underpinned everything Komsomol did — long-winded meetings and set-piece ceremonies, he found tedious. Regular flag-waving Komsomol demonstrations and marches, played out before audiences who agreed, he considered somewhat pointless. Why demonstrate when everyone agrees with you?

Ilham's experience of life as *Homo Sovieticus* — Soviet Man — was therefore quite different from the child of an ordinary citizen. In many ways, however, this would be his grounding, the beginning of his education that would only be complete during post-independence times. Through his formative years as a child, he spent much time with and around Heydar. The older Aliyev was a phenomenon. He possessed the personal charisma, that unmeasurable magnetism that is apparent in the likes of Margaret Thatcher, Bill Clinton and Jacques Chirac. People like this have an undefinable essence that draws people into their world and allows them to convince others of their arguments… to lead.

Heydar emitted this magnetism. It is a once in a generation thing and is not genetic. But Ilham watched and learned. He was exposed to Heydar and saw how he worked at close hand, perhaps better than anyone. More than School Number 6, this was where the young Ilham was educated.

When it came to the business end of Ilham's academic years in Baku, a mind that retained information was a definite bonus. Ilham soaked up books, papers and lessons and kept it stored. He had to work, but slipped smoothly towards a pass.

Final examinations in Soviet schools were rigorous and comprehensive. A general secondary school diploma equated to a high school diploma in the United States. But where diploma pass levels in the West were increasingly fuzzy, under the Soviet system there was a tight strictness to exam marking and plenty of demands upon students. The Soviet system aggressively sorted the wheat from the chaff.

Ilham sailed through the examination period untroubled, while he and his parents were already looking beyond Baku to "what next".

At 16 years old there were decisions to be made. Not for the first time, the demands of family, and fulfilling a duty to state, would see him take the more difficult option available. The son of Heydar could not be an embarrassment. Ilham's father impressed upon him that examples where sons and daughters of party leaders drifted into an almost *nouveau riche* existence, would not be tolerated under his watch. Heydar expected Ilham to represent him. And Azerbaijan.

School Number 6 still stands in Baku today, perhaps one kilometre away from the office of the President of Azerbaijan. The school is in an election district that Ilham visits often. He passes by the buildings of School Number 6 a few times each year, invoking a flicker of nostalgia and a smile of recognition.

The school and office buildings may be little more than a kilometre apart in geographical terms. But the steep highs and deep lows that would carry him between them, would be a tough journey that would take three decades.

Chapter Ten

"Come to me, brother, to Moscow"

Do let's go to Moscow. We must go. Please!
There's nowhere in the world like Moscow.
— Anton Chekhov, Russian playwright

In 1147, Prince Yuri Dolgoruki, the Grand Prince of Rostov, invited the prince of a large mediaeval Russian state of the Novgorod Republic, to 'come to me, brother, to Moscow'. Prince Dolgoruki is considered the founder of Moscow.

So successful was Moscow that the town grew. In 1156 Prince Dolgoruki ordered the construction of a wooden wall to protect the town from invaders and common bandits. As the population grew, the wall had to be rebuilt several times to accommodate the fast expanding 'suburbs'.

A favourable locale on a branch of the Volga River contributed much to Moscow's prosperity. Over the next 800 years the town became a city, then a capital, then one of the world's most important metropolis.

By the time of Ilham's arrival in the city, metropolitan Moscow was one of the planet's largest urban areas. She was the political, economic, cultural, financial, educational and transportation centre of the Soviet Union, the heartbeat of an empire that, in 1991, spread over 22.4 million square kilometres. Whether they liked it or not, in the case of many of those who found the Soviet system oppressive, Moscow was the capital city for almost 300 million people.

In the summer of 1977, 16 year old Ilham arrived at Sheremetyevo Airport. The drive along Leningrad Highway into the city, to the family's Politburo home, was one he had taken often in the past. But Baku had remained home and visits to Moscow relatively fleeting. This time there was an air of permanence. He had come to study.

Ilham's decision to enter the Moscow State Institute of International Relations (MGIMO) was not unusual for an aspiring son of one of Moscow's grandees. Heydar wanted to groom his son for a future within the Soviet system. What was unusual was the way he would go about this. He had achieved grades sufficient to jump from Baku to Moscow a few years ahead of what was considered "normal". He would join the facility in his teens, when most of those who would study around him had turned 20 or more.

He had, therefore, set himself a stern challenge. Jumping ahead a number of years, at this stage of personal development, would stretch his abilities.

Ilham would have some benefits to offset this disadvantage. His father had become a candidate (non-voting) member of the Soviet Politburo in 1976. Heydar had a well appointed home in the city. He had several Volga and Zil cars at his disposal, and a staff.

One could never miss a member of the Politburo. The Volgas and Zils looked really stunning moving along the streets among the army of small cars, Zhigulis and Zaporojets, owned by common citizens.

Ilham would reap some benefits from his illustrious father, benefits that would help him during his time at the Moscow State Institute of International Relations (MGIMO). Among the elite of the Soviet system who were granted a place there, he would have one of the biggest homes, arrive for classes in a Volga or Zil, and not have to worry about money. His name may have also piqued interest.

Perhaps a lecturer would even go easy, believing that upsetting Ilham could lead to trouble with one of the most powerful men in the Soviet Union. But that was where the benefits ended. Heydar was a serious parent. Aside from the Director of MGIMO, lecturers and examiners, his son would answer to him personally.

Heydar was not the sort of man to let his son have it easy. He never allowed Ilham to float through his studies through nepotism, and believed it would be wrong that he attain position and be shown to be uneducated or ill prepared. That was not his style. He was scornful of others who allowed their children to take that route.

Beyond the walls of MGIMO, it was he who would judge Ilham's studies, and he was far more demanding on the young student than any lecturer.

The Moscow State Institute of International Relations was one of the highest regarded universities in the whole of the Soviet Union. The U.S.S.R. Council of People's Commissars established a Department of International Relations at Lomonosov Moscow State University in 1943. A year later the Sovnarkom transformed this department into a separate institution, MGIMO was founded, it is believed, on October 14, 1944. Among its grandees were scientist Yevgeny Tarle and Sergey Krylov, an author of the United Nations Charter.

"The Moscow State Institute of International Relations was an institution designed to shape generations of future leaders within the Soviet Union and Eastern Bloc," says Nataliya Kirillovna Kapitonova, Ilham's English Literature teacher during that period, and who still serves at MGIMO today. "Our alumni have shaped nations and held senior positions in dozens of nations, including the Foreign Ministers of Russia, Ukraine, Belarus, Kazakhstan, Slovakia and Mongolia."

This would be very important for the Soviet Union. In the early years after the end of World War Two, a shattered Europe was rebuilding and the two sides of what later became known as the Iron Curtain were competing. A new generation of Soviet diplomats was required, competent in foreign policy and international economics, and able to represent the nation within the new world order.

In 1944, MGIMO began its first scholastic year with 200 students, within three faculties — a School of International Relations, School of Economics and School of Law. This number would quickly grow, as did MGIMO's reputation and its scope. In 1954 MGIMO was integrated with one of the oldest Russian institutes — the Moscow Institute of Oriental Studies, successor to the Lasarevsky School. Four years later the Institute of Foreign Trade of the U.S.S.R. Ministry for Foreign Trade was grafted into MGIMO. Later a School of International Law and the School of International Journalism were added.

MGIMO quickly become an elitist institution. Rising stars of the party, government nomenclature and the cream of the Soviet Union's educational system found their way there. Yet the strength of its admissions policy also allowed the school to do what it was supposed to. MGIMO was the diplomatic school of the Soviet Union Ministry of Foreign Affairs, the primary outlet for preparing specialists in international relations and diplomacy.

"MGIMO was elitist in some ways. Yes," says Kapitonova. "But for future leaders, such as Ilham Aliyev, it was a place where a student was among his present and, more importantly, future peers. Students received educational experience and also gained valuable professional contacts that would serve them throughout their future professional lives.

"Each year, the very brightest youngsters from across the Soviet Union were admitted. There was a lot of talent across the country competing for a relatively small number of places."

Today, the institution's website says: "MGIMO University keeps in touch with numerous foreign universities and schools. The University serves as coordinator for universities in Russia and CIS countries for the following academic branches: international relations, regional studies, public relations and publicity. The cooperation with foreign universities of the USA, France, Germany, Japan, India and China aims to create common education areas..."

In the 1970s and 1980s MGIMO existed within a far more closed scope from which to draw its student body, but the predominantly Soviet elite was infused by the best and the brightest from Eastern Europe and other allied Communist countries.

Recent alumni, when Ilham arrived in Moscow, included future Russian Ministers of Foreign Affairs Sergei Lavrov and Andrei Kozyrev and OSCE Secretary General Ján Kubi. Among those at MGIMO during the same period as the future Azerbaijani President was Kirsan Ilyumzhinov, future President of the Republic of Kalmykia of the Russian Federation and President of FIDE, the 'World Chess Federation'. Also in classes during this time was Zhan Videnov, future Prime Minister of Bulgaria.

Ilham was, of course, no stranger to Moscow by this time. The Aliyev family visited the Soviet capital often when Heydar was a major player in Azerbaijan. His elevation to the Politburo meant that the family now had a permanent home. But this would be the first occasion that the teenager himself was to spend an extended period of time in a city that would go on to be an adoptive home for some years.

'If only we could go back to Moscow! Sell the house, finish with our life here, and go back to Moscow,' wrote Anton Chekhov, the famed Russian writer.

The city, grimly hung with dreary monolithic communist buildings in places, was also one of unique charm in others. City planners of that era were supremely diligent in their aims, but despite their best efforts it was a metropolis that refused to be crushed into the ruins of Soviet-era drudgery.

In 1984 Charles, Prince of Wales, famously described an extension to the National Gallery in London as a "monstrous carbuncle on the face of a much-loved and elegant friend". The Prince's term became widely used to describe architecture that was unsympathetic to its surroundings. Soviet Moscow was, tragically, a city of monstrous carbuncles.

This was a city in the midst of the Leonid Brezhnev era. He would serve as Secretary General of the Communist Party of the Soviet Union longer than anyone other than Joseph Stalin. The anti-Stalin period was still underway. In 1977, the year Ilham arrived in Moscow, the Soviet National Anthem's lyrics were amended with Stalin's name omitted. This was significant, but far more important for ordinary people was the pride that was held in Soviet achievements going forward. That February *Soyuz 24*, carrying cosmonauts Viktor Gorbatko and Yuri Glazkov, had docked with the *Salyut 5* space station. Moscow vied with Washington in the Space Race.

Back on earth, MGIMO had continued to churn out Soviet youth capable of leading the Eastern Bloc. The intake of students in 1977 was very much like any other. Many were young veterans of the army, who had served well and received recommendations based on their academic performance. Most of those in their early 20s were ordinary kids who had shone in secondary school, proven themselves in higher education and won a place there against the odds.

The new elite, destined for high places, mixed with others who had won places in a variety of ways. MGIMO was a melting pot of ethnicities and backgrounds. The one thing they all had in common was the taxing education that was to come.

An appearance of the name Aliyev on student rolls may have raised a few eyebrows. But for his part, Ilham is recalled as not drawing any attention to himself.

"It was not uncommon for the sons and daughters of people well placed in the system to throw their weight around, to hide behind their names and not engage at all," says Aleksandr Gurnov, a leading journalist at *Russia Today*, who was there during the mid-1970s. "This sort of person was the bane of the university. They were disruptive and they brought nothing to the table."

Even if he had wished to fit into that category, Ilham came from a family that expected more. Not that there weren't temptations given. Around MGIMO there was also a social buzz.

"There were discos and parties. I was learning journalism and he was learning to be a diplomat, so we moved in different circles, but I saw a lot of him and we became friends," says Gurnov. "I remember that he was a gentleman, all the girls used to like him because he was a man. He had moved from childhood to manhood, without the period of being a juvenile in between."

Yet the social life that surrounded life at MGIMO was a sidebar to the more serious pursuits.

"It is a misconception that you could go to university in the Soviet Union and not do your homework," says Gurnov. "Even if you were a golden boy."

From interviews from faculty and staff at MGIMO, a picture emerges of a quiet, unassuming student without airs. If you did not know his surname, or were not aware of his links, Ilham would never press the issue.

"Ilham really studied and could never have been accused of taking it easy," says Gurnov. "He studied hard, achieved good marks and was very smart. This is what I remember of him."

The Azerbaijani got on with student life as well as he could within the confines of being the son of the Soviet Union's top Azerbaijani and highest placed Muslim.

According to those who knew him, Ilham made friends quickly, although he was somewhat shy and reserved.

Many new students had not been to Moscow before, so he became one of those who, informally, took on the role of assimilating newcomers into the vast city. Ostankino Television Tower, then Europe's tallest tower, Shukhov Tower, the North River Terminal, the Tsentrosoyuz building and Bakhmetevsky Bus Garage were on the agenda for most people visiting the Soviet capital. What Ilham was interested in were the city's cultural treasures. The Tretyakov Gallery, Pushkin Museum of Fine Arts and the State Historical Museum were just a few of the places that he spent time wandering around during those first few months. The museums and art galleries of Moscow fascinated him. In the weeks before classes started, he spent much of his time looking around, getting a feel for the Soviet capital.

That early summer period of 1977, when Ilham arrived in Moscow, was punctuated by the death of Elvis Presley at 42 and news of Steve Biko's death in police custody in South

Africa. But while the summer went on and the countdown to classes continued, Ilham's thoughts turned from exploring his surroundings to the scholastic year.

The MGIMO library contained over half a million books and magazines in Russian and more than 30 foreign languages. The library included the Museum of Rare Books which boasts a collection of 21,000 rare books and manuscripts, many in Azerbaijani or relating to Azerbaijan.

He could be found there a lot. The library was — and still is — an extraordinary collection. The Museum of Rare Books was a regular haunt of his. He went through several books each week from the main library collections, covering a variety of subjects.

Under Soviet rule, particularly during Joseph Stalin's reign, modern Azerbaijani writers were not in favour, but within the collection were tomes by the Azerbaijani masters Pur Hasan Asfaraini, whose Persian and Turkic ghazals are arguably unequalled, and Khurshidbanu Natavan, considered one of the best lyrical poets of Azerbaijan.

Then classes started.

"He was shy and not very talkative," says Kapitonova. "It was a long time before I understood why. When he entered MGIMO he was just 16 and the youngest student. But he quickly emerged in academic terms."

Kapitonova and her colleagues were charged with turning out students ready to be diplomats. Ilham had opted to specialise in Great Britain and, as MGIMO's resident expert, would spend much of his time under Kapitonova.

The course began with an intensive programme to learn English. As this went on, the course shifted from being taught in Russian to English.

"We covered British history, British culture, the country's political system and its political culture," she says. "Looking back, I would like to tell interesting anecdotes about Ilham, but there were none, he was just very studious and got on with his work."

She observes that around the facility there were "boys and girls from the elite who had too much money and would not care" but that "Ilham was not one of them, he worked, which he did not have to."

Kapitonova and her colleagues took the 15 or 16 students specialising in Great Britain from World War One until contemporary times. She adds that the syllabus was less skewed by rhetoric, although understandably taught the Soviet view on international history. The political science aspect was of particular interest to Ilham.

"The British system is old, but I noticed that Ilham enjoyed studying it as there are old and strange elements to it," she says. "The British system is interesting because of its many quirks."

For the next five years, he immersed himself in British life, culture and the political system. He learned fluent English. He wrote papers on British History and British Foreign Policy. There was extensive research requirements on students, exams, theoretical work and lectures grew increasingly deep on different aspects of the syllabus.

"His marks were excellent," she says. "And he was a very popular young student."

Towards the end of the programme, he started working on a comprehensive thesis titled *'The British Anti-War Movement of the 1970s and 1980s'.* After successfully defending this, he reached the end of his period as a student at MGIMO.

"I was his teacher," says Kapitonova, "so there was some distance between us. But I know many people who worked and studied at the institute who much admired him."

As well as those MGIMO alumni who have gone on to high position in governments, the university boasts hundreds serving in diplomatic positions across the world. Having completed his five years at the university, Ilham was beginning to look around him and the possibilities that lay ahead.

Chapter Eleven

The Making of a First Lady

Most people who meet my wife quickly conclude that she is remarkable. They are right about this. She is smart, funny and thoroughly charming. Often, after hearing her speak at some function or working with her on a project, people will approach me and say something to the effect of, you know, I think the world of you, Barack, but your wife, wow!
— Barack Obama, American statesman

In November 2005 the *London Times* reported on a surprising development in Baku. Writer David Mattin wrote:

> *We have grown accustomed to glamorous First Ladies. Usually, though, we look to the U.S. to provide them: Jackie Kennedy; more recently, Hilary Clinton and Laura Bush. But the world's most glamorous First Lady at the moment has an unfamiliar name.*
>
> *Mehriban Aliyeva is the wife of Ilham Aliyev, President of Azerbaijan since 2003. In a country where conservative Islam is widespread, Aliyeva, 41, is something of a surprise. Her designer dresses are set off by dramatic sunglasses, and the mother of three has posed for Vogue. All that glamour, though, is combined, it seems, with formidable ambition. A qualified physician, Aliyeva stood for parliament in Sunday's general election…*

In 1932 Mohammad Ali al-Abid was elected as the first President of Syria. He was an enlightened and intelligent man, a student of the prestigious Galatasaray Lisesi, who went on to study in Paris, served as the Ottoman Empire's ambassador to Washington and travelled through the U.S., England, Switzerland, France and Egypt before World War One. He served as Syria's Minister of Finance before becoming President. He was fond of French literature and economics, and spoke and read in Arabic, English and Persian. But however educated and 'open' he remained constricted by the norms of his society.

On June 11, 1932, the day of his inauguration, his wife, Zahra al-Yusuf asked if she could attend the official function at the Presidential Palace. President al-Abid replied: "You attending a state function? Filled with men? That is impossible Zahra. What do you want people to say?"

But Zahra al-Yusuf was no shrinking violet and unwilling to remain idle. Born into Damascus aristocracy, she too was educated, wished to fulfill a positive role and refused to take no for an answer, even from the President. She began to push the envelope, take on civic duties and gradually began to play a greater role in public life. Al-Abid ended his tenure as President of Syria in December 1936, and passed away three years later, but during his Presidency and beyond it, even after he died, his wife served. She formed and had an active role in several charity organisations, such as Goutte de Lait, and headed the Syrian Red Crescent and Syrian branch of the International Red Cross. She was later presented with the Red Cross Medal of Honour in Gold, the first Arab woman to win such an accolade.

If Zahra al-Yusuf steam-rollered herself into an active and productive public role, the 20th century saw few further gains. While role models such as Jackie Kennedy emerged elsewhere in the world, in the Muslim world the 'al-Yusuf model' remained intact. First Ladies in the East were confined to low-key roles heading charity organisations, providing gravitas to intellectual forums and taking on official ceremonies. Al-Yusuf's achievements can be seen as a great step forward against a backdrop of 400 years of the Ottoman Empire, where women were completely segregated from public life.

Women were sidelined from power, in male-dominated societies, and those that found themselves positioned to contribute were handicapped by restrictive convention.

But towards the latter years of the 20th century that started to change. Names such as Sheikha Moza bint Nasser al-Missned, wife of the Emir of Qatar and Queen Rania Al Abdullah of Jordan emerged.

Sheikha Moza does not try to discard her Muslim identity, or encourage her people to clamour towards Western values. Instead she champions national identity. She is quoted as saying: "People tend to believe that to be modern you have to disengage from your heritage. But it's not true. We don't see the global citizen as someone with no identity, but rather, someone who has confidence and is proud of their culture and history — and open to the modern world."

Queen Rania became the youngest queen in the world when she acceded in 1999. She too revolutionised her society, while enchanting the world with her eloquence and elegance, showing a new side to Muslim leaders that the rest of the world had never seen. She was ranked as the third most beautiful woman in the world by *Harper's & Queen* magazine and number 80 in *Forbes'* list of Most Powerful Women in the World. She, too, has toured the world speaking on behalf of Jordan and defending women's rights in the Arab and Muslim World. She made world headlines by appearing on the Oprah Winfrey Show in 2006, breaking stereotypes of Arab women.

All have been pioneers, paralleled on their defining path by the likes of Sheikha Sabeeka bint Ibrahim Al Khalifa of Bahrain, Sheikha Fatima bint Mubarak of the United Arab Emirates and Emine Erdogan of Turkey.

In the case of Sheikha Moza and Queen Rania there are some very apparent parallels. In addition to being leaders in their respective societies, they were born into ordinary families, seemingly never destined to follow their husbands into power. They are highly educated, met their husbands by coincidence and married men perhaps never destined to rule their countries. The Emir of Qatar deposed his father and King Abdullah of Jordan was a surprise late appointment as Crown Prince by his father during the last few days of his life.

In recent years another name emerged on that list, drawn from a similar scenario to the aforementioned trio, one who was related to Mir Jalal Pashayev. Known by his pseudonym Mir Jalal, he was one of Azerbaijan's best known writers. His books *Resurrection Man, Manifest of a Young Man, Where Are We Going* and his 1984 best seller, *People of the Same Age,* contributed to a glowing reputation. A professor at the State University of Baku, his satirical short stories, taking apart Soviet bureaucracy, made him famous.

Mir Jalal Pashayev had three sons and two daughters. Of those Hafiz Pashayev became one of Azerbaijan's most notable diplomats and scholars and academician, Arif Pashayev, claimed for himself a doctoral degree in physics and mathematics and emerged as Rector of the National Academy of Aviation in Baku.

Arif Pashayev married Aida Imanguliyeva, a renowned philologist and one of Azerbaijan's leading Arabists. Aida

Imanguliyeva was a well-known scholar of Oriental studies and a skilful connoisseur of Arabic literature. The scientific heritage of Imanguliyeva is still being studied to this day, and numerous scholars of Oriental studies in Azerbaijan are graduates of her school. They lived in Baku quietly, building a family. On August 26, 1964, the couple had a daughter. She was named Mehriban, an older sister to Nargiz.

"Mehriban was a quiet girl, who grew up with an unusual dedication to her studies," says Hafiz Pashayev. "She was always at the top of her classes."

The future First Lady of Azerbaijan gravitated towards medicine and already had her eye on this direction when, in June 1982, she graduated from Secondary Public School No. 23 in Baku, claiming a Gold Medal. Within months, 18-year-old Mehriban Pashayeva joined the student body of the Azerbaijan Medical University on Bakikhanov Street in central Baku.

Records show that she was a studious member of the university, with an exemplary attendance record. There was strict competition for a limited number of places within Azerbaijan Medical University, which boasted a long record of alumni going on to top class careers in Azerbaijan and the Soviet Union.

After excelling there, she was admitted to Ivan Mikhaylovich Sechenov Moscow Medical Academy (MMA), the oldest Soviet medical higher educational institution.

Leaving Baku for MMA would put the young Azerbaijani medical student in the same vortex as an Azerbaijani lecturer based at the Moscow State Institute of International Relations (MGIMO). Ilham Aliyev had become a lecturer at MGIMO.

Moscow is a big city. According to the 2002 census the population of the Moscow region was 10 million. Even in the 1980s it was one of the biggest cities in the world. The chances of two people meeting were a lottery. Although both worked and studied in the Soviet capital, it was in Baku that their paths crossed.

"I saw Mehriban at a few social events, for the first time at a classical music concert at the Azerbaijan State Philharmonic Hall," says Ilham. It turned out that Aida Imanguliyeva and Zarifa Aliyeva knew each other.

"I introduced myself and everything grew from there. I think, looking back, that I knew from very, very early in the relationship that she was the one."

In 1984, Ilham and Mehriban were married. On July 3, 1986, the couple's first child, Leyla, arrived.

"The arrival of Leyla changed my life," says Ilham. "A child gives you a new perspective. In my job today, as President, that perspective is forged through the prism of being a husband, a father and, indeed, a grandfather."

Another Azerbaijani expatriate for whom Leyla changed a great deal was Heydar.

His place within the Soviet system was in flux following the appointment of Mikhail Gorbachev as Soviet leader, who was looking to promote liberals in order to usher in the era of *perestroika*. But amid the tough political battles at the Kremlin, Heydar suddenly had a potent diversion; his first grandchild.

In political terms, the First Deputy Prime Minister of the Soviet Union was embroiled in what amounted to the very beginnings of the final collapse of the U.S.S.R.. Yet he discovered that politics and national events mattered just a little less after Leyla arrived.

The couple continued their quiet academic lives at MMA and MGIMO while bringing up a family. Indeed, throughout much of 1988 Mehriban managed to complete her diploma, with honours, while carrying their second child, Arzu.

Juggling motherhood and a career, Mehriban had decided to specialise. She joined the Eye Diseases Scientific-Research Institute, founded in 1973 as the All-Union Research Institute of Eye Diseases, a step towards becoming an ophthalmologist, a medical doctor who specialises in surgical eye care.

The Eye Diseases Scientific-Research Institute was at the head of eye care in the entire Soviet Union, boasting 150 beds and seeing around 80,000 patients a year. It was challenging, demanding, and called upon those working there to become acquainted with up to 6,000 different eye diseases connected with short-sightedness, far-sightedness, astigmatism, keratoconus, nystagmus and others.

The Eye Diseases Scientific-Research Institute was run by academician Professor M. M. Krasnov, possibly the Soviet Union's leading ophthalmologist, to whom some of the most extreme and challenging optical cases were referred, drawn from a population of 293 million in 1991, the third most populous nation after China and India.

At the Eye Diseases Scientific-Research Institute, Mehriban immersed herself in issues like the creation and development of new methods of diagnostics and treatment of various eye diseases and the application of new technologies to clinical practice, as well as training of hospital doctors from throughout the Soviet Union and Eastern Bloc.

For sometime, life remained wonderfully sweet and simple for Mehriban Aliyeva and her growing family. But then, in 1990, Mikhail Sergeyevich Gorbachev ordered his troops into Baku. Everything would change after this, setting the family on a course that would lead them back to Baku, via Turkey.

On January 21, 1990, in the wake of the Gorbachev massacre, Heydar made a sorrowful address at the Azerbaijani Embassy in Moscow. As a result of this, Ilham would be forced from his position at MGIMO. By early 1992, Ilham had used an instinct for private enterprise and launched the business that was to prove such a success.

But post-Soviet Russian society was in tatters and difficult to live in. The family eventually left Moscow behind, shifting to Turkey. That year Mehriban resigned from the Eye Diseases Scientific-Research Institute and moved with her husband to Istanbul.

In April 1994 Mehriban was at home when her husband received a fateful telephone call from his father summoning him back to Azerbaijan. Life was set to change dramatically. What she could never have known was that this call from her father-in-law would set in motion a chain of events that would, in time, propel her husband into politics and then the Presidency, and see her own career path take a quite unexpected turn.

Chapter Twelve

New Zealand... or not

One looks back with appreciation to brilliant teachers, with gratitude to those who touched our human feelings. The curriculum is so much necessary raw material, but warmth is the vital element for the growing plant and for the soul of the child.
— Carl Jung, Swiss psychiatrist

When famed Irish playwright George Bernard Shaw visited New Zealand a reporter asked him his impression of the place and, after a pause, Shaw is said to have replied: "Altogether too many sheep." The indigenous people of New Zealand, the Maori, named their lands Aotearoa, commonly understood to mean 'The Land of the Long White Cloud'. Noted for its rugged beauty, the country is isolated, situated close to 2,000 kilometres south-east of Australia across the Tasman Sea.

The relationship between the Soviet Union and New Zealand was one that was forged during World War Two. From a New Zealand perspective, it was a relationship based on the suffering of its own. New Zealand servicemen endured appalling conditions and risks as part of the Arctic convoys that brought vital supplies to the Soviet Union at the height of the war.

Russia's significance to the islands led to the establishing of a legation in Moscow on April 13, 1944. But the relationship quickly soured during the early stages of the Cold War. In 1949 New Zealand withdrew its diplomats.

In 1973 Socialist Prime Minister Norman Kirk initiated renewed links. He established an embassy in Moscow, stating that the Soviet Union was a world power whose views had to be taken into consideration. He also stated that the Soviet Union was an increasingly active participant in Asian affairs.

During the 1970s, engagement between Moscow and Wellington grew markedly. After World War Two America had exerted influence over New Zealand, which, along with Australia, formed the ANZUS security treaty in 1951. But times were changing. New Zealanders had grown increasingly independent and aware of their own quite distinct culture and the government was asserting its distinct foreign policy agenda. In 1985, the same year that Azerbaijani student Ilham was preparing to finalise his Ph.D. in Moscow, New Zealand had made some startling moves.

The ANZUS treaty, once fully mutual between Australia, New Zealand and the United States, was weakening and America in particular would be infuriated by Wellington. In February 1985, New Zealand announced that it would refuse nuclear-powered or nuclear-armed ships access to its ports. Soon after Washington announced that it was suspending its treaty security obligations to New Zealand pending the restoration of port access, but Wellington would not back down and in June 1987 would become a Nuclear-free zone, the first Western-allied state to forge such status.

The easing of a formerly tight relationship between New Zealand and America was something that the Soviet Union was determined to build upon. By 1985, renewed diplomatic relations between New Zealand and Soviet Union were a dozen years in the making. Wellington, while not in play, was a degree less pro-Western and, perhaps, set to become somewhat instinctively neutral. The socialist administration of Prime Minister David Lange was viewed as amenable.

In Moscow, that year, there was also change. The Ministry of Foreign Affairs administered the diplomatic relations of the Soviet Union. Once the Soviet Council of Ministers agreed diplomatic recognition of a state, the Ministry established embassies and consulates, provided core staffing and served as a conduit for formal communications. A Soviet ambassador serving abroad would be regarded — as per international law — as the personal representative of the Head of State of the Soviet Union.

The Ministry of Foreign Affairs had grown under the consummate diplomat and politician Andrei Gromyko. He would serve as Soviet Foreign Minister from 1957 until mid-1985. Gromyko was an expert negotiator and to his political enemies was nicknamed 'Comrade Nyet' for his non-committal negotiating style. One famous story was told of Gromyko leaving a Washington hotel and being asked by a reporter: "Minister Gromyko, did you enjoy your breakfast today?"

His response was: "Perhaps."

After the passing of Leonid Brezhnev in November 1982, much had changed. Yuri Andropov had served as Head of State for 15 months, and Konstantin Chernenko for barely a year. Upon his passing, on March 11, 1985, the Presidium of the Supreme Soviet of the U.S.S.R. went into a huddle again to pinpoint a new leader. It was Gromyko who nominated Mikhail Gorbachev for the Communist Party General Secretary's post.

But ironically Gromyko was quickly replaced as Foreign Minister. Gorbachev appointed Eduard Shevardnadze to the position, consolidating Gorbachev's circle of relatively young reformers.

Shevardnadze set about modernising and upgrading the ministry, making major personnel changes. The Ministry of Foreign Affairs was organised into geographical departments and administered to reflect Soviet concerns. Departments and administrations of the ministry included geographical ones, dealing with the regions of Europe, Latin America, Asia and Africa, and functional ones, dealing with such concerns as international organisations and cultural affairs. Shevardnadze restructured some of the geographical and functional departments, mainly by grouping countries into categories reflecting modern world realities.

This modern pragmatism involved the Soviet Union's foreign representation targeting nations not within her traditional sphere but those that were 'inclined' towards Moscow. Or at least those not firmly in Washington's sphere.

Engaging nations such as New Zealand involved putting in place a diplomatic representation that was modern, forward looking and progressive.

During the early months of the post-Gromyko period, many of the old style ambassadors were moved on and attention was paid to staffing highlighted embassies with a young progressive cadre of fresh faces. The stiff, Soviet diplomatic corps of old would change quickly, starting with sweeping changes in embassies that served nations which could be influenced. New Zealand, which was not geopolitically important, but was taking a less pro-Washington stance, was one of these.

The embassy in Wellington was one of those targeted for a new generation of Soviet diplomats. In 1985, the Ministry started casting around, looking for bright new graduates who would become the backbone of the country's diplomatic services for the next decades.

Shevardnadze was a man of action. He wanted change. Immediately. Within weeks of his appointment as Minister of Foreign Affairs, officials from the department were sent out to Moscow's leading educational institutions seeking students with "the right stuff."

There were an immediate 50 positions to fill, students who would go straight into the diplomatic training programme and, within months, start to be assigned to key embassies around the world, those targeted for renewal. Among those institutions whose students came under review were Lomonosov Moscow State University, U.S.S.R. Academy of Sciences, Moscow Institute of Physics and Technology, Rostov State University, Moscow State University of Economics, Statistics and Information Sciences and the obvious Moscow State Institute of International Relations.

By the early summer of 1985 Ilham successfully obtained a Ph.D. in history with a dissertation titled '*The Anti-War Movement in Great Britain and the attitude of political parties in the 1970s and 1980s*'.

It was time for him to begin thinking about what next.

"After I graduated from the university I was hoping to continue on a research path and I was supposed to go to work in one of the Azerbaijani universities. This was how I mapped out the next few years," he says.

At the same time, MGIMO was undergoing some scrutiny. Around this time, the Ministry contacted the university and asked for a brief to be produced on suitable students. There were no specific parameters, only that they were on the look out for some interesting recruits who would be fast tracked into the diplomatic service. Ilham had done very well. He was an obvious choice.

Things were changing in Moscow. Gorbachev was suspicious of those he viewed as the Brezhnevite old guard. His *perestroika* was yet to surface, but a fresh gloss on the Soviet Politburo, Gorbachev believed, was required. It would take some time before the levers of power were sufficiently in his hands in order to clear out those Gorbachev did not like, but the winds of change were already blowing through the Kremlin. Gorbachev had begun targeting potential rivals and personally organising intrigues that would destabilise them politically.

Aware of the political and organisational weight of Heydar Aliyev, Gorbachev directed the first strokes against him. As a result, Heydar was not the rising star he was under Andropov and Chernenko.

Foreign Minister Shevardnadze was. Which is why the Foreign Ministry's campaign to unearth diplomatic talent threw up a strange name. The Minister reviewed many of the case files of those students thought promising and allowed an offer to be made to the son of Heydar Aliyev.

The first Ilham knew about this was when invited to a meeting at the Ministry of Foreign Affairs. It was explained that he was a promising candidate for a diplomatic career, one of a new generation of ambassadors-in-waiting.

"I was invited to take up a post with the Soviet Union Embassy in New Zealand," he says. "It was an intriguing offer. I was honoured."

New Zealand had appeal. Ilham had grown up to the backdrop of his father who was one of the dominant personalities of the Soviet Union. It was his time to distance himself, in a career that the Foreign Ministry assured him would lead to a quick rise up through the ranks to an ambassador's post.

Yet within a week another challenge was also on the horizon. For eight years MGIMO had been the centre of his life. Armed with a Ph.D. in history, he was an asset that they did not wish to lose.

Times were changing, quickly, with a new era creating, it was clear, a more open Soviet Union. The universities were encouraged to renew themselves, modernise and have a far more internationalist view. Between the end of the 1984/85 scholastic year and the beginning of the 1985/86 scholastic year the arrival of Gorbachev set a transformational tone.

Considered one of the brightest of his generation in MGIMO, despite a shy nature Ilham was thought by the faculty to have all the hallmarks of being someone who was able to communicate his depth of knowledge. As MGIMO began the long road to modernity, which would take a decade or more to achieve, the 24-year-old Azerbaijani was seen as an ideal recruit. The same week as the Ministry of Foreign Affairs made their approach with an offer of a new career, beginning 16,500 kilometres from Moscow, there came a second offer — one that would keep him in exactly the same location.

Lecturer is the name given to those who teach in their first permanent university position, usually academics early in their careers. They lead research groups and supervise postgraduate students as well as lecture courses. Over time, natural progression would ensure that when vacancies opened up within a given department, an experienced lecturer could become a professor, a position typically held by only a couple of those employed in a given department. MGIMO invited Ilham to stay on and take on a post as lecturer. During the course of their time as a lecturer, those wishing to progress in academic terms would accrue a strong publication record and through experience gain prowess in teaching. A senior lecturer, on the way to a professorship, would need a period when they should show strong research ability, as well as sound teaching and administrative skills.

Most lecturers at MGIMO had a Ph.D., and indeed it was considered a prerequisite of the job if the lecturer had designs upon a career as a senior academic. In as little as a handful of years, Ilham could return to Baku not just as a Ph.D. holder but, potentially, as a professor, able to command just about any relevant post he wished in Azerbaijani academic circles. It was an inviting offer.

"After many years at MGIMO, I had roots in Moscow, but also I really enjoyed my time at the university. The people were top quality, the faculty was well run and the students that had followed me into MGIMO were so dedicated and focused," says Ilham. "It was humbling that those in senior positions thought that I was capable of inspiring the people who followed me."

For a few days Ilham considered the options before him. He agonised over the issue. The prospect of serving in New Zealand, and the challenge presented by MGIMO, both fascinated him. The Ministry had given him hardly days to decide if he wished to become a diplomat, while both the educational institutions were preparing their teaching staff for the new scholastic year. He had no time for procrastination.

In the event, he would plump for MGIMO and life as a lecturer. The diametric shift from student to teacher, within the same facility, was quite a change in emphasis. Ilham completed his Ph.D. and left MGIMO. A few weeks later he reported back to take up a teaching role.

"It was strange to be on a different side of the lecture, giving instead of receiving, but, although there was some trepidation, I found that it came naturally," he says. "It helped that this was a subject that I did, and still do, find compelling, and passing on knowledge was very rewarding."

"A teacher affects eternity. He can never tell where his influence stops," said journalist, historian and academic Henry Brooks Adams, while Lebanese writer Khalil Gibran stated that: "The teacher who is indeed wise does not bid you to enter the house of his wisdom, but rather leads you to the threshold of your mind."

"Ilham was a natural leader in the lecture hall, and an inspiration to his students as he brought his classes to life," says Nataliya Kapitonova, his former teacher. "Why do we choose this profession? We are driven by our passion to change lives and make a difference. Even during those days MGIMO tried to ensure that our educators had a vision of what it took to succeed as a teacher."

Ilham quickly found his feet and within a couple of months of the beginning of the scholastic year found a rhythm. Several of his former students recall a sympathetic figure. Others a hard taskmaster, but one who was fair.

Several of his former students, interviewed for this book, recall that he had high expectations and that he would brook no silly excuses when it came to deadlines. Yet at the same time he was not one of those lecturers who turned up, spoke and left. He was a nurturing influence upon his students.

Although he was on the opposite side of the classroom, life for Ilham continued in very much the same mould as it did during his student years. The pressures of politics — and his father's place within the Soviet hierarchy — would intervene and provide their own set of challenges at times. But for the most part Ilham continued his career path quietly. He taught classes and enjoyed the challenge of leading research groups that pushed the boundaries of common knowledge. It was a testing and challenging time, something which satisfied him greatly. Ilham loved what MGIMO represented and lived on the satisfaction he took from his job. But politics — the family business — would never remain far away. Ultimately the price of politics would be his career, in more ways than one.

Chapter Thirteen

Baku Bloodied

The soldier pulled up his gun as we froze. I waited for him to shout a warning. But nothing came. Seconds later my sister fell. She was hit in the chest. Moza was nine, a child. I pulled her from the cold of the sidewalk and held her to me. I knew she was dying. I looked up. The soldier sneered and swore at me, calling me a Muslim dog.

— Sergina Shurko, resident of Baku

On the evening of April 8, 1989, the Patriarch of Georgia, Ilia II, made an address to thousands of Georgians gathered in the Rustaveli Avenue area of Tbilisi. The people were angry. Moscow was widely perceived as undermining the growing pro-independence movement by using Abkhaz separatism. Divide and rule.

The people were furious, but it was clear that Colonel General Igor Rodionov, Commander of the Transcaucasus Military District, was encircling the protesters with troops and tanks. Tensions were rising. Patriarch Ilia appealed to the people to go home.

Shortly before dawn the following morning Soviet armoured personnel carriers and troops moved in to disband and clear Rustaveli Avenue, using force. One of the first victims was a 16-year-old girl, who was beaten to death. By sunrise, the death toll would be 20 and hundreds of others were injured.

Perhaps the Georgians were naive. After all, when it came to dissent their distant and uncaring leadership in Moscow had a history written in blood.

The Hungarian Revolution of 1956 had been ruthlessly put down with estimates of 2,500 killed and 13,000 wounded. Led by Alexander Dubcek, the Prague Spring of 1968 had briefly bloomed and then been mercilessly crushed. On the night of August 20, 1968, armies from the Soviet Union, Bulgaria, Poland and Hungary invaded Prague, around 200,000 troops and 2,000 tanks. Some 72 Czechs and Slovaks were killed, 702 severely wounded and another 436 were slightly injured. In the aftermath of this, a wave of emigration saw some 300,000 people leave Czechoslovakia.

Three decades later, the leader of the Soviet Union had worn a different face to Leonid Brezhnev, who presided over Hungary and Czechoslovakia.

Gorbachev publicly acknowledged that his *glasnost* and *perestroika* initiatives were forged from Dubcek's 'Socialism with a human face'. According to author Mark Almond in his book *Uprising: Political Upheavals that have Shaped the World*, in 1989, when asked what the difference was between the Prague Spring and his own reforms, Gorbachev stated bluntly, "Nineteen years".

But by the time that two decades stretched between Prague and events in Tbilisi, Gorbachev was ready to personally reach into the Brezhnev playbook.

April 9 is now remembered as the Day of National Unity in Georgia, while in political terms this marked the beginning of the end of Moscow's hold over the nation. The people had rallied around Georgian opposition to Soviet power. A session of the Supreme Council of Georgian S.S.R. condemned the occupation and annexation of Georgia in 1921.

On March 31, 1991, Georgians voted overwhelmingly in favour of independence from the Soviet Union and on April 9, 1991, the second anniversary of the tragedy, Georgia proclaimed its sovereignty.

From events in Hungary and Czechoslovakia, indeed from their own experiences in 1956 (on March 9, 1956, between 80 and 150, youths were massacred when local authorities lost control over the armed forces when they demanded independence), they should really have been able to anticipate Moscow's response. Georgian protesters circa-1989 were guilty of hopelessly underestimating Moscow's willingness to oppress.

Indeed, 'Tbilisi Syndrome', a state of denial as to Moscow's willingness to crush dissent, extended across the Caucasus to nearby Azerbaijan.

"Proclaiming a state of emergency in Baku and sending the army to the city was the biggest mistake of my political life," said former Soviet President Mikhail Gorbachev in 1995.

Hindsight changed the viewpoint of the West's former darling, although, in a statement released on February 3, 1995, he stated: "Before the troops arrived in Baku, the Azerbaijan Supreme Soviet and other political bodies were paralysed, dozens of people had fallen victim to extremists, power had been toppled by force in some regions, a 200-kilometre section of the Soviet border with Iran had been destroyed, and a state of emergency had been declared to prevent arbitrariness and robbery."

Gorbachev contends that; "the measures taken in the prevalent condition of the time prevented greater dangers."

That may be a politician's view, but for the family of Moza Shurko, those of the other 130 people cut down by Soviet bullets, and indeed the nearly one thousand unarmed civilians who were injured, such an expedient political diagnosis would be hard to draw. Allahshukur Pashazada, the most senior cleric sitting on the Spiritual Board of Muslims of the Caucasus dubbed Gorbachev a "merciless killer" in the wake of the event, demanding that the Soviet leader be hauled before an international court to answer charges of crimes against humanity.

On January 20, 2010, President Ilham Aliyev of Azerbaijan visited Martyrs'Alley in downtown Baku. His country ground to a halt while he led it in mourning. Twenty years earlier, on January 20, 1990, Soviet troops stormed Baku on Gorbachev's orders in a flawed attempt to save Communist rule and put down Azerbaijan's independence movement. The flaw sat not just in the killing itself, but in the predictability that Azerbaijanis, many of whom still supported Moscow, would shift their support behind those who spoke of independence.

The seeds of January 1990 had been sown two years earlier, on February 20, 1988, when Armenia's National Council of Nagorno-Karabakh defied international law by voting to unify that region with Armenia. Tensions rose, skirmishing began. In 1968 Martin Luther King Jr. had commented: "Hate begets hate; violence begets violence; toughness begets a greater toughness."

And in Azerbaijan the spiral that he was referring to became quickly apparent. Violence in the city of Sumgait, third largest city in Azerbaijan, north of Baku, saw 26 ethnic Armenians and six ethnic Azerbaijanis dead, many injured, and dozens of homes vandalised and looted. Sumgait would begin a trend, the opening salvo of a programme said to have been planned in Moscow. Armenian Eduard Grigoryan was widely named as head of the practical end of the operation.

Several more attacks were made on Azerbaijanis, most notably a bloody breakdown of civil society which occurred in the Armenian town of Spitak.

Soon, large numbers of refugees were leaving Armenia and Azerbaijan as violence escalated against the minority in each country. Inter-ethnic conflict grew. Gorbachev's hurried 1989 proposal for enhanced autonomy for Nagorno-Karabakh within Azerbaijan satisfied neither Armenians or Azerbaijanis, leaving the situation to simmer further.

When a joint session of the Armenian Supreme Soviet and the National Council, the legislative body of Nagorno-Karabakh, announced — illegally — the unification of Nagorno-Karabakh with Armenia, Azerbaijani refugees from the region, and those displaced from Armenia, protested and demanded their rights. There were some clashes with the Armenian community.

Moscow intervened. A director of *Radio Liberty*'s Azerbaijani Service later reported:

> *For several days, those 26,000 troops cracked down on protesters, firing into crowds without warning and killing more than 200 people. At least 700 were injured. Moscow declared emergency rule, which lasted for more than a year. Thousands of Popular Front members and sympathisers were arrested, imprisoned, and tortured.*
>
> *I remember that cold, windy January night well. I was keeping vigil with some friends on one of the main roads leading from the airport into the city.*
>
> *I couldn't get in touch with my parents, who had gone into the city in hope of finding me. Later I saw my father's tears for the first time in my life; he and*

my mother had gone to the morgues in search of me, finding instead the bodies of dozens of dead lining bloodstained corridors. They saw the bodies of women and children, of Azeris, of Tatars, of Jews, of Lezgins, of Russians. All of them ordinary citizens of Baku.

I remember walking the streets as the sun rose that morning, seeing tanks and armoured personnel carriers topped with young soldiers with guns at the ready. The country was in a state of disbelief…

Later, I remember the mass burial of hundreds of victims at Baku's Shehidler Khiyabani (Martyrs' Alley). Millions attended the funeral. The harbour was clogged with small private boats blaring their horns. Azerbaijan was united like never before. The era of the Soviet Union was over.

The traditional 40-day mourning period was marked by a national strike in honour of those who had stood up and sacrificed their lives for freedom. Factories ground to a standstill and people stayed home from work.

Soviet officials tried in vain to spin the tragedy. Soviet President Mikhail Gorbachev defended the invasion by citing the supposedly imminent danger of Islamic fundamentalism in Azerbaijan.

Speaking today, the boy in the photo holding an image of his father, Siraj Kazimov, does not falter when asked whom he views as responsible for what he and his siblings have suffered — Gorbachev. His father was an engineer on the Baku city metro.

"It took several years for my mother to die. But I can tell you that she was never the same after my father was murdered. She died of a broken heart," he says. Now in his mid-20s, he recalls the story of his mother and relatives frantically searching hospitals and morgues, desperate for news. He also remembers the moment he heard that an aunt had discovered the remains of his father.

"There were so many bodies, the authorities were keeping them in cold storage fridges normally used for food," says Kazimov. "Afterwards the government helped. We were given an apartment and my mother received a small pension. But my sister, my brother and I have never really recovered. Gorbachev's actions have left my family shattered.

"I will carry this with me until I die. And there are hundreds like me in Baku."

Chapter Fourteen

A Stain on Humanity

All humanity is one undivided and indivisible family, and each one of us is responsible for the misdeeds of all the others. I cannot detach myself from the wickedest soul.
— Mahatma Gandhi, Indian Philosopher

"It was a peaceful, peaceful place," says Lord Raymond Hylton. "People had not had problems with their neighbours. The Armenian families in Khojaly joined Azerbaijani families for Muslim celebrations, like Eid. At Christmas, Azerbaijani families shared in their neighbours' Christian traditions and gave gifts. That was how things were." Interviewed in the House of Lords, Lord Hylton remains gently neutral on the issue. He has visited Baku, Yerevan and parts of Nagorno-Karabakh.

Thousands of miles from London, an Azerbaijani pensioner sits in her new government-provided home in Sabirabad, a few hours outside of Baku. The house is basic, but far better than the tents and later shacks that provided shelter for the remnants of Kasumova and her family in the wake of Khojaly, and later when being driven out of Nagorno-Karabakh altogether.

Her family having suffered enough, she recalls: "My next door neighbour was Armenian. She was in my home every day. It was the same for everyone in Khojaly. We heard of the problems between Baku and Yerevan, but it seemed so far away as there was nothing but a desire to live together, and live peacefully. We wanted to be left alone and get on with life."

The Armenian assault on the town of Khojaly, in the early months of 1992, was the most notorious event in a long running dispute between Armenia and Azerbaijan over Nagorno-Karabakh.

Originally a town of approximately 7,000 people, predominantly Azerbaijani, situated on one of the main routes through Nagorno-Karabakh and in possession of the enclave's only airport, Khojaly was, militarily, the tactically significant town in the area. To the south-west of Khojaly was Stepanakert (Khankendi), the capital of the Nagorno-Karabakh region and a base for Armenian and Russian forces from the days of the Soviet Union. With numerous smaller Armenian settlements in the surrounding countryside, the majority of the population in the area was ethnic Armenian.

Shelled sporadically by Armenian forces since 1988 the population of Khojaly had been reduced to approximately 3,000, as a result of people fleeing from the conflict, but it was at the beginning of 1992 that events took a turn for the worse heralding disaster for the Azerbaijani population. In the months preceding the notorious attack, Khojaly became more isolated from the outside world. Utility supplies, such as electricity, were increasingly interrupted for longer and more frequent periods, the roads to Agdam to the north-east were blocked making supplies of essentials such as food, water and medicines only possible by a few flights into the airport. Even these deliveries became increasingly more and more difficult due to Azerbaijani aircraft coming under fire from the surrounding area.

In January of 1992 an independent American journalist, Thomas Goltz, was in Agdam and, becoming aware of the growing influx of refugees, secured a ride on one of the aircraft attempting to supply Khojaly. Rated to carry 24 persons the Russian built Mi-8 'Hip' helicopter was actually carrying 50; together with aid, weapons and ammunition. The aircraft was badly overloaded, necessarily slow, and therefore an extremely vulnerable target. In the two months prior to this flight, Thomas reported, two dozen helicopters, three a week, had been hit by ground fire, including two complete kills. Unsurprisingly his aircraft was also hit with a round through the fuel tank but was fortunate enough to survive the attack. He went on to say that:

> *On arrival there were no working phones in Xodjali (Khojaly), no working anything: no electricity, no heating oil and no running water. The only link with the outside world was the helicopters and those were under threat with each run. The isolation of the place became all too apparent as night fell.*

A small group of Azerbaijanis, containing only a few professional soldiers, were attempting to defend the airport perimeter with sporadic firefights taking place all through the night. One first hand account of the background to the coming atrocity states:

> *On February 25th, at approximately 7.30pm, Elman Mammadov, head of the Khojaly Executive Board, was informed by outposts that Armenian Armed Forces had been spotted moving towards Khojaly from all directions. Amongst these invaders were officers, troops and tanks of the former Soviet Union's 366th Motorised Infantry Brigade who were also stationed in Stepanakert. In the months preceding*

this attack several deserters from this regiment, who were originally from Turkmenistan, had taken refuge in Azeri towns to escape the reported beatings and cruel treatment they had received at the hands of Armenian and Russian officers, allegedly due to their being Muslims.

The disintegration of the Soviet Union had resulted in a degradation of centralised discipline and control of their military forces allowing, by default, greater local autonomy and freedom to seek allegiances and align themselves with whomsoever they chose. They had chosen Armenia.

The scene was now set. A military lacking command. A client state which was happy to adopt what amounted to a well-armed militia. A territorial gripe that had not just been simmering for generations, but one which had been exploited by Moscow to divide and conquer its distant regions. The fate of Nagorno-Karabakh in the early1990s was, perhaps, inevitable. The *Boston Globe* ran an article on March 16, 1992, highlighting the activities of the 366th stating:

Troops of the former Soviet army are continuing to fight and die in Nagorno-Karabakh, despite claims by the Commonwealth of Independent States' high command that they have been withdrawn… described as volunteers, fighting for cause, not high salaries… there is Yuri Nikolayevich, a cheery but cautious lieutenant colonel said to have been the deputy commander of the 366th regiment. Yuri Nikolayevich still wears his uniform. He refuses to give his full name or talk about his current role. Armenian officials say

> *that Yuri Nikolayevich went over to the Armenian fighters last week with a large part of the regiment's military hardware.*

Ethnic tensions and the prior history of these forces appear to be major contributory factors in the way events were to unfold in Khojaly:

> *[another Russian Officer]... refers to the Azerbaijani fighters as "dukhi", the Soviet army slang for Afghan mujahideen. "Most are savages," he says. He believes that Islam has to be checked here in Karabakh. "If not," he says, "I'll have to fight them in Belarus." And he is now training Armenian Karabakh's first border unit, made up, he says, of Armenians who had served in the Soviet airborne, marines and border forces...*

The period of massacre began with sustained shelling of Khojaly between 10.30pm and 11.00pm on the evening of February 25. The heavy weapons of the 366th Russian regiment proved devastating and a series of fires engulfed the town over the course of several hours. Following the bombardment, armoured personnel carriers, tanks and troops moved on the town. The airport, defended by a small group of Azerbaijani special police (OMON) with few heavy weapons, was no match for the invading force and the first target to fall. Once troops and vehicles started moving into the increasingly beleaguered town, the occupants of Khojaly had little choice but to flee, either to the north-east in the direction of the main town of Agdam or to surrounding Azerbaijani villages where they hoped they may find shelter.

In the early hours of the morning of February 26, witnessing surrounding houses go up in flames, some Azerbaijanis made the decision to flee. The majority of residents, however, remained, taking shelter in basements until about 3am when further members of the civil defence forces began to evacuate and encouraged others to follow. The weather at the time was extremely cold, reaching-10 degrees celsius in surrounding areas. Forests and mountains were covered in deep snow and people, in desperation, were fleeing into the night completely unprepared and with little or no protection from the harsh elements.

As these completely vulnerable citizens, interspersed with armed members of the civil defence force, attempted to make their way through freezing forests to the, hopefully, safe haven of other villages and Agdam, many were to meet a violent death, or capture and mutilation, at the hands of Armenian forces, some waiting in ambush at likely emergence points. The reports of what happened next are many and varied but share a common theme of indiscriminate killing, brutality and mutilation, with no regard for women, children or the elderly.

No words can express better the full horrors of those days than those of the international press. Britain's *Independent* newspaper recounts one survivor's experiences in an article dated June 12, 1992:

> *"To escape, the townspeople had to reach the Azeri town of Agdam about 15 miles away. They thought they were going to make it, until at about dawn they reached a bottleneck between the two Azeri villages of Nakhchivanik and Saderak. None of my group was hurt up to then... Then we were spotted by a car on*

the road, and the Armenian outposts started opening fire," Mr Sadikov said.

Mr Sadikov said only 10 people from his group of 80 made it through, including his wife and militiaman son. Seven of his immediate relations died, including his 67-year-old elder brother.

"I only had time to reach down and cover his face with his hat," he said, pulling his own big flat Turkish cap over his eyes. "We have never got any of the bodies back."

The first groups were lucky to have the benefit of covering fire. One hero of the evacuation, Alif Hajief, was shot dead as he struggled to change a magazine while covering the third group's crossing, Mr Sadikov said.

Another hero, Elman Mammadov, the Mayor of Khojaly, said he and several others spent the whole day of 26 February in the bushy hillside, surrounded by dead bodies as they tried to keep three Armenian armoured personnel carriers at bay.

In attempting to escape through the forests and mountains some refugees died of exposure, ill prepared for the sub-zero temperatures. Elman Mammadov reports further:

That year the winter was quite severe. The forest was covered with snow. Many people were barefoot, without any warm clothes on, since they didn't have time to bring anything with them. Just imagine they had to cross an icy cold river and then walk through a snowy forest. Many died from exposure; others ended up with severe frostbite.

...About two to three kilometres away from Agdam, near Nakhchivanik, we reached the end of the

forest and found ourselves in a large open area. What we didn't realise was that it was an ambush — the Armenians were waiting there in trenches for us. They knew that any survivors would have to pass that area. By that time, it was already early morning and just starting to get light.

In a situation like that, there's no time to think about what to do. A few of the other men and I tried to cover the others by firing our weapons. We divided into several small groups and took our positions. We told everyone to run across as quickly as possible. The Armenian armoured machines got closer and closer and then opened fire. So many innocent people died in that trap; a few lucky ones managed to escape.

There were ten men in our group, and five were wounded. Only four of us had guns, so we knew we wouldn't be able to break out of the encirclement. The other survivors had already crossed the front line, and we were left behind with the Armenian military forces. If we moved, we would have to face the Armenians again.

We decided to hide ourselves in a small forest nearby. We stayed there for 24 hours.

There are many consistent accounts of the Nakhchivanik incident in particular. A report in *The Sunday Times*, March 8, 1992, gives corroboration from other witnesses:

It was close to the Armenian lines we knew we would have to cross. There was a road, and the first units of the column ran across then all hell broke loose. Bullets were raining down from all sides. We had just entered their trap.

> *The Azeri defenders were picked off one by one. Survivors say that Armenian forces then began a pitiless slaughter, firing at anything that moved in the gullies. A video taken by an Azeri cameraman, wailing and crying as he filmed body after body, showed a grizzly trail of death leading towards higher, forested ground where the villagers had sought refuge from the Armenians.*
>
> *"The Armenians just shot and shot and shot," said Omar Veyselov, lying in hospital in Agdam with shrapnel wounds. "I saw my wife and daughter fall right by me."*

Helicopter attempts to reach survivors were usually frustrated by Armenian ground fire but in the days to follow the scale of the slaughter was to become ever more apparent. International reporting was limited, but nevertheless it was there. On March 3, 1992, the *New York Times* stated:

> *...dozens of bodies scattered over the area lent credence to Azerbaijani reports of massacre. Azerbaijani officials and journalists who flew briefly to the region by helicopter brought back three dead children with the backs of their heads blown off. They said shooting by Armenians had prevented them from recovering more bodies. "Women and children had been scalped," said Assad Faradjev, an aide to Nagorno-Karabakh's Azerbaijani Community Governor. "When we began to pick up bodies, they began firing at us."*
>
> *Reports of trucks filled with bodies coming into Agdam abound from many journalists and eyewitnesses. More disturbing is the mutilations that appear to have*

been carried out to bodies, some whilst the victims were still alive. Tales of people being scalped, with ears missing, skin removed from faces.

On the same day as the *New York Times*, the *Washington Times* added: "Azeri television showed pictures of one truckload of bodies brought to the Azeri town of Agdam, some with their faces apparently scratched with knives or their eyes gouged out." According to the *Independent* on June 12, while the dead were still being counted, some statistics had emerged about the nature of the killings. This article stated:

Officially, 184 people have so far been certified as dead, being the number of people that could be medically examined by the republic's forensic department. "This is just a small percentage of the dead," said Rafiq Youssifov, the republic's chief forensic scientist. "They were the only bodies brought to us." Of these 184 people, 51 were women, and 13 were children under 14 years old. Gunshots killed 151 people, shrapnel killed 20 and axes or blunt instruments killed 10. Exposure in the highland snows killed the last three. Thirty-three people showed signs of deliberate mutilation, including ears, noses, breasts or penises cut off and eyes gouged out, according to Professor Youssifov's report.

The official death toll from Khojaly is 613 dead, of which 106 were women and 63 children. Eight families were wiped out, 487 wounded, 130 children lost one parent and 25 lost both. Some 150 people went missing and 1,275 were taken hostage. These figures are almost universally accepted. Reports from those taken hostage, some held locally, some transported back to Stepanakert, were of brutal treatment and varying levels of time in captivity.

Events in Khojaly triggered condemnation and investigations from Human Rights groups including Amnesty International, Helsinki Watch and the Moscow based Memorial. The wider conflict resulted in four UN Security Council Resolutions regarding cessation of hostilities and withdrawal of forces. Four resolutions were adopted by UN Security Council in 1993 (30 April — No. 822, 29 July — No. 853, 14 October — No.874 and 12 November — No. 884).

According to the UN the conflict as a whole generated more than one million refugees, ending up in huge camps in Azerbaijan with little immediate hope of returning to Nagorno-Karabakh. The UN estimated approximately 300 Azerbaijani people drowned in the Arax river on the border of Iran and 10,000 were surviving in a makeshift tent city 10 miles from Iran.

The *Boston Sunday Globe* on November 21, 1993, recorded this merciless attitude:

> *A 40 year old accountant, sitting with friends in tent No. 566 on a recent day, explaining how the Armenians seized her village in less than a half hour, forcing the entire population toward the river in a chaotic scramble for survival.*

The ongoing dispute over the region cost lives counted in the thousands. 'Khojaly' distilled the essence of that conflict, full of hatred, into a brutal few days still sharply remembered today by many. The term 'massacre' hardly seems to do justice to these horrors. Massacres occurred frequently in World War One when massed infantry were cut down wholesale by enemy machine gun fire, but these events were performed by men in uniform 'A' seeing only figures in uniform 'B' that were, in turn, intent on the destruction of 'A'. In Khojaly all the victims were civilian. Similarly, aircraft crew carrying out the carpet bombing of European cities during World War Two had a remoteness from the mayhem they created.

There was no such remoteness and distance in Khojaly. The fatal injuries and disfigurements to women and children were up close and personal, gratuitous violence when no such actions were called for if the true objective was simply to secure a small airport town. It was highly unlikely that fleeing refugees would be somehow converted into an effective force and able to retaliate.

"Extermination," in other words, genocide, seems so much more appropriate.

Chapter Fifteen

Career Change

Success in business requires training and discipline and hard work. But if you're not frightened by these things, the opportunities are just as great today as they ever were.
— David Rockefeller, American banker

On January 21, 1990, Heydar Aliyev made no bones about where he apportioned blame for the massacre in Baku. He stated:

> *Regarding the events that happened in Azerbaijan I think that they contravene human rights, principles of democracy, humanity and the building of a state of law in our country... I think that there were opportunities for political settlement of the problem in Azerbaijan. But the leaders of Azerbaijan and U.S.S.R. didn't use those opportunities. They had opportunity to prevent attacks on the border. They knew that three months earlier people put forward their demands regarding the border line. But nobody tried to talk to them and to conduct explanatory work. I repeat: there are opportunities to ease people's anxiety.*
>
> *I think the behaviour of people who took that decision was politically wrong. They made a political mistake. They just did not realise the true circumstances in the Republic, didn't know the psychology of Azeri people, didn't have contacts with various segments of*

population. They couldn't even imagine that this issue will result in such a tragedy.

They had to foresee it and take appropriate steps, to consider what is more important and needed. By the way there is information that lots of militaries are also killed. I would ask, was that the fault of the ordinary Russian guy, who was sent by a wrong decision of the supreme party government of U.S.S.R. to put down a so called revolt in Azerbaijan?

If it was necessary they could use forces which already were in Azerbaijan. The government of Soviet Azerbaijan who made such a decision should bear the blame. Those who misinformed the supreme political government of U.S.S.R. should also be blamed. I consider that the supreme government of the state did not have timely and objective information. The government was misinformed and as a result such a decision was made. All who are involved in this tragedy should be punished.

Heydar Aliyev's statement effectively implicated Mikhail Gorbachev. It was a dramatic challenge and placed, in the public domain, the Soviet President as a culpable authority for a massacre. Under Gorbachev's *perestroika* programme there was expected to be openness, but for the most part this did not extend to publicly implicating the President in the massacre of innocent people on the streets of Baku.

It was a challenge that Gorbachev could not ignore.

Heydar Aliyev was already sidelined. His enforced 'retirement' was about as much as Gorbachev could do under the law. The statement crossed boundaries, but it did not break laws. A little more harassment by the authorities was possible. The surveillance of Heydar could be made more intrusive and his isolation could be made tougher as people were leaned upon to sever ties with him. For his impudence, Heydar would become a social pariah as more people than ever avoided contact with him in order to protect their own positions.

Heydar Aliyev understood this and never took it personally when people avoided him or severed friendships. He understood politics within the Soviet system and knew that it was impossible for many people to go against an establishment that could take away their jobs and livelihoods on a whim. But there were others who took a brave decision to defy the system and maintained their friendship and contact with him. He never forgot those who took such risks.

If Heydar Aliyev himself could be punished only so far, the Kremlin looked for his soft points. One of those was his son. At this point Ilham had enjoyed several years as a lecturer at Moscow State Institute of International Relations.

"I was happy there and enjoyed imparting knowledge to succeeding years. There were a lot of brilliant students who had a strong desire to learn," he says.

It was a fulfilling period that had seen him emerge as an academic of note. But that was about to end. There was retribution in the air. Vladimir Kryuchkov, the KGB head, was pure old school and always had time to deal with dissenters. Within days of his father's statement Ilham received a terse note which stated it had been decided to terminate his position at Moscow State Institute of International Relations with immediate effect.

An unsigned, three line letter on MGIMO letterhead would end an extended association that had seen Ilham emerge as an academic and educator. It was an unexpected and bitter event — but not one that he did not anticipate as a worst case scenario in the circumstances. Yet it was a hammer blow to someone who had dedicated himself to MGIMO and its students.

"It was a shock, yes," he recalls with a shrug.

Now there was a practical concern. Ilham had a family to feed and these were changing times in the Soviet Union. Events in Baku were indicative of a wider change in the crumbling nation.

Failed attempts at reform, a stagnant economy and war in Afghanistan had led to a general feeling of discontent, especially in the Baltic republics and Eastern Europe. Greater political and social freedoms, instituted by what was to be the last Soviet leader, created an atmosphere of open criticism of the Moscow regime. Gorbachev's efforts to streamline the Communist system were much needed, but ultimately proved impossible for him to maintain control. He unleashed a cascade of events that eventually resulted in the dissolution of the Soviet Union. On March 15, 1990, weeks after the Baku tragedy, Gorbachev was elected as the first President, simultaneously as the constitution was amended to deprive the Communist Party of political power.

But *perestroika* and *glasnost* led to the Kremlin losing its absolute grip. The failing occupation of Afghanistan, and especially the mishandling of Chernobyl, which Gorbachev tried to cover up, ruined his credibility. In general, dissatisfaction increased and the entirely positive view of Soviet life which was at the centre of national propaganda was rapidly dismantled.

In the wake of Baku and other events, rumblings began across the empire which would lead to the Communist governments of Bulgaria, Czechoslovakia, East Germany, Hungary, Poland and Romania being brought down in 1991 as revolution swept Eastern Europe.

Upheaval in Eastern Europe spread to nationalities within the U.S.S.R. that resented Soviet oppression, which in turn reawakened simmering ethnic tensions, such as that in Nagorno-Karabakh.

After years of Soviet military build-up at the expense of domestic development, economic growth was at a standstill. A vast trade gap had emptied the coffers of the union, leading to the Soviet system teetering on bankruptcy. Economic liberalisation had not helped. Another Gorbachev mantra, *uskoreniye*, meant speeding-up of economic development, while *perestroika* referred to political and economic restructuring. But hidden inflation and all-pervasive shortages aggravated the situation, with corruption creating a successful black market that undermined the official economy. Reforms made some inroads in decentralisation, but failed to dismantle the crippling fundamentals of the old and discredited Stalinist system.

Government spending increased when it could least afford, as the administration was engaged in propping up an increasing number of unprofitable state enterprises. Untenable consumer price subsidies also sucked out what little revenues there were, at the same time as tax revenues declined, as independently-minded republics withheld tax revenues in the name of autonomy. Decentralisation caused production bottlenecks and the half-cut system in its place was unable to cope. The economy was crashing, causing crippling unemployment and throwing millions into poverty. State institutions lost their subsidies and collapsed, taking with them the rest of the teetering economy.

Life for Ilham would now take a diametric change in direction. The education system was also in financial trouble. The Soviet education budget was slashed and years of under-investment meant that the system was quickly stressed, almost to breaking point. No-one was recruiting, either in Russia, or in Baku, where much the same was happening. Universities were scaling down to cope with the crisis, laying off staff and cutting places for students. Among those already in the system there was a massive drop-out rate as students could not afford to live amid steep increases in housing and utility prices.

From a noted lecturer in one of the Soviet Union's most renowned educational institutions, Ilham was now touting around a CV that, however impressive, was superfluous in a sector that was radically downsizing.

Coupled with that, there was a growing realisation that "the system" was also against him.

"I applied for many jobs in Moscow, and indeed elsewhere, but it became clear that I was on a blacklist somewhere. Several people even told me 'I would like to give you this position, but I am not allowed to'," he says. "It was quite depressing."

Even when Ilham left the realms of the educational industry there was the same response. Where there were jobs, in place was an invisible barrier that a few people quietly acknowledged to him that this was on government orders. Amid the collapse of the Soviet Union, the administration remained as petty as ever.

"So I decided to go into business privately," he says. "There was no other option if I was to feed my family."

From academia to entrepreneurship. It was a hugely risky transformation. Hailing from the heart of the Communist Empire, Ilham had no experience of private enterprise. Neither did just about anyone aside from those with fingers in the Black Economy. Before the emerging private sector lay a bewildering concept, underscored by a market with little history of such a thing. Another private sector growth area was the development of private businesses *de novo*. Small-scale enterprises became the norm, many street vendors setting up. These two had ties into organised crime, either as a part of mafia scams or through the payment of protection fees to criminal gangs. Prior to most official privatisation, some 40 per cent of the Russian non-agricultural workforce were employed in the private sector. Private construction firms were becoming widespread.

The early stages of private sector development in the post-Soviet Union were accompanied by recognised 'waves' of entrepreneurs. Between 1987 and 1989, at the very beginning of this shift in social culture, many of the entrepreneurs who owned and led cooperative firms had illegal incomes, often through ties into criminal gangs and Mafia. Next to get in on the act were high-level civil servants, who used their positions to dominate the second wave of entrepreneurs, between 1989 and 1990.

By the time that Ilham was assessing the possibilities before him there was a third wave underway, characterised by directors and managers of state-owned firms, who took the opportunity to privatise 'their' enterprises to their own advantage or to establish new businesses based upon the same failing state companies. Insider knowledge, influence-peddling based upon political positions and vast criminal ties underpinned the new economy as the Soviet Union crumbled.

Despite the dark undercurrents that accompanied much of this new private sector there were opportunities for someone with a good idea and a deft approach.

Trade and services in general were under-supplied during the Soviet era. In 1988, in America, the cradle of consumerism, there were 61 retail shops per 10,000 citizens. That same year Russia had only 20 per 10,000 citizens, and of that figure a majority were antiquated old state-run outlets.

Retail was clearly set for a bonanza. Yet the economy was shot, the masses suffered and struggled with disposable income. A shop, or chain, even in Moscow, would have to stand out in an increasingly competitive environment.

Serving retail through import was another option and presented many opportunities. Surprisingly, the former Azerbaijani academic turned his attention to fashion.

It is hard to speak about fashion in the Soviet Union. The production of clothes, as any other industry, was in the hands of the State. So there simply was no choice in terms of what to buy. Stylish clothes from the West, as any other foreign goods, were forbidden. People daring to wear such clothes, if they could somehow obtain them, were called *Stilyaga* (Russian for 'dandy', but with a very negative connotation).

But worse than the name calling that a fashionista could expect was official repercussions. The KGB, the much feared State Security Committee, came down on such people and those looking too fashionable were considered dangerous to society. As for women, they could not look too attractive either as this was also considered a threat to state security. Those young women who paid too much attention to their appearance were considered unsatisfactory and were generally barred from joining the Komsomol (Young Communist League) and, as a result, would have a problem with getting a job or ensuring that their names were well placed on state lists, such as the housing list. In the Soviet Empire every person needed to be a member of the Communist Party on some level in order to get anywhere. A fashionista would be hampered for looking a little too "pretty" or be judged to look a little too "western".

Within these strict moral parameters, Soviet Union fashion could be called "Soviet style". But just as *perestroika* had changed many things, it also allowed people to reject this dowdy and dated look.

In the 1990s, fashion is typically referred to as the decade of 'anti-fashion', characterised by minimalist styles, and many overlapping, often contradictory trends. On the streets of Moscow "Soviet style" was replaced by grunge fashion, made popular by Seattle-based band Nirvana and its lead singer Kurt Cobain. The grunge look lasted until the end of the decade. Another innovation that would have been punishable under the old system was navel piercing, which became a trend, along with the tight lycra or black leather mini skirt, inspired by Michelle Pfeiffer's performance as Catwoman in the 1992 film Batman Returns and singer Victoria Beckham's catsuits in several Spice Girls videos.

Seeing all these changes on the streets of Moscow, and on visits to Baku, Ilham sensed that the fashion market could only grow as younger generations embraced the new liberalism. Yet at the same time there were now many Russians, or residents from elsewhere in the Soviet Bloc, in a position to afford top brands. For everyone ready to spend on a pair of Versace jeans, a Prada tie or Giorgio Armani suit there were tens of thousands who could not hope to reach such levels.

The answer was to manufacture at home in the hope of producing quality clothing, in western styles, but significantly cheaper. Admitting to knowing little about women's fashions, he began to study men's styles. While fashion designers had been working on women's fashion collections for some time, the 1980s saw the first emergence of couture culture for men. Designers such as Vivienne Westwood, Anne Klein and Jean Paul Gaultier first presented a new type of business wear, the 'Power' suit, which quickly moved into mainstream fashion.

Some of the designers of the 1990s that promoted international dress fashions included Michael Cors, Isaac Mizrahi and Oscar De La Renta. These fashion artists, along with Calvin Klein, Ralph Lauren, Bill Blass and Donna Karan all influenced fashion around the world.

The more the former-academic learned, the more he saw an opportunity. Western influences were everywhere in the former Soviet Bloc, and men were gaining a quick understanding of what was 'hip' in places like New York, London, Paris and Milan. They wanted to look good, every bit as much as the women.

The term metrosexual was first coined by journalist Mark Simpson to describe the single man with a penchant for shopping and, in general, the 'good life'. Russia and the Soviet Bloc were now full of wannabe metrosexuals. It was not until 2002 that metrosexuality became recognised as a lifestyle when Simpson penned an article that introduced David Beckham as a noteworthy metrosexual. But they were there before that nonetheless.

Someone like Beckham was the real thing, a genuine metrosexual with a wardrobe full of designer labels. But to a majority — including a big majority in Russia — metrosexuality would come at a price that meant a few corners being cut. In order to get there one needed the right kind of sweaters, button-down shirts, suits, jeans and classic pants.

Supplying menswear into an increasingly sophisticated Russian market was a niche. The Azerbaijani businessman was one of the first. Within six months of leaving MGIMO Ilham opened a small factory just outside Moscow.

"It was hard to adapt to the free market, but you did what you had to," he says. It was not the most modern plant, situated in the premises of a bankrupt garment firm, but Ilham had done his homework well and brought in modern garment systems that would allow the company to produce jackets, suits, pants and shirts made of silk, linen, ramie, cotton, polyester and blended fabrics. The company opened with a handful of staff, but this grew.

Suddenly, following 14 years in which he acquainted himself with the intricacies and foibles of history, Ilham had learned a great deal about fabric, collar style, jackets, number of buttons, single breasted or double breasted and other details that made up suit styles. He was happy to leave style decisions to his paid talent, the designers, but nevertheless took a hands-on approach.

In the 1990s, less than a year after his departure from MGIMO, Ilham's sales team fanned out across Russia with a 'middle ground' product — dozens of smart western styles, a variety of quality fabrics and, most importantly, well manufactured. Backed up by an array of shirts and many styles of ties, this 'middle ground' approach found fertile ground. His menswear swept into the market and, within weeks, the company was struggling to fulfill a burgeoning order book. New staff were being taken on each month as the company worked to expand its manufacturing and supply operations.

"My father used to say, 'Let them see you and not the suit. That should be secondary'," commented Cary Grant, but he was well out of step in post-Communist times.

"[Lenin] was no dandy," wrote his biographer Robert Service. "While wanting to remain tidy, he did not enjoy shopping for clothes; he got others to do this for him — or rather he wore his clothes until such time as one of his relatives became sufficiently exasperated to buy a new suit or a pair of shoes for him."

According to Service, Lenin was a bit of a neat freak. "He hated untidiness — and he admonished family members if they failed to keep their buttons neatly sewn and their shoes repaired."

Lenin's dress markedly changed after arriving in Russia to lead the "proletarian" revolution. Gone were the worn, heavy mountain boots. He often donned a suit purchased in Switzerland, but added the worker's cap to his attire. The cap was actually not popular attire among the Russian working class, but rather the cover worn by turn of the century painters. Lenin's suit and cap combo became his signature. It was a class statement that "distinguished him from *[other politicians]* and their solemn Homburg hats."

Swiss couture was every bit equalled within the bowels of Ilham's relatively small factory. As proof of this, within weeks of the sales operation getting underway thousands of units were leaving for wholesalers and some of the larger retailers across the country.

New styles also rolled out in 1992. A double-breasted classic suit, vintage British suits with just a single button row down the front, Italian cut suits tailored, clean and well-pressed and the American suit, a style that is more casual, wider at the shoulders and a straighter line along the sides.

All these were in huge demand, along with their accessories, shirts and ties. A pair of the big names of Soviet era shopping, as they sought to survive and upgrade themselves, quickly began to be major outlets for the new enterprise.

Two stolid Russian department stores had one thing in common throughout the grey Soviet era: they rhymed with 'glum'. But GUM and TSUM, once notorious for empty shelves, grim customers and grumpy staff, were attempting a retail revival. Both became customers.

Therefore the fertile market began to expand. With his many contacts, Ilham's firm quickly found orders coming in from Azerbaijan, while Russia quickly became one nation on an export list that included many of the former Warsaw Pact states, like Poland, Czechoslovakia, Bulgaria, Ukraine, Belarus and others.

Western fashionistas would be in for a surprise. The former Warsaw Pact countries were no longer the land of shapeless shifts and ill-fitting polyester shirts. The collapse of Communism had given free rein to Russians' traditional creativity and love of self-adornment. "Only two countries, Russia and Italy, have a similar mentality. We really love to decorate ourselves," says Natalia Vinogradova, President of the Russian Association of Fashion Houses.

Ilham's decision on what markets to probe would prove very well founded. Within a year of opening its doors, the factory had grown in size and would continue on the same positive trajectory. Expansion, when it came, took Ilham beyond Soviet borders for an extended period for the first time. While his business was thriving, employing many Russians and making an impact on the economy, he personally grew tired of the bad feeling created by his name and the problems that were now apparent in Russia itself.

In August 1991, Boris Yeltsin had won a global name having set himself as a modern democrat in defying a coup by government elements opposed to *perestroika* and Gorbachev. Yeltsin swept to power with a wave of high expectations when he was elected President of the Russian Soviet Federative Socialist Republic with pandemic corruption, economic collapse, and enormous political and social problems hitting Russia.

One would have thought that those in government would have had more to worry about than persecuting anyone with the surname Aliyev. But there was still resentment toward Heydar Aliyev among many in the higher echelons of the Yeltsin administration, those with a leg still in the dim Soviet past. Many even blamed Heydar for what they saw as his part in the demise of Soviet hegemony in speaking out so openly and condemning the government.

The many problems led Ilham to consider what next. Inside 18 months he had created an international business that generated export revenues for Russia, created jobs, and fed a market that helped to prevent the Russian economy soaking up more imports. But expansion meant opportunity. A factory near Moscow was positioned excellently for the Russian market, but the inherent problems of the era meant that exports were becoming harder to shift, mainly because of collapsing infrastructure but also because of the corruption and crime that was spreading and becoming endemic.

Beautiful and imposing Istanbul is the only city in the world that is situated on two continents — Europe and Asia. It is a megacity, the cultural and financial centre of Turkey, located on the Bosphorus Strait and encompassing a natural harbour known as the Golden Horn. Because of its strategic location Istanbul has served as the capital city of the Roman Empire, the Byzantine Empire and the Ottoman Empire. The city was also in the midst of a major economic and social boom that would see the population more than triple during the quarter century between 1980 and 2005. In 1992 it stood at around nine million people.

With a huge domestic market in Istanbul and Turkey, and tremendous links with the rest of the world, the city was an ideal base for a business expansion, out of Russia. There was the common culture linking Azerbaijanis with Turkey and with much of the region. The term Turkic represents a broad ethno-linguistic group of people including existing societies such as the Azerbaijani, Karachays, Kazakhs, Tatar, Kyrgyz and Turkish people.

Because of this there was a familiarity that made Istanbul attractive to Ilham. The city was rich and colourful in terms of its social, cultural and commercial activities. Opera, ballet and theatre continued throughout the year. During seasonal festivals, world famous orchestras, choral ensembles, concerts and jazz legends flocked there to play for packed houses. Cultural events dominated a very attractive social landscape.

So it was, in 1993, the Aliyevs moved to Turkey, which would briefly become home while shuttling in and out of Russia.

Outside of Istanbul, from a nondescript office, he built a second operation that dealt with clothing. This acted as an international sales office for produce manufactured in Russia and resulted in a broad import segment for clothing going into the former Soviet Empire.

Life was good. Ilham studiously avoided events at home, which had catapulted his father back into the political fray. Instead, he was doing business, enjoying his family, unchattelled from the burdens of surname problems and the miseries that accompanied life in Russia at that time.

In many ways, this period in Turkey would prove a seminal time. Out of the Soviet system. Out of Russia. Out of the long-shadow of a political giant. He would spend his time on realisation of ideas.

It would be a period that was all too brief. In April 1994 he was working in the small office that was in his home when a telephone call came from Azerbaijan. It was his father, Heydar. Nothing unusual. Father and son made it a point to speak every week.

Only this time the call was something different. It was a telephone call that would change the direction of his life forever.

Chapter Sixteen

Events at Home

Nearly all men can stand adversity, but if you want to test a man's character, give him power.
— Abraham Lincoln, American statesman

Azerbaijan declared its independence from the former Soviet Union on August 30, 1991, the first nations to recognise her independence being, intriguingly, Turkey, Israel, Romania and Pakistan. Ayaz Mutallibov, former First Secretary of the Azerbaijani Communist Party, almost by virtue of his Soviet authority, became the country's first President on September 8, 1991. Mutallibov was elected in a single-candidate nationwide election.

But his would be a short-lived tenure, dogged by Nagorno-Karabakh and a nation in collapse through economic mismanagement. Mutallibov is remembered by most people in Azerbaijan as a weak-willed and self-important man, with inexperienced political perspicacity. While giving preference to short-term effects in political processes, Mutallibov lost his influence and support.

Within days of the Khojaly Massacre, the National Assembly of Azerbaijan forced Mutallibov to resign. Just nine weeks later, the Supreme Council of Azerbaijan, which was dominated by the former Communist Party of Azerbaijan, ordered Mutallibov's recall as President to replace the temporary leadership of Yaqub Mammadov.

But his restored Presidency did not last. He attempted to suspend scheduled Presidential elections and ban all political activity, which prompted the opposition to organise resistance and take power. Armed forces led by the Azerbaijan Popular Front (APF) swept into Baku, took control of Parliament and Azerbaijan State Radio and Television, seizing power and leaving Mutallibov to flee to Moscow in exile, where he remains until the present day.

On May 17, 1992, Isa Gambar was elected Chairman of the National Assembly, making him Acting President ahead of national elections on June 17, 1992, which brought Abulfaz Elchibey to power.

Abulfaz Aliyev, leader of the APF, had assumed the nickname of Elchibey, meaning 'noble messenger' in Azerbaijani and he made history as the first non-Communist President. He defeated six other candidates and won 54 per cent of the vote. But he, like Mutallibov, would only hold the position briefly.

Elchibey's government had struggled to hold the levers of power with any credibility. They had promised to reverse military failures in Nagorno-Karabakh, which had seen the Khojaly Massacre followed by abject military defeats in Shusha and Lachin. His government's much touted counter offensive saw Azerbaijani forces reclaim around half of Nagorno-Karabakh within months, reaching to within a few kilometres of Shusha. But that was a high tide mark and the effort quickly collapsed due to rampant incompetence and corruption among politicians and high ranking members of the armed forces. The charge of treason was being directed at a great many people.

Abject failure in Nagorno-Karabakh caused a collapse in Elchibey's support and, coupled with increasing and widespread corruption and incompetence in general, there was growing unrest. The people, it seemed, had finally had enough in June 1993, one year into Elchibey's Presidency. There was increasing anarchy in the country. Journalists criticising the government were being beaten, industrial enterprises ground to a halt and political groups formed their own armed militias.

Ganja, Azerbaijan's second-largest city, named Kirovabad during Soviet times, was the main industrial centre of western Azerbaijan. Ganja had been swamped with tens of thousands of refugees from Nagorno-Karabakh, and been far closer to the action as the military had been swept from Azerbaijani territory, not once, but twice.

Ganja's economy was dominated by aluminum, porcelain, instrument making, furniture, textiles and other industries, all of which suffered in general through the post-Soviet economic malaise, but had been further hindered by government mismanagement and corruption. Anger had grown to breaking point in Ganja. An armed insurrection in the city first ousted the national government there, and then started to move toward Baku. The armed forces stood aside, unwilling to fight to save a discredited government. With his support dwindling, Elchibey fled to his native village of Kalaki in Nakhchivan.

Elchibey was formally deposed by a national referendum in August 1993, but a new power was already established in Baku, one that would change everything for Azerbaijan and replace turmoil with much needed stability.

After his ouster from the politburo in 1987, Heydar Aliyev had endured three long years in KGB forced isolation. He had suffered a reported heart attack and was not in rude health, but in the wake of his infamous statement in 1990, and the loosening of the KGB's grip, had sought to return home.

Almost immediately after this appearance in Moscow, Heydar officially renounced his membership of the Communist Party of the Soviet Union. He wrote:

> *I am informing you that I have decided to withdraw from the Communist Party of the U.S.S.R. I want to state that, in this decision, I am not just following fashion, but that it is a result of my evaluation of the hardships, happenings and the many disappointments that I have lived during recent times. The following reasons compelled me to take this step:*
>
> *The very idea of leaving the Communist Party crossed my mind after the military aggression against the people of Azerbaijan, committed in January 1990, under the direction of the leaders of the Communist Party of Azerbaijan and U.S.S.R. During the events of January hundreds of people were killed and wounded. I condemned those inhumane events, which contradicted the Constitution and basic law, and I expected that the Central Committee of the Communist Party of the U.S.S.R. and Azerbaijan would solve this case and punish the criminals involved.*
>
> *I pulled myself together and waited. But, in response to my speeches, attacks were arranged against me in media organs of the Communist Party. All my attempts to refute baseless charges against me in the same media failed. The main achievement of 'Perestroika' and 'Glasnost' have shown itself as one-sided.*
>
> *Six months have now passed. Yet the criminals, who are widely known to everyone, are still not punished. On the contrary, they are supported in efforts to conceal their guilt. They believe that time will pass, and that their role in this tragedy will be*

forgotten. But time has proven that crimes against nations are never forgotten — or forgiven — even as decades pass...

Secondly, my decision is based upon the hypocritical, bifrontal policy of the Community party, appeasing the Armenian nationalists who have held Nagorno-Karabakh Autonomous Region for more than three years. This region had been taken from Azerbaijan...

Thirdly, I can see that in times of democracy, political freedoms and pluralism in Azerbaijan, the national movement for democracy is being choked by the Communist Party of Azerbaijan, with the support of the Communist Party of U.S.S.R..

...I was against, and I am still against, the new Union Treaty as proposed by Moscow. It is impossible to have several sovereign countries within the framework of one sovereign state. All former Soviet Republics have to be given true political and economic freedoms, independence that is important so they may revive their national forms.

...All above mentioned facts force me to take this final step and declare my withdrawal from the Communist Party of U.S.S.R., notwithstanding that making such a decision was a very difficult task for me. I have grown in the Communist Family and my whole adult life has been related to the Communist Party. In 1943, when I was only 20, I bound my life to the party of Bolsheviks. I believed in values of Communism with all my heart, and participated in implementation of its plans.

But now all these beliefs are dead. All those countless declarations regarding the renewal of the

> *party, and renewal of the union of republics, are lies. We have to say openly to the people that the Communist experiment and the way of socialism have failed, and that the union of republics, which was created and maintained by means of violence, is now set to collapse.*
>
> *I realise all the difficulties that I will face because of this declaration, and can foresee every sort of attack and moral pressures that will be set against me. But an unbiased analysis of Communist Party's past had brought me to the conclusion that I have declared above...*

Hardly had ink dried upon this indictment of the Communist system than Heydar Aliyev decided to return to his homeland of Nakhchivan. He had enough of Moscow and, having defied the Communist Party openly, was ready to defy the KGB. He made no secret that he was intending to depart from Moscow, almost challenging the collapsing "system" to stop him.

Moscow was preoccupied and this did not register. Baku was not. Power brokers in the Azerbaijani capital did not want Heydar Aliyev back in their orbit, even if he claimed that he was not interested in politics. Many observers thought the veteran politician was heading back to vie for power.

"Absolutely my father wished to return to Nakhchivan and live a quiet life," says Ilham. "He was not in the best of health and was not ready for the cut and thrust of politics. He was tired of Moscow and tired of politics. He wanted to live peacefully among his own people."

Not everyone was buying into that story. Ayaz Mutallibov, appointed First Secretary of the Azerbaijan Communist Party on January 24, 1990, four days after the massacre and later to be President, did not like the idea of the former giant of Azerbaijani politics on his doorstep. Mutallibov pressed his 'apparatus' into service, in order to 'lean' on Heydar and convince him to remain in Moscow.

"We heard from Baku that Heydar Aliyev would not be welcome," says Ali Hasanov, today Head of the Department of Public-Political Issues in the Presidential Administration. "There were a series of menacing threats and plenty of dark insinuations that all would not be well if he tried to return."

Heydar heard these words, but was stoic. He had been away for too long. He was not in the rudest of health. He wanted to be home and to be among 'his' people, not trapped in Moscow among strangers and the turmoil. He and several aides booked a flight home on July 20, 1990. Without wishing to do so, Heydar had thrown down the gauntlet.

The battle lines were drawn. High noon was upon both sides.

Even as the group left for Sheremetyevo International Airport messages were being received, advising them to stay put. If he was nervous, Heydar did not show it. He is recalled smiling and speaking to well-wishers in the departure lounge, fellow Azerbaijanis who recognised their former leader. His relaxed demeanour, according to Hasanov, came from a sense of peace as to what would happen next.

"He was ready to die, I think, if that was what was to come," he says. "Heydar Aliyev was isolated and out-on-a-limb in Moscow. Staying there, away from what was dear to him, was a worthless exercise and he would have been prepared to die instead of remaining where he was."

The flight took off from Sheremetyevo International Airport that morning ahead of a three hour flight to Baku.

Heydar had made his intentions clear. After just a few hours in Baku, a connecting flight would take him to Nakhchivan and a self-imposed exile. On the ground in Baku, however, Mutallibov and his administration read the situation somewhat differently. He believed that Heydar Aliyev was preparing to storm Baku.

"That was nonsense," says Hasanov. "There were five of us, Heydar Aliyev and four others. Heydar Aliyev had made no public or private announcements, other than to condemn those responsible for the massacre and call for their punishment. Not a word had passed his lips calling for an overthrow of government or seeking public support to rise up."

"He wanted to get back to Nakhchivan and live quietly," says Ilham, who was left behind in Moscow looking for a job after his dismissal from MGIMO.

As news filtered through to Baku that Heydar was on the flight, the government in Baku acted. The airport was partly closed off and a security cordon thrown around its parameter. During the three hour flight of the Tupolev aircraft, a dozen buses of government supporters, mainly old-style Communist rabble rousers, were driven to the site. Police marshalled them to a site approximate to a remote apron, well away from the bleak Soviet terminal.

By late morning the Tupolev aircraft landed and taxied to its parking bay. On board, Heydar had completed a flight of autograph signings and chats with crew and passengers. Even those who had demanded to know why he had so publicly turned his back on Communism had been won over. Those who wished to chat learned that he wished to retire gracefully and quietly.

"There were a few angry people on board, who demanded to know what he was doing," says Hasanov. "But he explained that, like them, he just wished to be at home, and that he did not have some revolutionary scheme."

Most of the 100 or so passengers on the flight had filed towards his seat during the flight. Heydar, for so long isolated from people by the grip of the KGB, revelled in the social intercourse. In many ways it took his mind off the unknown quantity of what was waiting for him in Baku. He and his party were full of tension, not knowing what fate was ready for them in Baku.

That sense of well-being ended within minutes of landing. The Tupolev taxied far from the terminal, to an isolated spot, and those on board quickly became aware of shouting and chanting from outside the aircraft. On the port side of the aircraft several hundred angry looking men were assembled. They were in an ugly mood.

On board the aircraft, Hasanov remembers that there was outrage among the passengers as to what was obviously being planned.

"There were angry voices, people cursing the men and calling out that Heydar Aliyev had every right to return if he wished," says Hasanov.

As a passenger staircase was put into place men outside surged forward, wild and excitable, calling loudly for him to "go home" and bellowing insults toward him. Tempers grew inside the aircraft.

The four men with Heydar considered what to do, how to protect him when there were hundreds in the ugly mob. But offers quickly came. One man they did not know stood in the aisle and shouted: "They should not do this. I will stand by Heydar Aliyev. Who will stand with me?"

A handful of others stood, offering to form a human shield to prevent him from harm. Eventually a dozen men, most of them unknown to him, escorted the 67 year old through the angry mob and to a car nearby. Several sustained cuts as protesters lashed out, but Heydar reached his car without injury.

Thanks to the help of these strangers he made it out of the airport and, within 24 hours, reached home to his beloved Nakhchivan.

It was, perhaps, inevitable, that Heydar would not remain idle and that people would come calling. One profile of him states: "Aliyev reinvented himself as a moderate nationalist" and set himself up for a speedy political return.

But those close to him are adamant that power was no aphrodisiac to him and not something he craved.

"No, he had no plan beyond getting to Nakhchivan," says Ilham. "He had been a victim of politics in Moscow, and in view of what he had come to realise as the truth, felt sorrow for his part in the Soviet Union. Politics were anathema to him at the time. He had no interest."

If Mutallibov had believed that then he may have left well alone. But he did not, and wanted to avoid the risk. Hardly had Heydar unpacked his bags in Nakhchivan when, through a series of envoys, Mutallibov privately chided Heydar for returning and warned that he would brook not a single word of criticism.

What was the catalyst to Heydar Aliyev dabbling in politics one cannot say. But he was incandescent with rage at what he saw round him, the virtual collapse of the nation. He would not be strong-armed into remaining quiet. Least of all by a figure whose ability he doubted and less still by a man who, through intermediaries, was issuing menacing threats.

Plato had stated that: "The price of apathy towards public affairs is to be ruled by evil men." Heydar considered Mutallibov an incompetent and corrupt leader. Even if he did indeed resist the call to serve, he was quickly sucked back into the fray.

At 67 years old, depending on whom you ask, Heydar plotted to, or reluctantly, found himself elected as Nakhchivan's representative to the Supreme Council of Azerbaijan S.S.R. in Baku, in the dying days of the Soviet Union. He was critical of the regime and the Communist Party.

It was an odd transformation. In 1969, Heydar Aliyev was appointed by Leonid Brezhnev to the post of First Secretary of the Central Committee of Azerbaijan Communist Party and he had ended his time within the Soviet system in 1987 as First Deputy Prime Minister of the Soviet Union.

Now, as a regular member of the Supreme Council he was in the unusual position of being a voice in the opposition. For months he had ignored Mutallibov and his proxies, before deciding to leave Baku. Again, there is suggestion that this was amid coercion and threats.

Either way, Heydar Aliyev returned to Nakhchivan, unbroken, yet unwilling to accept that the dregs of the Communist Party remained on in Baku, clinging to power for as long as they could, stealing as much as they could, while taking as little responsibility as they could, for the country as a whole, and for the disaster that was Nagorno-Karabakh in particular. He was elected Chairman of the Supreme Council of Nakhchivan Autonomous Republic in 1991 and would see that his homeland was as comfortable as possible in trying times. One crisis came in May 1992, when Armenian forces shelled the Sadarak region of Nakhchivan. The Armenians invaded Nagorno-Karabakh and then repelled the subsequent attempts by Azerbaijani forces to liberate the region.

After Mutallibov was unseated in Baku, life got no better under Elchibey. Indeed, it became markedly worse. Armenia enforced a blockade of Nakhchivan in response to a blockade organised against it over Nagorno-Karabakh. For the Azerbaijani people of Nakhchivan times became progressively harder due to the economic squeeze and post-Soviet economic malaise. Far from plotting a return to Baku, Heydar Aliyev was now concerned with holding this small entity together and maintaining some measure of normality.

In Azerbaijan, however, events were coming to a head. Discontent had reached a peak on June 4, 1993, when Elchibey dispatched his Presidential Guard to Ganja in an ultimately failed attempt to suppress an army rebellion led by Colonel Surat Huseynov. Over 60 people died, which only served to heighten anger directed towards the government and saw more sections of the armed forces join Huseynov. A former director of a wool factory, Huseynov had become popular during the years of the Karabakh war as a leader of armed forces. Now, however, he used his men in a brazen coup attempt.

On June 5, a small aircraft landed at Nakhchivan Airport containing an envoy from Elchibey. He travelled into Nakhchivan City with a message, imploring Heydar to return to Baku and prevent the collapse of the government. He declined.

On June 6, the same aircraft flew into Nakhchivan a second time. Huseynov's rebels were still moving. Elchibey's support was ebbing. Baku was in flux. He implored Heydar to reconsider. A second time Heydar Aliyev refused.

On June 7, the same aircraft was again parked in Nakhchivan's small airport. This time there was a delegation from the government. Huseynov and his men were approaching the outskirts of Baku. Elchibey implored his fellow Nakhchivanian to return to the national capital. For a third time, Heydar heard the arguments, but insisted that he wished to have no part in the crisis.

By June 8 the noose was fully around Elchibey. No element of the Azerbaijani armed forces was ready to defend him. Baku's police force had stood aside and most of those around the President had melted away. Besieged in the President's Office he came to accept that there were no options remaining and prepared to leave. But if history records Elchibey poorly, it should also record that even as he considered his own fate, he also considered that chaos would erupt on the streets of Baku without a President in place and with rebel troops bearing down upon the city. That afternoon he dispatched his closest lieutenants on an aircraft headed for Nakhchivan. Their brief was not to come back without Heydar on board.

That morning, Heydar met with the delegation from Baku and heard the shocking news that the President was preparing to leave Baku and that the nation was facing an absolute power vacuum that could lead to any of the worst possible scenarios for Azerbaijan.

Heydar Aliyev, they said, had no option but to travel to Baku immediately.

Rebellious troops were on the outskirts of Baku and Heydar's aircraft landed in the capital Baku. It was quite a contrast from his first 'homecoming'.

A couple of years earlier he had been portrayed as a danger to national security and hundreds of hooligans had been bussed to the airport in an effort to intimidate him into turning around and returning to Moscow.

On this occasion, several thousand chanting supporters greeted Heydar, chanting his name and besieging him to claim power. Perhaps the only similarity was that the 70 year old needed a bodyguard again. But instead of protecting him from physical harm, on this occasion it was required to stop the throng of supporters from attempting to touch the man now being held up as Azerbaijan's saviour-in-waiting.

Within days, Heydar Aliyev had gripped the levers of power. Rebellious troops were placated by his appearance and returned to their bases. He became Chairman of the Azerbaijani Parliament on June 15, 1993, which allowed him to assume Presidential powers under the constitution.

Within 10 weeks, on August 29, a national referendum formally ended the Elchibey era and cleared the way for Heydar to stand in a fresh Presidential poll.

He and two other candidates stood in Presidential Elections held in October 1993, that would inject some much needed stability into the Azerbaijani political system. Voter turnout was about 90 per cent, of which a reported 99 per cent voted for Heydar Aliyev. Many international observers declared the elections biased because no major opposition candidates ran and reported that the mass media favoured the eventual winner and barely reported on the campaigns of other candidates. However, the people had confidence in him and believed that he could save the country from the chaos.

Chapter Seventeen

Home in Baku

No man will ever bring out of the Presidency the reputation which carries him into it. To myself, personally, it brings nothing but increasing drudgery and daily loss of friends.
— Thomas Jefferson, American statesman

Ilham Aliyev never sought public life. If the Soviet Union had not collapsed he may have gone on to be a diplomat. If Mikhail Gorbachev had not sent his troops into Baku to massacre innocent people in 1990, prompting a chain of events that saw Ilham terminated from a much loved job, lecturing at Moscow State Institute of International Relations, he may have even stayed there.

As it was, the son of the towering figure that was Heydar Aliyev had been content to take the knocks as he emerged into the post-Soviet private sector. There was a Russian adage that summed up the attitude of the people to their Communist system. *'They pretend to pay us, and we pretend to work'* went the saying.

All that had changed. Embracing capitalism had been a struggle. Under Boris Yeltsin, first President of the Russian Federation, structural reforms resulted in hyperinflation, declining GDP, industrial collapse and a banking crisis. A strained economy sat on the brink. Banks closed, investor confidence was lost and prices skyrocketed.

But against this backdrop Ilham had done well for himself in the new private sector. Markets throughout Eastern

Europe, and especially Russia, soaked up products from his factory outside Moscow and his imports into the market had been equally successful.

Spreading his time between the family home in Turkey, his clients and a production facility in Russia, and travelling elsewhere when required, it was a quiet, contented life that a few years earlier, under the Soviet system, would have been impossible. Even when Heydar was at the peak of his powers, the benefits of a larger than average house, several Zils and other tokens of power were surely offset by the miseries of the late-Soviet period. All that was now in the past.

"We were comfortable and happy. I contemplated little else as it was a good period of my life," he says.

Yet that is not to say he was aloof from the events that were shaping the world. On January 14, 1994, U.S. President Bill Clinton and Russian President Boris Yeltsin signed the Kremlin Accords, which ended the pre-programmed aiming of nuclear missiles toward each country's targets, and also provided for the dismantling of the nuclear arsenal in Ukraine.

The Balkans were in crisis, February of that year seeing the Markale massacres, when Bosnian Serb army mortar shells killed 68 civilians and wounded about 200 in a Sarajevo marketplace, while two months later the Rwandan Genocide began in Kigali. Elsewhere TV tycoon Silvio Berlusconi won the Italian general election and South Africa held its first fully multi-racial elections, marking the final end of apartheid. On May 10 Nelson Mandela was inaugurated as South Africa's first black president.

An avid newspaper reader, Ilham followed world events and often discussed them at length with his father. Heydar, now in power in Baku, was dealing with a world in flux as well as the many challenges which faced Azerbaijan. Several times each week the pair spoke, turning over world events, Ilham's business and the challenges that were demanding so much from Heydar. The latter, of pensionable age in most countries, was holding together a nation that had been hurtling towards collapse. There was much to talk about.

The year 1994 was designated as the 'International Year of the Family' by the United Nations. It was the year that Ilham would make the supreme sacrifice for his family.

In October 1993, Heydar Aliyev had been sworn in as President of Azerbaijan. It was a nation in turmoil: a shattered economy, chaos on the streets, social problems and a picture dominated by a disastrous inability to defend Azerbaijan's borders. Then there was the prospect of an oil deal.

In an expansive interview with Russia's *Literaturnaya Gazeta*, former President Abulfaz Elchibey recalled of his days that "...Almost 2,000 wells in Azerbaijan were not working at that time because of technical obsolescence and the shortage of funds..."

Heydar had needed to act quickly. As early as 1990 the government of Azerbaijan began negotiating a possible oil deal with the British oil giant British Petroleum and others. Both sides saw that there was chance to earn large profits from the deal. Azerbaijan needed desperately to redevelop its obsolete oil drilling and refinery equipment. By this time production had fallen to 1900 levels and was declining at a rate of six per cent per year. For Azerbaijan the political benefits to come from an agreement were obvious — independence and hard currency, which mattered greatly in the post-Cold War environment.

The whiff of those billions also caused massive attempts at corruption. During the Ayaz Mutallibov Presidency there was talk of herculean efforts to conclude a speedy deal, at a rate of knots that led to questions why. Russian firms clamoured to get a slice of the pie, while foreign multi-nationals stayed on the fringes.

Oil wealth is often a breeding ground for corruption. According to anticorruption campaign group *Transparency International*, billions of dollars are lost to bribery in public purchasing, citing the oil sector in many nations as a particular problem.

The security vacuum of this period bears comparison with Iraq more than a decade and a half later. A failure of central control, chronic discord and the temptations of 'black gold' led to scams that ran from the bottom to the top of the industry and government.

The country's most lucrative sector, the Azerbaijani oil industry had grown weak. Criminals used a number of methods to defraud the industry, including the manipulation of fuel pump gauges and incorrect measurement of tankers' contents — both of which resulted in an undeclared surplus that was then to be sold on the black market.

Oil smuggling operations were so brazen that they were virtually carried out in the open as the police and local politicians were in the pocket of those running the scams. Some pipelines were peppered with illegal taps, allowing thieves to top up their loads at will.

There were also claims that only 60 per cent of trucks carrying oil products from Azerbaijani wells to other areas reached their destination, while others had their valuable cargoes skimmed.

But what monies were reaching government were also reaching a higher level of corruption. Millions of dollars each month disappeared due to kickbacks, bribes and rampant use of shell companies.

During the Elchibey Presidency the problem became endemic. While the President's own integrity was not necessarily in doubt, the coalition of political forces he stitched together within his government understood that their time may be short — and got to work quickly with their noses in the corruption trough.

Azerbaijan certainly did require foreign investment in its oil sector, but the way it was sculpted within government negotiations at that time effectively gave away swathes of the Azerbaijani oil fields. There was more than a whiff of a few decision makers getting rich with the national economy receiving much too little in return.

By the time of Heydar's arrival there was already an inconceivable deal on the table, one that would require renegotiation. The previous administration was interrupted on the cusp of negotiating away Azerbaijan's oil riches.

Of course, this was just one of the many problems that beset Heydar Aliyev during his early days in power following the October 1993 Presidential Poll. But it was one that would set the tone, not only for his years in power, but for many future generations and, indeed, for Azerbaijan for decades to come.

"President Aliyev understood that this was it, what he did with the nation's oil wealth would define him," says Natig Aliyev, Minister of Industry and Energy. "Within days of assuming power he had taken advice as to the status of oil negotiations, the contract that was on the table and began to consider Azerbaijan's options."

Adds Natig Aliyev: "His mind was incredibly honed and sharp and although he was not a lawyer, he himself combed through the contract and came back to us with a list of questions. The contract was the length of a Baku Central telephone book, yet he found the many weaknesses himself and came to the conclusion the whole enterprise was a sham on the side of Azerbaijanis."

The new Presidency began to tackle the many travails facing it with concurrent housekeeping. From top-to-bottom the administration contained Communists and Nationalists. He did not care for labels, aside from those of any political persuasion that were thieves and profiteers. Without emptying the government and causing wholesale instability, it was time for the cancers to be cut from the patient in order to bring about some degree of reform. From judges and senior policemen, the military, to civil servants, those holding positions in state-owned companies, and ministers, there were many changes to be made.

He would begin the long transition to democratic government, while attempting not to conduct a witch hunt that deflected attention from important issues such as Nagorno-Karabakh and the economy.

"A clean-up was overdue, and desperately needed," says Minister of Foreign Affairs Elmar Mammadyarov. Azerbaijan was to confront its Communist past with Heydar insisting that those in the new administration would not set out to settle old accounts, but to pursue a project to implement justice in a free country.

"He was acutely aware that rooting out corruption would not complete the transition from Communism; and that there was a risk that a programme would perpetuate a sense of injustice," says Mammadyarov.

But he understood that failure to fight the corruption caused by Communist rule, and the ease with which former apparatchiks found places for themselves in the Azerbaijani government would put the nation at risk. The new government replaced a number of top managers at state-controlled companies which were implicated in deals with ex-functionaries. Professors, judges and civil servants, among others, were either served up a warning as to their conduct, or replaced altogether.

Yet in those first few months in power Heydar Aliyev struggled to draw within his closest circle enough men and women who he knew and trusted implicitly. Especially in those early days of his Presidency, there were enemies all around. Azerbaijan had gone through two heads of state in close order, and there were still those who believed that manoeuvring could unseat a third, and open the door for their own elevation.

"You cannot underestimate the unsettled atmosphere, even though President Heydar Aliyev seemed to be a safe pair of hands, a good bet to see out his tenure," says Ali Abbasov, Minister of Communications and Information Technology.

Yet there was big money involved. Mutallibov and Elchibey had been chased from office. Some near the pinnacle of power would be quite happy to seize upon the instability to remove a third President and install themselves and their coterie in positions that could see them become millionaires, or even billionaires, inside a single five-year term of the Presidency.

Heydar needed to be careful. The decisions he made within the first months would not be measured in poll ratings, like in London, Washington or Paris. Instead, his successes and failures would be measured in how likely it was that there was a coup plot. It was government under the shadow of the barrel of a gun.

Heydar had begun to cherry pick those he felt he could trust and draw them into a tight inner circle. Yet the situation, and the scope of the job of running Azerbaijan, deemed it necessary that it was a big circle. Oil was both a curse and a blessing. He needed help.

Elchibey's administration had been on the cusp of a deal with an international consortium on a "Joint Development" contract for the 'Azeri', 'Chirag' and deep-water sections of the 'Guneshli' field. The terms of this contract, in Heydar Aliyev's view, were disastrous for Azerbaijan.

On January 10, 1994, he issued a decree dictating the structure of a national oil company for land and sea, oil and gas exploration production, creating the State Oil Company of Azerbaijan Republic (SOCAR).

Arguably no department was more important to the present and future of Azerbaijan than SOCAR, which had potential to quickly become one of the largest oil companies in the world *if* — and it was a big *if* — a suitable deal could be forged on 'Azeri', 'Chirag' and 'Guneshli'.

The combined Azeri-Chirag-Guneshli field was said to have potential to reach production of 150,000 barrels of crude per day.

Some believed that after being offered the "deal of the century" by the Elchibey administration it was questionable if the major oil companies would now enter into fresh negotiations on production sharing agreements (PSAs) at what would be far less advantageous rates to them than before.

This enormously consequential task would fall to those closest to the President. Natig Aliyev, former President of SOCAR and the current Minister for Industry and Energy of Azerbaijan, was one of those who Heydar Aliyev considered implicitly trustworthy. The President knew others personally in the Azerbaijani oil industry who would be able to guide and point him in the right direction.

Among those was Khoshbakht Yusifzade, an old school oiler who had risen through the ranks to be one of the most noted oilmen in the former Soviet Union. He was well known to Heydar during his previous incarnation as head of the Azerbaijan S.S.R. and continued to be a key source of knowledge. Another with input was Azerbaijan's ambassador in Washington, Hafiz Pashayev, an influential figure who knew how Washington worked and was familiar with all the prominent players in America's oil industry.

During the early months of his Presidency, Heydar Aliyev succeeded in consigning the unsigned oil agreement to the shredder and bringing the oil majors back around the table. The British, Russian and American governments, BP, Pennzoil, Amoco, Lukoil, Statoil, Unocal, McDermott International, Turkish Petroleum and a host of others, were all engaged in a complex and protracted set of negotiations in a deal worth tens of billions.

"Heydar Aliyev could have remained President for half a century but the outcome of these contract talks, within months of assuming the position, would have defined his legacy," says Natig Aliyev. "It was that important to Azerbaijan. So much was at stake, it was frightening."

The administration was stretched and SOCAR was under intense pressure.

Heydar had come to realise that he needed another safe, reliable pair of hands in the organisation, a bridge between SOCAR and him personally. One candidate for the position formed in his mind.

It was an unspoken rule between the President of Azerbaijan and his businessman son that they spoke on the telephone at least once each week. Often it was more. When commitments allowed, Ilham occasionally spent time in Baku. Most of his business interests did not involve Azerbaijan and his home was in Istanbul. No word had ever been exchanged between them that involved changing that.

Then came *that* call in April 1994. When it came to work, Heydar was always direct and certainly to the point. Instead of a casual chat, on this occasion he began by stating that he felt Ilham should return home without delay and evoked a vision of what he required his son to do. The future of Azerbaijan was on the line over the success or failure of SOCAR's work. He wanted Ilham there.

"I listened and agreed straight away," says Ilham. Pressed as to whether he took time to consider the offer he replies: "Not for a second. It was my duty — to my father and my country. There was no decision to make."

Within days Ilham had set in motion an unstoppable chain of events to dispose of his business and to prepare for a permanent return to Baku. The business was doing well, so a buyer was quickly found from the many industry contacts he had developed. Selling the company he built from scratch, at a relative knockdown price for immediate disposal, may have been galling. But that was if Ilham had time to consider it. Amid the turnaround of dropping one life, to pick up another, there were few moments to consider any loss.

Within 10 days of the President of Azerbaijan placing that fateful call to Istanbul, Ilham was picked up for the short flight home to Baku. Leaving behind him his wife and children, in order to slowly complete arrangements for the whole family to shift their lives, he arrived in the Azerbaijani capital without fanfare, quietly. There was no trumpeting his arrival, no reporters or photographers. Just a single car awaiting at the airport and the short drive to the Presidential residence, where Ilham would stay until he could sort out a permanent home.

The drive into Baku was not unusual. Ilham returned home perhaps a dozen times each year. But on this occasion it was different. The sun was setting over Baku in spring. The trees were turning green after a long winter. Wild flowers were pushing their way upwards at the side of the road. It was a pretty sight.

But the airport road took the car past the derelict oil rigs and stagnant lakes of disregarded oil. The malaise that the Soviet-Era had left behind was easy to see but would be hard to overcome. SOCAR was a new beginning, but it came with a troubling legacy. Ilham pondered what was ahead.

Like many Azerbaijanis, Ilham knew the history and rudiments of the industry for oil was intrinsic to the fibre of the country. He knew from his brief telephone call that he was being asked to take some sort of role within a new future, but quite what role, he was unsure.

"Heydar Aliyev was delighted to have at his side someone else who he could trust implicitly," says Natig Aliyev. "During a difficult period it was a source of comfort that he had another pair of eyes and ears, not only in SOCAR, but within his sphere in general, who he could rely upon for advice and support, and someone who would tell him things straight."

Within days a Presidential Decree was issued that appointed Ilham as Vice President of SOCAR. It came as a surprise to many, some of whom were unaware that Ilham had been called home to take up an official position. For Ilham this would initiate a fresh, demanding phase in his life. Oil, part of his history, and that of every Azerbaijani, was now to become his profession. It was not easy.

Coupled with this was the fact that his role would be to participate within SOCAR's new round of negotiations with the international oil companies, attempting to forge an extraordinary deal that would underpin Azerbaijan's future — or sign it away in what would have been one of the biggest betrayals in human history.

"The appointment of Ilham Aliyev as SOCAR's Vice President in May had drawn the President closer to the country's oil company at a time when a tight relationship was required.

"Ilham was not an oilman either, but he learned quickly and was a vociferous reader," says Yusifzade. "There was a lack of confidence in SOCAR after what had happened earlier. Within weeks of Ilham's arrival that confidence returned. Ilham would serve as a bridge."

Chapter Eighteen

Hard Talk in Houston

In plain Texas talk, it's 'do the right thing'.
— Ross Perot, American billionaire

During the summer of 1836 two New York businessmen, John Kirby Allen and Augustus Chapman Allen, purchased 6,642 acres of land with the intention of founding a city. The brothers named their city after Sam Houston, a popular general at the Battle of San Jacinto, the decisive battle of the Texas Revolution, who was elected President of Texas in September 1836.

Soon after Columbus discovered America, Spanish explorers had ranged into the territory and the region became well known to early invaders and settlers. The bayous and flat lands were trodden by Spanish explorers, French traders and Anglo frontier adventurers.

In 1763, the Treaty of Paris eliminated the French from Texas, replaced by the English. In 1803, the Louisiana Purchase led to a flurry of arrivals. In the early 1820's colonists began settling land grants. The original Texas colonisers, 297 families in all, became known as the prestigious 'Old Three Hundred'.

Shortly after San Jacinto, the Allens offered a widow of one of the 'Old Three Hundred', $5,000 for a half a league of land (a league expresses the distance a person, or a horse, can walk in one hour of time, usually about 5.5 kilometres). Offering land for sale at one dollar per acre, they dubbed

Houston the 'great interior commercial emporium of Texas'.

A gusher, 90 miles to Houston's north-east, erupted on January 10, 1901 and ushered in the Texas oil boom and the petrochemical age that changed the course of the city's history. Within a few months the city emerged as the distribution centre of Spindletop crude. By the end of the year, a refinery had been built and about 50 industrial plants in the city had converted to oil-fuelled energy systems.

By 1906, around 30 oil companies and seven banks had opened in the city. Construction of the city's first 'skyscrapers' began. By 1949, 268 oilfields operated within a 100-mile radius of Houston.

By the time that Ilham and his team flew into Houston Intercontinental Airport in June 1994, Houston was the fourth-largest city in the United States and the largest in Texas, recognised worldwide for its energy industry with five of the six supermajor energy companies having a large base of operations there, including ConocoPhillips, Exxon-Mobil, Shell Oil and BP.

While Houston could trace its oil history back barely a century, Ilham could point to his nation's heritage steeped in the black stuff. In 1877, Charles Marvin, the American meteorologist, observed there was conclusive evidence that for more than two millennia oil had been exported from the Absheron Peninsula. According to Marvin, chief of the U.S. Weather Bureau after 1913, Absheron, on which the Azerbaijan capital of Baku sits, had provided fuel to Iran, Iraq, India and other countries, well before the time of Jesus Christ or the Prophet Mohammed.

This was reported by historians and travellers like Abu Ishaq Ibrahim ibn Muhammad al-Farisi al-Istakhri, Ahmad bin Yahya Balazuri, Abu al-Hasan Ali ibn al-Husayn ibn Ali al-Mas'udi, Marco Polo, the Venetian traveller who visited Azerbaijan in the second half of the 13th century, and Adam Olearius.

Polo, who gained fame for his worldwide travels, recorded in the book *Il Milione*, that the Absheron Peninsula was dotted with oil wells. He described the output of those wells as being hundreds of shiploads.

In the 17th Century, Turkish traveller Evliyya Chelebi, recorded that: "Baku fortress was surrounded by 500 wells, from which white and black acid refined oil was produced".

Azerbaijani oil was used for lighting, in medicines, for arms and as a religious source, fire being the focus of Zoroastrianism. Followers of Zoroaster worshipped the eternal fire.

In 1683, an Engelbert Kaempfer, Secretary of the Swedish Embassy to Persia, visited Baku and in his subsequent report noted a "flaming steppe" that "...constitutes peculiar and wonderful sight, for some of the fissures were blazing with big fires, others with quiet flame... others emitted smoke or at any case perceptible evaporation that was sending off a heavy and stinking taste of oil. It was occupying the territory of 88 steps in length and 26 steps in width."

Oil extraction was still, to some degree, a cottage industry. In general, people dug shallow water wells, perhaps just a few metres deep, in order to extract the oil they needed for domestic use and then some for sale. Probably the first recognisable oil well in a modern sense was dug by a resident of the Absheron Peninsula in 1594. The man, named Nur Oglu, dug down to thirty-five metres and was rewarded with a good flow of oil that he could sell.

By 1806, three decades before John Kirby Allen and Augustus Chapman Allen arrived in Houston, and almost a century before that first gusher, records show that there were 50 'oil wells' dotted around Absheron. By 1821 there were 120. Imperial Russia, of which Azerbaijan was a part, produced 3,500 tonnes of oil in 1825 and doubled its output by the mid-century. A hungry pipeline took Azerbaijani oil from the Caspian to the Black Sea port of Batumi.

Yet even by the middle of the century, despite a growing trade in oil, the vast majority of wells were just two or three metres in depth. The exceptions showed the direction that the industry was taking. In a village called Suraxani, not far from the boundaries of Baku, there was one well recorded as being 12 metres. The wooden structure that stood over the well, to accommodate the increasingly technical drill, "looked like an upturned pyramid". The modern oil well was slowly being born.

From this and other 'big' wells, there was still production of less than a dozen barrels a day. Oil was stored in stone-lined holes near to the wellhead, and when sufficient oil was produced would be sold on to the state.

In 1870, still three and a half decades before Houston's 'gusher', the oil industry supported 14 oil stores in Baku and an increasingly mechanised world was hungry for Azerbaijani black gold.

Baku was finally able to meet that demand in 1872. It was the year of the *Mary Celeste*, famously discovered abandoned in the Atlantic Ocean. Ulysses S. Grant was in the White House, Queen Victoria on the British Throne, Adolphe Thiers had become the second President of France and Alexander III was Emperor of Russia.

The Old World was, in a matter of speaking, ended by an event which happened quietly and without fanfare in Absheron in 1871. That year a more mechanised well was dug. This was capable of producing 50 barrels per day, a revolutionary forward step.

A year later, the same system had spread throughout the peninsula. Oil production went through the roof. By 1913, there were 3,500 wells in and around Baku. Statistics show that in 1900, the Baku region accounted for a vast majority of Imperial Russia's oil production, and in turn Imperial Russia accounted for half the world's oil production. In 1878, Ludvig Nobel (part of the family from which the Nobel Awards are derived) and his company Branobel transformed the industry by commissioning the first oil tanker and launching it on the Caspian Sea. At that time the industry did not rely on huge pipelines in order to deliver vast amounts of black gold to an increasingly oil hungry world.

Azerbaijan's autonomy within Imperial Russia, and especially during her brief years of independence, would have made her rich as the world became increasingly mechanised. But the boom years abruptly ended. In 1920 the Bolsheviks captured Azerbaijan, the starting point of nearly seven decades under Moscow's yoke. Under the Communist system all private property — including Azerbaijan's booming petroleum sector — was confiscated and placed at the service of the wider state.

Azerbaijan's oil industry was directed towards the Soviet Union — its wealth and the money this generated being spirited away from Baku, with little returning. Azerbaijan kept much of the Soviet Union running throughout these long Communist years, and underpinned Soviet success in helping to win World War Two, but Azerbaijan was rewarded with few of the fruits of the oil wealth it provided for the union. Even fundamentals, such as investment in the oilfields and in petroleum industry technology, were ignored as Moscow plundered. The bare minimum was spent in order to maintain capacity.

Intensive geological and geophysical mapping during the 1950s and 1960s resulted in the Caspian's oil-and-gas bearing structures being determined. Thereafter Moscow rushed to tap into this reservoir as cheaply as possible. Production reached its peak in 1967 with 414,000 barrels per day. Gas production increased steadily. Guneshli (1979), Chirag (1985), Azeri (1988) and Kapaz (1989) oilfields were tapped. The Azeri-Chirag-Guneshli field was the last significant oil achievement of the Soviet Era.

By the time of the collapse of Moscow's empire, the lack of investment was taking its toll. To Western oilmen, the industry in Azerbaijan looked like something out of the history books. The Azerbaijani oil industry was decades behind its Western counterparts by every measure.

Houston, for example, had become known as the world's oil capital. Baku was no better than a backward cousin.

"Azerbaijani oilmen were the best in the world, they had to be, for while Western oilmen had a wealth of technological know-how behind them, ours worked with old fashioned equipment and methods," says Khoshbakht Yusifzade, Vice President of SOCAR. "It was proven that a newly independent Azerbaijan sat on massive reserves, but at that point it would have taken a generation for the nation to limp along and develop these resources ourselves."

Under Mutallibov and Elchibey attempts had been made to rectify this — as quickly as possible — by looking to western technical expertise. Elchibey's administration had rushed to negotiate with Western oil firms. One particular uncompleted deal concerned the Chirag field, today part of the Azeri-Chirag-Guneshli field. When Elchibey was unseated, Chirag was being negotiated away for an investment of $21 million over six years, with all production during that period sold to the Azerbaijan government at market prices. It would have been a scandalous loss to Azerbaijan.

Later Chirag was packaged as part of Azeri-Chirag-Guneshli, owned by a consortium of firms, and when production commenced in 1997 with the Chirag Early Oil Project, just a single offshore platform was producing over 130,000 barrels per day (bpd), which fed millions into the national economy.

Chirag was one of several examples of the Elchibey administration's cowboy approach, one perhaps better suited to Houston a century earlier. If circumstances had not intervened, Elchibey had been due to sign his contract on July 21, 1993, locking Azerbaijan into a very poor deal. Self-interest, inexperience, weakness and not a little pocket-lining by those involved on the Azerbaijani side had underpinned the deal. Tens of millions in commissions, if not more, were allegedly involved.

"Instead of the Contract of the Century, which later emerged, the 1993 deal would perhaps have become known as the Backhander of the Century," says an Azerbaijani oilman, who was on the fringes of the negotiating process. "It was an incredibly corrupt process. Azerbaijan would have been beholden to the oil companies, with its oil belonging, lock, stock and barrel, to the West, instead of being pumped into the Soviet Union as before. Half a dozen people involved in the negotiation from our side would have become multi-multi-millionaires."

Ultimately, the same level of corruption and incompetence that was brought to oil negotiations, had been brought to bear in running the country. This would be the main factor in preventing a July 21, 1993, contract signing. The government blundered its handling of Nagorno-Karabakh, floundered on the economy and the people became tired of bloated levels of corruption.

"My father was not going to be bounced into a deal, let alone the one that was almost completed in the summer of 1993," says Ilham. "It was a brave move to suspend negotiations, because the pressure really was on."

Elchibey was a former Soviet dissident, a career politician, and the nuances of business and negotiation were lost on him. By contrast, Heydar Aliyev had succeeded within the old Soviet system, when one needed to be a lion to survive. Negotiation was second nature.

During those dark early days of his Presidency, when chaos and uncertainty swirled across Azerbaijan on so many levels, including Nagorno-Karabakh, among the many pressures on him was the nation's unsigned oil deal.

He decided to suspend negotiations immediately, for two reasons. Firstly, he was not an oilman. He did not know enough on the subject personally to make a judgment call. It was a complicated subject that needed consideration, especially as the short and medium term future of Azerbaijan would be dictated directly by the success of this deal. Heydar decided to pull together a committee of experts to forge a coherent Azerbaijani position.

Secondly, he was sending a message. It was a form of diplomatic language. By suspending, he drew a line under previous negotiations and signalled that the new government would not be bounced onto the course of its predecessor.

"He was a strongman, something that they would soon find out," says Natig Aliyev, former President of SOCAR. "The new government, and the new President, were on a completely different tangent."

Azerbaijan formed a committee of foreign experts. This group would conduct negotiations with oil companies. The State Oil Company of the Azerbaijani Republic (SOCAR), which had led the 1993 negotiations, would initially remain on the sidelines, until the new President could shape the organisation.

This foreign committee did much to shape the new President's stance. The unsigned deal was, as had been suspected, a crime waiting to happen. Azerbaijan's policy would be altogether more hardline.

Using the deliberations of these experts as a guide, on December 4, 1993, SOCAR sent the foreign oil companies a file detailing Azerbaijan's new perspective on the matter, backed up by facts and figures, and dictating that the old deal was dead.

"The President called for all parties to begin again with a fresh page," says Yusifzade.

The oil companies were not impressed, and let the Azerbaijan government know their disquiet. Eventually, for a second time, negotiations got underway between Azerbaijan and some of the world's biggest oil firms, among them BP Exploration, Amoco, Lukoil and Exxon.

"By now the President was up to speed on the dynamics of the Azeri, Chirag and Guneshli oilfields," says Natig Aliyev. "The tougher line he demanded in negotiations with the oil companies paid dividends."

During 1994, in the conference rooms of Baku and the various oil capitals of the world, a new deal was slowly forged. Perhaps too slowly. The President was not satisfied. Some parties were perceived to be dragging their heels, attempting to force Azerbaijan into a corner. As a result some domestic voices were raised that Azerbaijan should go it alone. Others questioned the leadership of SOCAR.

"The President wanted to be closer to negotiations, to have a stronger hand, and to see the deal being led, from the Azerbaijani side, by someone closer to him. This was, after all, a contract that would define Heydar Aliyev the President," says Natig Aliyev. Hardly four months after the Presidential Decree that appointed him Vice President of SOCAR, Ilham flew into Houston on what appeared to be the last leg of a protracted re-negotiation process.

His introduction to the industry had been perhaps the most challenging period of his life. Months of learning the industry from the inside and getting to grips with the finer points of current negotiations.

Initially, the new SOCAR Vice President shared his office with Yusifzade, arguably Azerbaijan's foremost industry expert.

Adds Yusifzade: "He soaked up information and details like a sponge and was pretty much up to speed on the salient issues within six weeks. Then he was tasked with assuming a role within the small negotiating team."

Azerbaijan's so-called committee of experts was now in a lesser role and the Azerbaijani team took on a forward involvement. It was a tough, mentally demanding task, complicated further by the disputed status of the Caspian and the demands of negotiating with a consortium of multi-nationals, with all their competing individual demands and stances. Russia was scrambling to assert itself and the pressures exerted from Moscow hung heavy over much of the process.

"There was a pressure to conclude a deal quickly, as this would have speedy and enormous benefits for the country," says Natig Aliyev. "Yet there was the competing pressure to get the best long-term deal possible."

But despite the many pressures and competing factors, gradually a deal came together. In early September, SOCAR's negotiating team flew to Houston for what seemed to be an opportunity to 'cross the t's and dot the i's'. Hopes were high, and Ilham left behind him in Baku a huge burden of expectation.

"It seemed that this would be the final round of negotiations and that a contract was virtually ready," says Hafiz Pashayev, who joined the Azerbaijani negotiating team from Washington.

But there was a shock in store.

Chapter Nineteen

Contract of the Century

To keep a lamp burning we have to keep putting oil in it.
— Mother Teresa, Indian missionary

The end of the Soviet Union had put the Caspian Sea and its vast oil and gas wealth into play. Negotiations related to the demarcation of the Caspian had only just begun among the littoral states bordering the oil-rich sea — Azerbaijan, Russia, Kazakhstan, Turkmenistan and Iran. In Azerbaijan, a working group was organised under the directive of the President, and this would steer Azerbaijan's claims. Azerbaijan was the only country advocating the sectorial division of the Caspian, while several others engaged in a 'land grab', issuing wild claims and demands that were greatly in excess of anything they had previously had in their possession.

Heydar Aliyev ordered that the State Oil Company of the Azerbaijan Republic (SOCAR) engage only in the exploration and development of deposits in the Caspian Sea, based on the sectorial division of the Caspian as determined in 1970 by the U.S.S.R. Ministry of Oil, the last delimitation of the Caspian undertaken by Moscow. SOCAR did not expand on the sectorial boundaries that were determined for Azerbaijan in 1970.

As negotiations were underway between the five, it was clear that opinions diverged quite dramatically. Again, Azerbaijan took a lead. Heydar's policy was that the five needed a quick, clean agreement that would enable them to begin exploiting the wealth that was there. Russia, the most outspoken of the group, had an economy in freefall and desperately needed to move on with developing the Caspian. Iran's economy was moribund. Azerbaijan, Turkmenistan and Kazakhstan, all newly independent, could strengthen their fledgling economies with petro-dollars. It was, conventional thinking went, in everyone's interests to divide the Caspian and get on with it.

But conventional thinking on the Caspian competed with strategic thinking. Some of the five made their demands and attempted to blackmail the others by dragging their heels on an agreement, in the hope that those perceived as weaker would give in.

The new President's strategy was to let the others argue their positions while he stated that SOCAR had its boundaries, as set in the 1970s, and that it would base its sea boundaries with Iran on the Astara-Hasangulu line, which was accepted as the boundary line separating the former Soviet Union and Iran.

Azerbaijan would remain willing to talk, but he was not going to set his negotiators the task of arguing any preposterous claims based on trumped-up concepts. Nor, he declared, would his nation budge from the basic principles which were his red line positions.

Others tabled various suggestions. One was that any exploration that took place anywhere in the Caspian should be jointly owned by all five littoral states. Iran went on to — creatively — state that the Caspian be equally divided so that each would receive 20 per cent, without any relation to their actual border on the sea. It made no sense and was unrealistic.

Azerbaijan stated its position and remained consistent. With that as a basis, the country could begin to negotiate with Big Oil. Several other nations, their claims and new claims causing inconsistency, floundered when it came to discussing their nominal Caspian territories with oil companies.

That is not to say that there were not unresolved problems facing Azerbaijan, only that the stability in Baku's position was to pay dividends. Perhaps the biggest matter that would concern the Azerbaijani side was hydrocarbon resources that overlapped the median line between countries. Azerbaijan and Turkmenistan were one such case over the Kapaz field, though differences between the two were small. Not enough to prove problematic in the long-term, and not a stumbling block with the oil companies.

Even then, and the Caspian issue would drag on endlessly, the majority were leaning towards a concept that deposits and structures that fell on a median line should be divided equally between both parties that shared it, regardless of whether the deposit fell more on one side or the other. Years of wrangling remained ahead.

The stability of Azerbaijan's position meant that the nation was well positioned for its discussions with the oil companies. Demarcation was not a hot potato, but nevertheless would be the subject of indepth discussions during negotiations towards an oil deal.

By the time of their arrival in Houston for talks with the oil companies, the Azerbaijan negotiating team was confident. The consortium they were dealing with had floated a contract, the result of months of talks and discussions. Everything seemed positive.

After several days of meetings with the final points of the agreement reached, the Azerbaijani party waited in their hotel for the proposed final contract to be delivered. The team, headed by Ilham Aliyev, Natig Aliyev, head of SOCAR, and Hafiz Pashayev, Azerbaijani Ambassador in Washington, remained in contact with Baku.

Heydar Aliyev, always noted for his late nights in the office, had ordered that he be called at any time, at home or office, with an update when the contract arrived, and when it was approved. The Azerbaijani team of retained oil lawyers were on stand-by to comb through the document.

At last it was delivered. Within hours of receiving the sizeable document they would be ready to give their verdict. If everything was in place, a preliminary agreement would be signed, ahead of a planned official signing ceremony in the Azerbaijan capital a few weeks later.

Yet there was a shock in store. The draft contract was delivered, more or less as agreed, but with one important deviation. A clause had been inserted that the contract would come into effect only when the boundaries of the Caspian had been finally agreed by the five littoral states in a binding treaty. In effect, this clause would finalise the deal, but hold off its initiation indefinitely. Azerbaijan's future would be held hostage to the vague notions of its four Caspian partners. Azerbaijan would be at the mercy of others, several of whom were seemingly ready for the long haul in dragging out negotiations on final status of the Caspian in order to achieve territorial gains.

The shocked Azerbaijan negotiating team could not possibly consider a clause that placed untenable power in the hands of others, especially one that would in effect suspend actual investment and work on the Azerbaijani oil fields.

A day after the draft was delivered, Ilham and the Azerbaijan negotiating team sat around a Houston conference table with their opposites from the oil industry. They sat on the cusp of a multi-billion dollar investment in the oil fields, an advance of hundreds of millions of dollars that would flood immediately into national coffers. The contract would ensure that Azerbaijan's petro-dollar income would progressively rise, further infusing the economy and handing the government the ability to build the nation as a whole. It was, in short, a document that would breathe life into Azerbaijan. It was vital. Yet the final status of the Caspian could (and would prove to be) years off. Azerbaijan could not afford to sit on its hands endlessly and wait for some form of agreement. Doing so would be like playing Russian Roulette with the future of the nation.

Heydar, consulted extensively by telephone, was equally adamant. During a conference call with the negotiating team in Houston, he stated: "...We need schools. We need hospitals. And we cannot wait for some elongated negotiations on the Caspian that will ultimately make not one bit of difference to our territory. Our children cannot wait..."

The following day, during a tense, knife-edge meeting, Ilham explained the Azerbaijan position. He reiterated that Azerbaijan had settled its territories along internationally accepted lines, lines that would not change. Then he demanded that the offending clause be withdrawn — and both sides get to work.

"When Ilham Aliyev finished, there was silence and those in the room, even the lawyers, took in a collective deep breath," says one who was there from the Azerbaijan side. "It was a pivotal moment."

Three and a half years of arduous negotiations had led to this single decisive juncture. Perhaps the very existence of Azerbaijan rested on what happened next. A collapse of the deal would be catastrophic. The schools and hospitals which the President had alluded to the previous evening may never arrive.

As the Big Oil consortium learned that Azerbaijan would not delay the contract, they responded by stating that the clause stayed. No matter that both sides stood to make billions, the oil companies wished to lock Azerbaijan into a contract and then sit back and wait.

"Five or ten years. No-one knew how long the final status of the Caspian would take," says Dr Mana Saeed Al Otaiba, former UAE Oil Minister and five times Chairman of OPEC.

The oil companies were willing to wait. Azerbaijan simply could not afford to. The Azerbaijani team had two choices. Buckle and give in to Big Oil's demands. Or walk. The latter involved the most dramatic of circumstances. Azerbaijan would leave the negotiating table and walk away from a $30 billion contract that had the scope to mend a country that was crippled.

"Ilham Aliyev was polite, but firm. He stated that Azerbaijan could not accept a delay and then excused himself and the SOCAR team from negotiations," says the same source. "He was not in any way rude, but firm, leaving no doubt as to Azerbaijan's willingness to leave the contract on the table."

"Frankly, it was a big risk, going into the Caspian with such an investment, at a time when several of the littoral states were being intransigent," says one of those who sat in the room on the side of Big Oil. "But we did not expect the Azerbaijanis to be so adamant."

It is difficult to understand how the Azerbaijan negotiating team must have felt as they packed their briefcases and walked out of that oak panelled conference room. They marched towards their cars in silence, each and every member of the group was probably reeling from what looked like an abject failure. They were walking away, rightly or wrongly, from the definitive moment in the then brief history of independent Azerbaijan.

"It was a shock. Of course. We were more than deflated, we were in shock," says the Azerbaijani source.

The hotel was only a few minutes away by car. But the occupants of the cars carrying the Azerbaijani negotiators travelled in silence. The weight of history was, perhaps, on their shoulders. The schools and hospitals, and all the other infrastructure that the country needed so badly, now looked a pipe dream.

"I realised that if we agreed on that, then there would never be a beginning to the contract," says Ilham. "We needed foreign companies, we needed to develop our oil industry, but if we agreed to that paragraph, then it would mean it would never start. That provision in the contract would see the contract effectively begin when the status of the Caspian was resolved, and that was a long way off.

"Indeed, it is not resolved today. Where would Azerbaijan be now, if we had agreed upon that clause?"

In the hours that followed their departure from negotiations, the team went for their 'Plan B'.

In Baku, the President placed a call to his counterpart in the White House.

Just having turned 47 years old, the new President Bill Clinton had been in power for hardly seven months. He was the third-youngest President when entering office, after Theodore Roosevelt and John F. Kennedy. But a keen mind had seen the Governor of the small state of Arkansas get an excellent grip on foreign policy. He had spoken with his counterpart in Azerbaijan a number of times and, on occasional meetings with Hafiz Pashayev, the Azerbaijani

Ambassador in Washington, had proven to have an excellent knowledge of the Caspian region.

The transition of the former Soviet Union into independent states had begun the rapid development of U.S. trade and investment, certainly in Azerbaijan. The U.S. had quickly moved to establish diplomatic relations with Baku, and both had worked to establish bilateral frameworks for trade and investment. In the few months of Heydar Aliyev's Presidency, this relationship had warmed further.

Foreign firms had to deal with volatile business conditions, turbulent currency exchange rates and changing regulations, taxes and export and import regulations. But the benefits far outweighed the risks. In areas such as agribusiness, oil and oil processing equipment, telecommunications, transportation and healthcare, trade ties boomed. Agricultural products, which accounted for about two-thirds of American exports to the region stood at around $2.4 billion and were notably growing to Azerbaijan, as the country attempted to get its moribund agrian sector back on track.

Talks were underway between the U.S., EU and others, and Azerbaijan, to conclude trade agreements and investment and tax treaties, as well as intellectual property protection and business facilitation.

The U.S. Trade and Development Programme (TDP) was active in Baku, funding feasibility studies and training programmes. America's Eximbank had begun Azerbaijan-based short and medium term insurance, credit and loan guarantee programmes for exports, while Azerbaijan was a member of the European Bank for Reconstruction and Development, which directed most of its funding to the nascent private sector and privatisation of state enterprises, and supported improvements in infrastructure and the environment.

In short, Azerbaijan's economy was still in post-Soviet doldrums, the building blocks of future growth were being laid and the commercial relationship between the country and the United States, in particular, was burgeoning.

On a geopolitical level there was even more momentum. Azerbaijan's increasingly 'balanced' relationship with Russia ran parallel to closer Baku-Washington ties. Western geopolitical strategies in the 1990s were, to a large degree, based on securing alternative sources of energy and transport routes that would bypass Russia, while Washington's approach towards Iran, Azerbaijan's southern neighbour, strongly influenced development of U.S.-Azerbaijani ties.

Azerbaijan was the only major Caspian oil and gas producing country that exported almost exclusively to the West, while avoiding membership of OPEC or Russian-led cartels for exporting gas. Under its new President, the nation also became one of Eurasia's most geopolitically balanced states — and was therefore deeply important in a troubled region.

It was because of this relationship that Heydar was able to speak straight with Clinton — and to receive a credible response. Azerbaijan's intrinsic importance to American foreign policy in the Caspian, towards the former Soviet states, and Eurasia as a whole, meant that the American government would clearly find it within its own interests to ensure that Azerbaijan was stable and prosperous — and that could only be achieved with a coherent oil deal.

By the time that the phone lines between Baku and Washington were twitching with heavy conversation, Ilham Aliyev and Hafiz Pashayev were already in the air, taking a Delta Airlines shuttle from Texas to Washington. Located at 1000 Independence Avenue, the United States Department of Energy's overarching mission is to advance the economic and energy security of the United States.

By the time that the two Azerbaijanis landed at Dulles International Airport, located 26 miles from downtown Washington, they had a White House confirmed appointment with Hazel O'Leary, America's ground breaking Secretary of Energy.

The brilliant and formidable O'Leary was the first and only woman and first and only African American to hold the position. But she was far more than window-dressing in Clinton's cabinet, which he declared during his campaign should be diverse. She won early plaudits for declassifying Cold War-era records showing that the government had used Americans as guinea pigs in human radiation experiments.

The Azerbaijanis had one opportunity only. In their meeting they must persuade O'Leary of the merits of the deal, without the offending clause, and ensure that the American government would lean on Big Oil. Even then it was no slam dunk.

Clinton was demonised by the Republican Party and just months earlier his election had divided America.

Time magazine reported "…Representative Patrick McHenry of North Carolina, a conservative who keeps a bust of Reagan on his desk… (says) "To the average American who's struggling, we're in some other stratosphere. We're the party of Big Business and Big Oil and the rich."

By contrast the Clinton administration was in no way cosy with Big Oil. Even if the White House and Department of Energy was behind Azerbaijan, would Big Oil listen? In Washington, Ilham Aliyev and Hafiz Pashayev found Secretary O'Leary as responsive as they hoped. The deal was in everyone's interest, not least those of America, in geopolitical and economic terms.

The same evening, the two flew back to Houston. A follow up meeting with the same oil consortium had been arranged for the next morning. They had heard nothing from them. A sleepless night of trepidation followed, while in Baku the President remained in touch. No-one on the Azerbaijani side was under any illusion as to the importance of the impending meeting. If talks collapsed again, Ilham and his party would return home with nothing.

The following day, mid-morning, the Azerbaijani team filed into the same meeting room they had left so suddenly 48 hours earlier.

"There was considerable hope that some pressure from Washington would do the trick, but there were no firm indications," says one of the Azerbaijani negotiating team. "There was every chance that we would hear a reiteration of the same conditions to the contract and could perhaps have been on our way to the airport before the end of the day."

After the usual greetings and preliminaries, the tension was quickly abated when a lawyer for the oil companies announced, somewhat tersely, that after consultations with the U.S. government a decision had been made to drop the offending clause. Secretary O'Leary had made her feelings known on the issue. Given the strategic interests of the United States, which merged for the most part with those of Azerbaijan, Washington was heavily in favour of the immediate commencement of work in the Azerbaijani area of the Caspian. This was enough to ensure that the consortium quickly decided to drop the "final status" clause.

The impact of this development cannot be underestimated.

The Azerbaijani team was indeed flying out of Houston Intercontinental Airport that evening, enroute to Baku, but they were returning home as conquering heroes instead of vanquished negotiators. That made all the difference to the flight.

Over the next few weeks, as news spread like wildfire around Baku of Ilham's return, and a major deal that had been settled in Houston, preparations were made in Azerbaijan for the official contract signing.

"There was a feeling that something great was in the offing. People were on a high. The sense of achievement was palpable," says Rahman Hajiyev, Editor in Chief of a local information agency.

This feeling was perhaps most acute among those who knew the precarious state of Azerbaijan's fiscals. The nation's coffers were tight to breaking point, and the deal included a generous signing-on payment. Secondly, SOCAR figures showed that the investment that Big Oil would pump into Azerbaijan's oil fields would have a profound and — if not immediate — startlingly speedy impact in driving up the number of barrels per day that the nation could produce.

From 1990 to 1997 world oil consumption increased 6.2 million barrels per day. Asian consumption accounted for all but 300,000 barrels per day of that gain and contributed to a price recovery that extended into 1997. Declining Russian production played a role in the price. Between 1990 and 1996 Russian production declined over five million barrels per day. International markets, in the west in particular, would gobble up Azerbaijani oil.

Between Houston and an official contract signing, there was political work still to be done to shore up the deal. In mid-August Ilham Aliyev met with Rosemarie Forsythe, Director of Russian, Ukrainian and Eurasian Affairs, at the U.S. National Security Council. This paved the way for a visit to Baku by Madeleine Albright, U.S. Secretary of State. Soon after Heydar Aliyev met for talks with U.S. Vice President Al Gore on the sidelines of a population conference in Cairo, Egypt.

September 20, 1994, saw the culmination of three and a half years of sometimes arduous, and always testing, negotiations when Azerbaijan and the consortium signed the nation defining production sharing contract, the 'Azeri, Chirag and deep-water Guneshli International Contract No. 1.'

During a ceremony held at Baku's historic Gulistan Palace, SOCAR officially signed the document that would quickly transform Azerbaijan from its past as an under-funded Soviet oil producer, into a modern oil exporter. SOCAR would hold 20 per cent of the shares in the new consortium, while BP, Amoco, Pennzoil, Unocal and McDermott International of the United States, Russia's Lukoil, Norway's Statoil, Ramco of Scotland, the Turkish State Oil Company and later Delta-Nimi of Saudi Arabia would be partners in the enterprise.

At the event, BP's Managing Director, Lord John Browne said: "The investments will open new possibilities for Azerbaijan and will ensure the creation of thousands of jobs. It will be one of the greatest projects in the history of Azerbaijan."

As the size and scope of the contract became common knowledge, few would argue with Lord Browne's sentiment. It was certainly not PR speak.

"My personal feeling was that this moment brought us full circle," says Ilham. "Azerbaijan was the birthplace of the international oil industry. We had passed through an era of mismanagement and under investment. This deal would mark a sort of comeback. We would again be a leading global supplier of light sweet crude oil, with all the benefits that this brought to our nation and society."

As per the contract, Azerbaijan would receive some $300 million in bonus payments from the oil companies, including $80 million on confirmation and $70 million when the deal was agreed by the Milli Majlis (which Parliament duly completed on December 2). The contract included provisions for $7.4 billion investment over 30 years in the Azeri-Chirag-Guneshli field, which could rise as high as $13 billion. The partners in the deal stated that their estimates were that the field contained four billion barrels, some 511 million tonnes of crude. What was also important was the quality of the oil that Azeri-Chirag-Guneshli promised.

American Petroleum Institute gravity, known as API gravity, is the accepted industry measure of how heavy or light a petroleum liquid is when compared to water. An API gravity over 10 means that it is lighter and floats on water. Less than 10 means it is heavier and sinks. In general terms, oil with an API gravity below 45 commands the highest prices. Azeri-Chirag-Guneshli crude was considered to be among the lightest in the world, measuring 36.7 degrees average API gravity, comparable with high quality Saudi Arabian oil, which measures 34.2 degrees.

The impact of the deal on Azerbaijan could best be measured in scope. In 1994, the total Azerbaijani oil production stood at 160,000 barrels per day. As the oil companies began working on the Azeri-Chirag-Guneshli field, by as early as 1997 they were expected to be realising 40,000 barrels per day, rising quickly to 80,000 barrels per day. This alone would increase Azerbaijan's oil production by 50 per cent.

Yet as the field grew so did production. By 2009 this reached one million barrels per day, with peak production estimated to be 2012. According to *The Caspian: politics, energy and security,* Azeri-Chirag-Guneshli would produce some $80 billion in revenues for Azerbaijan.

"When you consider the raw figures, it gives insight into just what had been at stake in Houston. The deal was of enormous importance to rebuilding Azerbaijan after the malaise of the Soviet era," says Aslan Aslanov, head of Azertaj, the state information agency. "The nation would now have the means to begin on the road towards the 21st century."

Although it was impossible to accurately predict oil prices over ensuing years, according to some estimates, over the next three decades Azerbaijan stands to make around $80 billion from its oil revenues. During the signing ceremony, Heydar recounted the long and significant history of Azerbaijan as an international oil supplier and referred to oil as the "richest national wealth of the Azerbaijan Republic and Azerbaijani people". During the event he also defined the deal when he stated: "For Azerbaijan… this is the Contract of the Century…"

Pictured with his father, Ilham Aliyev in his teens. Soon after this image was taken he would leave for Moscow to pursue further education.

In the aftermath of Soviet carnage, the streets of the Azerbaijani capital were littered with bodies.

Millions on the streets of central Baku during the funerals of some of those cut down in the carnage. (above) Siraj Kazimov, son of one of those murdered, holds a portrait of his father.

Among the many students who passed through the doors of MGIMO were the future Foreign Ministers of Russia, Ukraine, Belarus, Kazakhstan, Slovakia and Mongolia, along with generations of leaders and top diplomats.

One of the darkest points of the Armenian invasion and occupation of Nagorno-Karabakh was the bloody Khojaly Massacre.

Heydar Aliyev (right) needed an ally whom he could trust implicitly, in a process that would affect the entire course of Azerbaijan's history.

Born into one of Azerbaijan's most prominent families, Mehriban Aliyeva would go from a career in medicine to First Lady of the country.

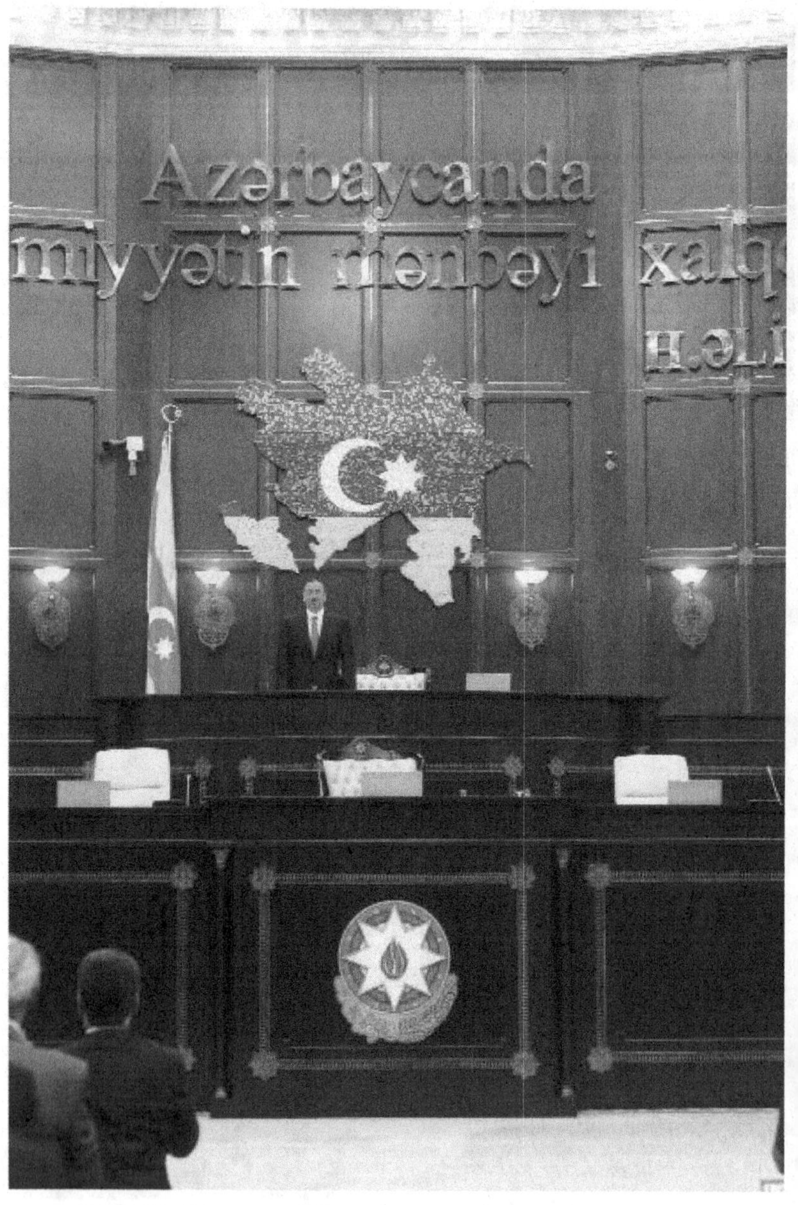

Ilham Aliyev addresses the Milli Majlis — Azerbaijan's Parliament and one of the most important institutions of the nation.

Chapter Twenty

Not an Apple

If liberty and equality, as is thought by some, are chiefly to be found in democracy, they will be best attained when all persons alike share in the government to the utmost.
— Aristotle, Greek philosopher

In December 1994, Azerbaijan's Parliament, the Milli Majlis, had ratified the Contract of the Century. But with this, the task facing President Heydar Aliyev and his nation was far from over. Ahead lay a challenge equally as demanding.

Two issues would absorb Ilham's time now. Primary was the need to deliver Azerbaijan's oil onto world markets. The Contract of the Century demanded the construction of a pipeline to carry Azerbaijan's oil to the west. This was set into a demanding timeframe, one that meant a flurry of geopolitical deal making. The first document relating to construction of the Baku-Tbilisi-Ceyhan pipeline was signed between Azerbaijan and Turkey as early as March 9, 1993, in Ankara. But now the serious work was underway.

Heydar Aliyev had set out to pump Azerbaijan's oil to the Mediterranean, via Turkey, where it would be loaded into oil tankers that would transport crude all over the world. He set off the project when initiating government-to-government discussions with Turkey's President, Suleyman Demirel. Turkey was very receptive.

The route of the proposed pipeline would create another drama. At its most convenient point between Azerbaijan's mainland and Nakhchivan, Armenia separates the two by just 40 kilometres. Nakhchivan borders Turkey. But Armenia, in pursuing its land-grab on Nagorno-Karabakh, excluded itself from any form of relations with Azerbaijan and the economic benefits that the pipeline would bring.

SOCAR had several other viable alternatives. South through Iran was the mothballed Iraqi-Turkish Mediterranean pipeline, tracing the Iranian border. An agreement for this was signed in March 1993. But politics made this unviable. A pipeline through Iran to the Gulf was the shortest route from a geographic standpoint, but there were major considerations that also dictated this unusable.

Another alternative for exporting oil was a proposal to rebuild an old pipeline through Georgia, to the Black Sea, from where ships could carry the oil out to the Mediterranean. But civil war in Georgia and its subsequent instability, had ruled out any likelihood of pursuing this option.

Lukoil, a partner in what later become known as the Baku-Tbilisi-Ceyhan pipeline consortium, pressed for a pipeline route through Russian territory to the Black Sea port of Novorossiysk, from where they proposed that tankers would transport oil through the Bosphorus to the Mediterranean. But Lukoil's existing pipelines were already busy with oil from Kazakhstan's Tengiz field. There were geopolitical pressures to avoid a Russian pipeline.

The best alternative, even if the most circuitous option, was an Azerbaijan-Georgia-Turkey route. This would be the most expensive, yet also the most politically expedient and therefore tenable. Georgian President Zviad Gamsakhurdia had been amenable to the concept, but passed away in office. His successor, Eduard Shevardnadze, a former

Minister of Foreign Affairs in the late Soviet Era, was equally amenable.

Yet, as with just about anything of significance in the Caucasus, the project was forged to a backdrop of furious geopolitical clamour. Ilham would be one of those closest involved in Azerbaijan's balancing act — to assert its own interest, while balancing the need for stable ties with her neighbours.

The Baku-Tbilisi-Ceyhan (BTC) project was in Russia's backyard. Baku-Tbilisi-Ceyhan would draw Azerbaijan closer to Europe and the U.S., so affecting Russian and Iranian economic and military dominance in the region.

What was abundantly clear was that Baku-Tbilisi-Ceyhan would weaken Russian influence in the Caucasus. In addition, the creation of an East-West energy corridor, independent of Russia, would weaken Moscow's influence. The project also constituted an important leg of the East-West energy corridor, gaining Turkey greater geopolitical importance.

BTC would diversify global oil supply. This was good for consumer states, as this guaranteed against a failure in supply elsewhere. But for critics of the pipeline — notably major suppliers, in whose interests it was to maintain control over the global supply — BTC was a direct challenge. Delivering BTC, while maintaining the difficult balancing act between all the region's competing powers, would be a delicate project.

"During this time we began to see the emergence of the diplomat in Ilham Aliyev," says Khoshbakht Yusifzade. "Of course, he had the best possible teacher in his father, yet diplomacy is a skill that comes from inherent skills and experience."

"Diplomacy is the art of letting someone have your way," wrote Daniele Vare, Italian diplomat and author, and in this case Azerbaijan needed to get its way while balancing the pressures of America, Russia and a host of others. That BTC survived amid competing political pressures is a testimony to the tenacity of the President and those who served him.

"If Azerbaijan's 'Contract of the Century' was a baptism of fire for President Ilham Aliyev, then the pressures of delivering BTC was a period when he honed his skills as a diplomat and a statesman," says Natig Aliyev.

With the primary political players gradually coming on board, behind the scenes work began on the vast logistics of the project, the geopolitical dynamics and stitching together the consortium that would operate the pipeline.

The project would encompass some 1,768 kilometres from the Sangachal Oil Terminal just outside Baku and wind its way across swathes of territory in Azerbaijan, Georgia and Turkey, coming to an end at the Ceyhan Marine Terminal (later named the Heydar Aliyev Terminal) on the south-eastern coast of Turkey. Around a quarter of the pipeline, 443 kilometres, lay in Azerbaijan, a seventh in Georgia, 249 kilometres, while 1,076 kilometres stretched across Turkey.

Between Baku and Turkey's coast, the engineering feats required were vast. The proposed pipeline would cross a number of mountain ranges at an altitude up to 2,830 metres, cross 3,000 roads, railways and utility lines — overground and underground — in addition to 1,500 rivers, brooks and streams, some as wide as 500 metres, including the powerful Ceyhan River in Turkey. The pipeline was to forge a corridor eight metres wide, with the pipe buried along its entire length at a depth of not less than one metre, and demanded a lifespan of 40 years.

It was a vast, herculean task which presented one of the biggest oil pipeline challenges ever undertaken. The primary partner in the enterprise was obvious. In addition to being a lead player in the Azeri-Chirag-Guneshli consortium, BP was arguably the world's leading pipeline builder. BP had a prolific pipeline record including the Trans Alaska pipeline system, the 1,287 kilometre pipeline stretching between Prudhoe Bay and Valdez, both in Alaska, the 169 kilometre Forties pipeline system in Scotland and the 829 kilometre Ocensa pipeline in Colombia.

Even before the signing of the Contract of the Century, Ilham and SOCAR were locked in negotiations with Turkey and Georgia, a handful of commercial partners, who would be brought into the pipeline consortium, as well as major banks and international financial institutions, in order to draw together the funding for a multibillion dollar project.

"It was a huge undertaking, pulling the pipeline consortium together, without which the Contract of the Century would have been worthless," says Yusifzadeh. "He worked tirelessly to pull together the many diverse strands of this deal. His experience in the commercial world was a big advantage."

The BTC project became "real" with the Ankara Declaration, an agreement announced on October 29, 1998, by the Presidents of Azerbaijan, Georgia, Turkey, Kazakhstan and Uzbekistan, the latter pair intending to link their exports into the route via supplementary pipelines.

By this point, Ilham had played a role in drawing together a multi-national consortium. BP, the pipe's operator, was also its biggest shareholder, with 30.1 per cent, while SOCAR held 25 per cent and smaller holdings were secured by Chevron, Norway's StatoilHydro, Türkiye Petrolleri Anonim Ortaklıgı, Eni/Agip of Italy, Total of France, Itochu and Inpex of Japan, America's ConocoPhillips and the Hess Corporation.

At standard capacity the vast pipeline would be capable of delivering one million barrels of oil per day and along its length it would require 10 million barrels to maintain delivery pressure. Oil from the Caspian would travel to Turkey at two metres per second, helped along by eight powerful pumping stations dotted along its route.

In addition, a finance consortium, comprising of the World Bank, the European Bank for Reconstruction and Development, the export credit agencies of seven other countries and a syndicate of 15 commercial banks had been pieced together to provide the $3.9 billion that would be required.

"The BTC pipeline was vital for our strategic and geopolitical interests," says Ilham. "The pipeline gave Azerbaijan an outstanding opportunity to become one of the world's leading petroleum exporters, on our own terms. That was what I found most satisfying."

With the Ankara Declaration, the formation of a pipeline consortium and the finance in place, work began on the second longest oil pipeline in the world, after Russia's Druzhba pipeline, which stretches some 4,000 kilometres from south-east Russia to points in Ukraine, Hungary, Poland and Germany, the largest artery for the transportation of Russian oil across Europe.

BTC was half the length of Druzhba, but nevertheless vast. Over ensuing months engineers would handle 150,000 individual joints of pipeline, each 12 metres in length, in total weighing over 650,000 tonnes of steel. The construction created 10,000 jobs during the building phase and 1,000 permanent positions in managing the pipeline during a four-decade lifespan.

To the backdrop of the great pipeline project, far more seismic things were occurring that would shape Azerbaijan just as markedly as the BTC or, indeed, the Contract of the Century. The question of Heydar Aliyev's democratic credentials will endure long into the future. A member of the Azerbaijan S.S.R. People's Commissariat for State Security (NKGB) from 1944, a Major General and one time Chairman of Azerbaijani KGB, and a former leader of Soviet Azerbaijan, had returned to politics stating that he saw the errors of the Soviet system. Was he wearing the clothes of a democrat, or actually a democrat?

"Heydar Aliyev believed in democracy for Azerbaijan," says Hafiz Pashayev. "But he would not pursue Western-style democracy in a hurried way that would open the door for instability. He believed in a transition."

The answer to his democratic credentials is more complicated than can be summarised by the 'yes' and 'no' schools of thinking. The collapse of Soviet Azerbaijan into independence had been tumultuous, destructive and deeply destabilising. In a couple of years he had personally ushered in some measure of order, but after three official Heads of State, and a couple of temporary measures, in less than half a decade of independence, this amounted to very little. Around Azerbaijan, competing interests continued to seek power and influence through a variety of means.

"He wanted democracy, but not at any cost. If pursuing this would allow the return of the bad-old-days and the bad-old-ways, he thought it prudent to build civil institutions slowly," says Ali Hasanov, today head of Department of public-political issues of the Presidential Administration. Indeed, speaking at Georgetown University, Heydar himself said: "Some people think we should be able to establish democracy in a short time, but that's impossible. Azerbaijan is a young nation and democracy is a new concept. The U.S. has been advancing on the path of democracy for a long time — more than 200 years. You've achieved a lot, but you're still working on it. Democracy is not an apple you buy at the market and bring back home."

All 15 republics that made up the Soviet Union would see the introduction of some form of Western-style liberal democracy, democratic principles became the dominant political *modus operandi*. It was a profound change which saw a variety of different degrees of success. Ironically, this came to a backdrop of unprecedented political unipolarity in the United States and much of the West. The West pressed the 15 republics to adopt Western political and governing norms and values, irrespective of the suitability and the maturity of these newly independent societies to adapt to these, or if they worked within wildly different social models, in order to counter any potential neo-Soviet entity from emerging.

"Prevailing thinking and historical analysis showed that liberal democratic states did not threaten each other the way non-liberal states did. Since the early 19th century this was the prevailing pattern," says Pashayev.

For America the Soviet collapse was an unprecedented opportunity to sow seeds of democracy and imbibe into the new 15 market economies an American view of how to build liberal democracy. As author Yevgeny Bendersky would later observe: "In hindsight, such a concept made political and economic sense. Soviet people, starved for political freedom, eagerly embraced democratic values in the first years after the fall of the U.S.S.R.. The majority of the population had vague concepts of how democracy should really work, but there was hope that once the democratic "floodgates" would open, the ensuing flow of political freedoms would usher in a new order of the day."

What did not happen from the start, and what is only now slowly becoming apparent, is that civil society in the former Soviet Union lacked proper education on even basic democratic principles. Newly found political freedom roughly translated into free elections for the majority of the people, but they knew next to nothing about other principles that are so crucial to a vibrant, working democracy. The importance of properly prepared civil society was demonstrated repeatedly in U.S. and UN efforts at establishing the rule of law in post-conflict societies around the world after 1991.

Autocratic executive rule was the tradition that most of the 15 states knew, and the only form of governance that a vast majority of their populations had experienced. Parliamentary-style democracy, checks and balances, separated legislative and judicial branches of government were unfamiliar and alien concepts.

It became apparent that many of the former Soviet states, and some within the broader Eastern Bloc, would struggle with the sort of speedy transition advocated by some in Washington, London, Bonn and Paris. Some would never make that transition at all. Replacing Moscow with an ephemeral concept of free elections was a huge task. Simply holding an election was far too simplistic.

Within Central Asia, Kazakhstan, Turkmenistan and Uzbekistan found themselves under Heads of State who had simply changed their job descriptions from first secretary of the Communist Party to Prime Minister or President. Tajikistan receded into civil war, while Kyrgyzstan moved smoothly into a relatively democratic system. Armenia grew a system that was democratic in outlook, but was dominated by deep and wide presidential powers.

These developments are viewed with hindsight. By the middle of the 90s, with independence still in its infancy, all these "new" nations were still finding their feet.

In Azerbaijan, the President inherited a position where his title held vast executive powers and felt he was in no position to dissipate the levers of state the office controlled. From Baku, like most of the Central Asia states, power traditionally came from top down. He was inclined to put stability first — and consider the quite real dangers of resurgent communist and nationalist trends — and think about multi-party democracy later. But he strove to ensure that there would not be the heavy-handed approach seen elsewhere.

His first electoral test came with Azerbaijan's Milli Majlis election of November 1995. The question was, would it be an opportunity for citizen groups and political parties to make themselves heard, or an opportunity for the President to create himself a legislative lap-dog?

Azerbaijan's Parliamentary body is the Milli Majlis, Azerbaijani for 'national assembly'. Framers of the constitution sought a body that would propose and debate legislation, and act as a check to the President. Section Five of the Constitution deemed that the Milli Majlis have 125 deputies. These would be elected through 100 single-seat constituencies and 25 through proportional representation. The Milli Majlis meets in legislative sessions twice a year.

However strong the hand of the President, the Milli Majlis remains relevant. Indeed, Azerbaijan's Parliament had played a (sometimes) chaotic yet powerful hand during the pre-Aliyev years.

A Law on Political parties was adopted in 1992, parties to be financed from the public budget. The President formed

Yeni Azerbaijan Partiyasi, the New Azerbaijan Party, in 1993. By 2009, some 52 political parties were registered. There is obviously a wafer thin line between a one-party state and multi-party democracy, and in Central Asia this mostly depended upon the intentions of the Head of State. Heydar Aliyev walked a line that attempted to balance both.

"Fostering a civil society, one capable of making educated and informed decisions, would take time," says Ilham.

Some say the fledgling President acquiesced to those demanding "democratic" changes. Others disagree. It was not so much acquiescence, as it was something that he saw was needed. The only disagreement between Heydar and those who wanted fully-fledged Western-style democracy was the speed that Azerbaijan would achieve a transition, and the eventual extent that Azerbaijani democracy would be identical in nature to 'Western' versions.

Azerbaijan, like all her neighbours, was unprepared, and perhaps incapable, of bringing the concept of Western-style democracy to fruition so quickly. The search for balance would begin to be defined through the nation's 1995 Milli Majlis election, Azerbaijan's first post-independence Parliamentary election.

With Heydar riding on a crest of popularity, there would be little surprise that the New Azerbaijan Party would make hay in this election. But the surprise of the poll came well in advance with the unveiling of the party's candidate list and a surprise announcement.

Heydar Aliyev created a surprise when he co-opted Ilham onto the New Azerbaijan Party ticket. Ilham chose to stand in the constituency of Garadagh in Baku.

It was with perhaps an assuredness that he would get kicked, in the form of foreign condemnation of the democratic process, that Heydar went to great lengths to bring the international community into Azerbaijan to view his nation's first election. The international community did not let him down.

The Vienna-based Organisation for Security and Cooperation in Europe (OSCE), states that it is "engaged in standard setting in fields including military security, economic and environmental cooperation, and human rights and humanitarian concerns." Its lofty ideal made OSCE well placed to join in monitoring efforts.

The President also invited in the Warsaw-based Office of Democratic Institutions and Human Rights (ODIHR) and the Electoral Assistance Division of the United Nations. These groups formed a 'Joint Electoral Observation Mission' which deployed some 120 international observers across Azerbaijan for the main election, and later 26 observers for run-off elections in 20 districts on November 26.

On November 12, 1995, Azerbaijan went to the polls in a landmark vote. In a country unused to an electoral process, a national election was a vast enterprise. The election saw the participation of 12 parties and over 1,000 candidates.

According to the Central Election Commission (CEC) figures showed that the turnout was 79.5 per cent. Of the 25 Milli Majlis seats distributed according to proportional representation, the Party of the Popular Front and the National Independence Party each took three.

Of the remaining 100 seats, contested by 386 candidates, 71 seats were decided without outright majorities. Others went to run offs because of minimum turnout requirements or problems with voting and were scheduled for repeat elections.

In Baku the election — which also encompassed voting on a constitutional amendment on which 91.9 per cent voted — was seen as a triumph. Just 871 days after Heydar had become President, amid the collapse of the previous administration, armed revolt, invasion and war, plus economic and social collapse, Azerbaijan had picked itself up, dusted itself off, and held the first national election in its history. Just managing to do that was a remarkable effort. A subsequent OSCE report stated:

> *Azerbaijan's election was multi-party, with many independent candidates and opposition parties actively participating. All candidates and parties received free air time on state television, which opposition parties used to criticise the government and put forward their own programmes. They also sought voter support through their own newspapers… the election law permitted observers and authorised representatives of political parties and candidates to monitor the voting and vote count…*

The Joint Electoral Observation Mission went on to conclude that the election did not correspond to internationally accepted norms, yet noted:

> *President Aliyev, who had stressed his personal commitment to free and fair elections, acknowledged that observers' criticisms were justified. But he maintained that the elections, though flawed, were a step forward. Aliyev has also pledged to continue Azerbaijan's democratisation, and to carry out the provisions of the constitution guaranteeing human and civil rights. The new constitution and the election have strengthened Aliyev, certifying his preeminence and assuring him of a supportive legislature. He has secured the status of New*

> *Azerbaijan, which he heads, as the ruling party. But he now has full responsibility for Azerbaijan, as he cannot blame policy failures or unfulfilled expectations on an uncooperative Parliament.*
>
> *...The election took place against a political background that, even by post-Soviet standards, has been unusually unstable, characterised by ethnic-territorial conflict, extra-constitutional changes of government and frequent coup attempts. Consequently, the election sought to create stable structures of government that would enjoy domestic respect and legitimacy, and, perhaps, to create a Parliamentary forum for political competition with clear rules of the game. By inviting the OSCE and the UN to observe the election, Azerbaijan's government also sought international recognition of its progress towards democracy...*
>
> *...President Aliyev repeatedly stressed his personal commitment to holding free and fair elections as an integral aspect of transforming Azerbaijan into a democratic, pluralistic society. Efforts to hold free and fair elections, however, took place in a complicated context of mutual distrust between the government and opposition parties...*

Thanks in no small measure to the overwhelming personal popularity of the President, New Azerbaijan now dominated the Milli Majlis. Among a swathe of new legislators was the member from Garadagh, Ilham Aliyev. In less than 18 months, Ilham had gone from leading a quiet life as a businessman to a Vice President of SOCAR and now a member of Azerbaijan's Parliament. Life had changed immeasurably, but the transformation from businessman to political leader was far from over.

Chapter Twenty-One

Parliamentarian

Parliament is not a congress of ambassadors from different and hostile interests; which interests each must maintain... parliament is a deliberative assembly of one nation, with one interest, that of the whole; where, not local purposes, not local prejudices ought to guide, but the general good, resulting from the general reason of the whole.
— Edmund Burke, British statesman

In 1201, King John of England granted a charter to the tin miners of Cornwall and Devon confirming their 'just and ancient customs and liberties'. In order to assert these, the tin miners of both areas met at Hingston Down. They referred to themselves as a Parliament which derives from words referring to conferences or discussions. The process of democratisation in England had actually begun a century earlier, in 1100, with the Charter of Liberties, in which King Henry I listed the powers of the monarchy under the law. But while the Charter of Liberties was limited in scope, it was King John's *Magna Carta Libertatum* that is recognised, today, as the starting point towards what we consider human rights, constitutions and other building bricks of modern society.

The 1215 *Magna Carta Libertatum* was written in Latin and means Great Charter of Freedoms in English. With this document King John proclaimed the rights to freemen, undertook for the monarchy to respect certain legal procedures and accept that his will could be bound by the law. Most importantly, it explicitly protected the rights of the King's subjects and supported what we know today as the writ of *habeas corpus*, allowing appeal against unlawful imprisonment.

The *Magna Carta Libertatum* set in motion the process that created today's constitutional law around the world, influenced the development of common law and many constitutional documents, including the United States Constitution.

King John's Parliament in Cornwall and Devon led to a national representative body. Model Parliament is the term used for the 1295 Parliament of King Edward I. This encompassed members of the clergy and aristocracy, seated with members from counties and boroughs. Each English county sent two knights, while two burgesses were elected from each borough. Each city provided two citizens. This composition became the model for later Parliaments, hence the name.

Edward I summoned Parliament together on November 13, 1295, proclaiming a writ of summons that stated "what touches all, should be approved of all, and it is also clear that common dangers should be met by measures agreed upon in common."

Parliamentary evolution resulted in the creation of a system of responsible government. Executive powers shifted, and different nations adapted systems that suited their own local conditions. A nation's form of government refers to how that state's executive, legislative and judicial organs are organised.

Democratic governments are those that permit the nation's citizens to manage their government either directly, or through elected representatives. This is opposed to authoritarian governments that limit or prohibit the direct participation of its citizens, such as the Soviet system.

Since the fall of the Soviet Union, democracy has begun to flourish around the world. As emerging nations struggle to identify themselves, they are also debating which form of democracy is best for them. Depending on the nation and its citizens, they may choose the more classic Parliamentary system or the less rigid Presidential system. They could also blend the two popular systems together to create the hybrid government that works best for national conditions.

The constitution of Azerbaijan was adopted by referendum on November 12, 1995 (same day as the seminal Milli Majlis election). It created a democratic, constitutional, secular and unitary republic, powers divided between the legislative, executive and judiciary, with the President as Head of the State. The Autonomous Republic of Nakhchivan is defined as an autonomous state within the Republic of Azerbaijan, which is an exclave from a geographical point of view.

Legislative power is deemed to be the responsibility of Milli Majlis, while the system is characterised by pluralism, the existence of more than one political party. Political parties participate through representatives in the legislative and local self-governing bodies.

The 1995 election was the first since independence was declared in August 1991. Prior to that the 360-member Supreme Soviet had sat, replaced by a 50-member National Council (Milli Majlis) dominated by former Communist apparachiks and unskilled people who entered politics during that period.

Nationwide elections were announced in April 1995, for a new, 125-seat National Assembly, a mixed majority-proportional representation system. The government was criticised for its refusal to register several opposition parties, including the prominent Azerbaijani Popular Front, while an initial ban on the Communist Party of Azerbaijan was lifted.

Eight party lists and 387 candidates were represented at the polls. Most parties supported Heydar Aliyev. Yet this was not unexpected given that he was riding high on a wave of personal popularity, viewed as the saviour of the nation and a man who would bring stability.

Polling day was monitored by observers from the Council of Europe and a joint OSCE-UN team. The voting outcome left 29 majority seats vacant in cases where the required minimum levels were not reached, thus necessitating a second round on November 26. There were 4.1 million registered voters and voter turnout in the first round was 86.05 per cent.

The OSCE Parliamentary Assembly had described Azerbaijan's election as 'neither free nor fair', while the Council of Europe reported the election was 'of a nature to harm the democratic character' of Azerbaijan, but added that this 'represented a first step towards a more democratic system.' Others took the event more in context. A Commonwealth of Independent States observer delegation and another grouping comprised of Turkish Parliamentarians made note of problems but thought these relatively minor and largely gave the election good grades, especially in the context of this being the first national election held in the country.

Addressing the first session of the Milli Majlis, on November 24 Heydar accepted that there were problems with the polls, and publicly acknowledged that many of the points raised by OSCE, the Council of Europe and others were justified. But he stated his belief that the election was a step forward and that the Milli Majlis would be both effective and, at times, a vibrant assembly where the new-to-Azerbaijan concept of political opposition could mature and that the opposition would begin to do its job.

Azerbaijan's first post-independence Parliament was a multi-party, multi-candidate affair. The Milli Majlis election of 1995 would be dominated by the New Azerbaijan Party. Yet the Milli Majlis would also be tooled with a vocal and visible strength of opposition Parliamentarians.

While the President would find a Milli Majlis dominated by his party and allies an amenable body, the governing party faced enough opposition, and a quality in opposition Parliamentarians, that it had vibrancy. Opposition parties would criticise the government and its policies at length — and vocally.

After round one of the election, New Azerbaijan held fifty-four seats, the Popular Front four seats, National Independence Party four seats, Democratic Independence Party two seats and there were one each for the Democratic Entrepreneurs Party, Citizens' Solidarity Party, 'Musavat' Party, Social Justice Party and 'Motherland' Party. There were 55 MPs who were officially non-affiliated, although a majority leaned toward New Azerbaijan.

"The 1995 election was a seminal moment in the history of modern Azerbaijan, a moment when we could begin to measure our democratic development," says Etibar Mammadov, leader of the National Independence Party.

Some around the President counselled against inviting in international monitors, understanding that no matter what occurred in the nation's first nationwide Parliamentary Election there would be rigorous criticism.

"He genuinely believed in the process of democratisation and although he understood that groups such as the OSCE and the Council of Europe would produce negative comment, he believed that we were on a learning curve," says Ilham.

The Azerbaijan President is quoted as saying: "These elections will be far from perfect. But they will get better."

While it was quite possible for foreigners, with their long standing democratic traditions, to be sniffy, there were undeniable positives from a national perspective. The Azerbaijan Supreme Soviet was a 360-man tool of Moscow. The 50-member National Council was a largely self serving and corruption driven instrument of post-independence administrations whose sole aim was to cling to power. The new Milli Majlis swept away much of that old power base. Instead of old style politicos, the impact of the elections was to bring to power a new generation of people from outside of the old ruling class.

According to statistics prepared by the Geneva-based Inter-Parliamentary Union (IPU), among this new generation were 17 engineers, 14 historians, 14 philologists, 12 physicists, 12 economists, 10 lawyers, 10 teachers, eight doctors, six agronomists, four chemists, four journalists, four biologists, three philosophers and three actors.

Within the Milli Majlis there were fifteen women MPs, 12 per cent of the whole 125-seat chamber. Data compiled by the IPU on the basis of information provided by National Parliaments in mid-2009 shows comparative data on the percentage of women in each National Parliament elected by direct suffrage. Nordic countries lead the way with 42 per cent women, while OSCE member states, including Nordic countries, stood at 21.3 per cent. Other regions monitored included Asia on 18.3 per cent, Sub-Saharan Africa 18.3 per cent, the Pacific 13.0 per cent and Arab states with 9.7 per cent.

Azerbaijan's 12 per cent, a decade and a half ago, a period in which the glass ceiling for women had further eroded but coming on the back of a masculine Soviet era, was nothing short of momentous. Even today, the IPU reports that the likes of Japan, Brazil and Sri Lanka (which had the world's first female Prime Minister) have lower proportions of female members within their chambers, and Azerbaijan hovered around the same level as Ireland and Greece. The United States posted figures of 16.8 per cent and in Westminster, the Mother of Parliaments, 19.5 per cent of members were women.

The duly elected representative for the constituency of Garadagh district would take his seat in Parliament amid a starkly different group of MPs that served in the old *majlis*. Among the deputies were five poets and five writers, a flurry of academics, and a new generation of politicians drawn — like Ilham — from outside the mainstream of Soviet Era politics. They were young and inexperienced, but what they lacked they made up for, in the eyes of the public, by not having roots in the Communist past.

"There was a belief, not just among deputies from New Azerbaijan, but among the whole *majlis* body, that we were heading in a fresh, purposeful direction," says Ilham. "There had been tensions during the election, normal political tensions, and although there were many diversions of opinion, there was an undercurrent in that we all knew we were here for a greater purpose."

Ilham had been back in Azerbaijan permanently for less than two years, lured to Baku by a request for help from his father. In that time, he had served as Vice President of SOCAR and played a fundamental part in the completion of the Contract of the Century.

"I was not fired by political ambition," says Ilham.

But as 1994 gave way to an election year, politics jumped on to the national agenda. Azerbaijan's Parliamentary elections dominated national life. From the political centre of Baku, to the remotest of remote villages, discussion centred on what next for government. Heydar Aliyev may have claimed a very one-sided Presidential Election in 1993, such was his personal popularity, but two years later Milli Majlis polls would define the direction that Azerbaijan would take.

The President had established the country and was tackling many of the issues that faced the nation. Much had been achieved. But a couple of years were nothing in the context of reversing the damage of the early independence years, and the corrosive period of the Soviet era. His job was far from over.

All signs were that Heydar retained his vast political base. His political capital at home was enormous and it was time to use it. His party, New Azerbaijan, was riding high in the polls. The opposition, led by the Azerbaijani Popular Front, which had transformed from a movement to a political party, and Musavat, had not achieved any semblance of national popularity and were ineffective. Therefore Heydar had a clear mandate to pursue his agenda for Azerbaijan.

Heydar Aliyev was a veteran politician. He was shaped by the cut and thrust of Soviet politics and knew that nothing could be left to chance, especially in an era where it was not the higher echelons of 'the party' to be appeased, but 4.1 million voters. He needed to ensure firstly that his own popularity reflected on the New Azerbaijan Party's polling fortunes, and then that he could rely upon the Milli Majlis to support his agenda as far as possible.

This would require ensuring that New Azerbaijan did as well as possible, and that those elected to the Milli Majlis shared his agenda. For even attempting this there were those nationally and internationally who would carp.

Creating a representative national *majlis* was hard enough. Those entrenched in power, the many hold-overs from the Communist era who had clung to power under Ayaz Mutallibov and Abulfaz Elchibey, had no inclination to support a reform agenda. That old adage of getting turkeys to vote for Christmas would seem appropriate.

And then there was the international comment that generally damned the election, and particularly Heydar's influence in the election. The same sources would be unlikely to condemn Bill Clinton, George W. Bush or Barack Obama as they utilised their position to ensure that mid-term elections were skewed, as far as possible to return Senators and Representatives from their respective parties, in order to support their own agendas.

Ilham was one of those who would support that agenda. But the MP for Garadagh was determined to make his presence felt. For every Gandhi, Bhutto, Chamberlain, Kennedy or Bush who served their country with honour, there were others drawn from the same stock who served only themselves and used their surnames to idle and profit. Some potentially brilliant young men and women from these dynastic political families squandered an opportunity to serve and follow in sometimes revered footsteps, and instead led less than blameless lives.

Ilham Aliyev would not be content to be one of those. He had made himself into an authority within the Moscow State Institute of International Relations, then, in a second career, capitalised on the collapse of the Soviet Union by creating a successful men's apparel business. Even when joining SOCAR he had shown himself not to be someone who was there to fill a chair. He was not the sort of personality to hitch a free ride.

"I wanted to represent the people who voted for me, for the party, and all the people of Garadagh, otherwise there seemed little point," says Ilham. "I saw myself first and foremost a representative of the people and accountable to those who elected me. If the members of the Milli Majlis of 1995 chose to remain in the mould of old style politicos then Azerbaijan would remain entrenched in the past."

It is not surprising that, in 1995, Ilham Aliyev gained 98.9 per cent of the 45,398 available vote from Garadagh district to become a Parliamentarian. The success of the first election and the support of the people were apparent.

In the new Milli Majlis, MPs would find their place as law-makers, government watchdogs, politicians, legislators, negotiators, policy analysts, public speakers and diplomats.

"I enjoyed the work," says Ilham. "Politics was not the most natural thing, but what appealed to me personally was that Garadagh needed help and its people needed a voice. Around me were many brilliant and hardworking people. With them in power the future of Azerbaijan looked bright."

Chapter Twenty-Two

The Lion in Winter

Today, more than ever before, life must be characterised by a sense of universal responsibility, not only nation to nation and human to human, but also human to other forms of life.
— Dalai Lama, Tibetan Buddhist leader

In May 1994, Ilham was appointed Vice President of the State Oil Company of Azerbaijan (SOCAR) and had proven himself during negotiations that led to the signing of the Contract of the Century. More and more, his father, the President, came to rely upon the safe pair of hands that his son represented. Ilham was not formally appointed, but quietly emerged as his father's chief advisor.

The 1990s represented a difficult period for Azerbaijan. The President had inherited a fractured nation, with crippling debt, failing health and education systems, a dispirited society and swathes of territory illegally occupied by Armenia.

Through sheer force of will, Heydar Aliyev was holding it together. His working days were commonly 20 hours. Every day represented an enormous battle. Yet the President was in his 70s — and not in the rudest of health. He was fighting on all sides as President and battling — personally — to remain fit. A safe pair of hands, on which he could rely implicitly, was all too welcome, especially during the early years of the Aliyev Presidency, when stability was still being re-established and there were still questions over loyalty.

Heydar is said to have survived a plethora of assassination attempts — according to some sources counted in double figures — during his decade in power in Baku.

A leadership figure for the President's agenda and the New Azerbaijan platform in the Milli Majlis, Ilham's ability to get things done quickly became appreciated. He had not lived in Baku full time for many years, since leaving for Moscow a shy 16 year old. But he returned a man, with plenty of life experience. A trained diplomat, a fluent English speaker and a successful businessman, he brought to SOCAR and the Milli Majlis an ability to turn his hand to most challenges, and a good track record. In those unstable post-Soviet times, he was unflinchingly loyal to his father, a trait that Heydar required as he sought to draw around him a coterie of confidantes and allies.

Ilham and his family settled back into life in Baku, in the hope that the travails of the past were over and that some semblance of stability in their home life could be established. The children found good school places and got to grips with their home country.

Yet for Ilham himself stability was undercut by the increasing demands of state.

Heydar also co-opted him onto the Azerbaijan National Olympic Committee (NOC). Subject to the controls of the International Olympic Committee, NOCs are responsible for organising their country's participation in the Olympic Games and promoting the development of athletes and training of coaches and officials at a national level. Today there are 205 NOCs. All 193 United Nations member states have NOCs, with Azerbaijan's recognised in 1993.

Bruce Jenner, the Olympic Decathlon gold medalist says: "I learned that the only way you are going to get anywhere in life is to work hard at it. Whether you are a musician, a writer, an athlete or a businessman, there is no getting around it. If you do, you will win — if you don't, you will not."

Azerbaijan government policy was that sports underpinned everything the country would want from its youth. Even in times of squeezed national budgets, efforts were made to improve crumbling sports infrastructure and get younger generations to embrace sport within their lives. But there was a deeper reason for this interest. Azerbaijan was a nation wounded by internal strife, politically polarised in places and bruised from Armenia's occupation.

DeMaurice Smith, Executive Director of the National Football League Players Association, says: "Sport… is at its best when it unifies, gives all of us reason to cheer, and when it transcends. Our sport does exactly that when it overcomes division and rejects discrimination and hatred."

As Smith observes, sports can be a tool to develop a coherent society and a unifying factor within a nation wounded by its recent history. Azerbaijan needed both. Ilham had to deliver.

Strasbourg also reached his desk. Today the Council of Europe, based in the French city of Strasbourg, covers virtually the entire European continent, with 47 member states. Founded on 5 May, 1949, by 10 countries, the Council of Europe seeks to develop throughout Europe common and democratic principles based on the European Convention on Human Rights and other reference texts on the protection of individuals.

Azerbaijan's accession to the body came on January 25, 2001. The country's Foreign Minister sits on the CoE's Committee of Ministers, while within the CoE's Parliamentary Assembly (PACE) Azerbaijan has a delegation of six representatives. Ilham headed this grouping.

Heydar Aliyev was pursuing a pragmatic balanced foreign policy. The country was in Russia's backyard, but also newly independent and intent upon forging good relations with the West. The Azerbaijani President maintained a constructive relationship with Moscow, but needed to strike a difficult geopolitical balance between East and West.

Azerbaijan cooperated with NATO and the European Union integration programmes, but becoming a full member of either was not on the agenda in Baku. What was, was an active and sometimes vociferous role in the Council of Europe. This was especially important as Azerbaijan attempted to further highlight the Nagorno-Karabakh crisis.

The Parliamentarians who make up PACE meet four times a year for week-long plenary sessions at the Palais de l'Europe in Strasbourg, to discuss issues and ask governments to take initiatives and report back. The body speaks for 800 million Europeans. PACE states on its website that it is "Greater Europe's democratic conscience".

Some 318 representatives sit in the chamber with each country, depending on its population, having between two and eighteen representatives, who provide a balanced reflection of the political forces represented in each national Parliament.

While Ilham's knowledge and experience were growing — not least from his experience in Strasbourg — his father was succeeding at home in Baku. The dark days of the mid-1990s were over and by the turn of the millennium stability had returned. But at the same time Heydar's health had become a concern.

In 1999 he had overcome a major heart bypass operation at the Cleveland Clinic in Ohio. Aged 76, he had fought his way back to health.

"Heydar Aliyev believed that his project was nowhere near complete," says one who served him closely during this era. "Through sheer mental strength, he got back to work as quickly as he could, dismissing health concerns. He felt he simply did not have time to lose, as there was much still to be done."

The Azerbaijan President was racing against the clock on several levels. Azerbaijan needed forward motion. His project needed time, and Heydar was aware of his own mortality. His age was against him, as was his health.

Between 1999 and the spring of 2003, Heydar Aliyev fought the ravages of time and ill-health, while steering what amounted to a renaissance in Azerbaijan. The nation was increasingly prosperous, stable and at peace with itself.

"He recognised that there was a long way to go," says another source, who worked in the President's Office and was familiar with the President's thoughts during that period. "A decade is a blink of an eye in the political life of a nation, particularly one that was being rebuilt from the ruins of the Soviet era."

On April 20, 2003, Heydar was forced to face the prospect that he would not be able to complete that project. The *BBC* reported of events that day:

> *The President of Azerbaijan, Heydar Aliyev, has collapsed twice during a ceremony broadcast live on state television, prompting new speculation about his health. Television showed Mr Aliyev clutching his heart and swaying as he addressed cadets from a military academy in the capital Baku.*
>
> *A statement from the Presidential press service later said he had merely lost his balance after suffering*

> *a drop in blood pressure and was now recovering well.*

At 76 years old, the lion of Azerbaijani politics was tired. His focus changed to making arrangements for continuity and securing what he believed was the legacy of the decade just gone. The function of his heart was increasingly impaired in its ability to supply sufficient blood flow and his old kidney problems were re-emerging.

The lion was now in the winter of his life. In July he was flown to Turkey for treatment.

It was nearly four months before, publicly at least, Heydar set in motion a narrative for the future. Under the Azerbaijani Constitution, the Prime Minister takes over as Head of State, pending elections, if the President dies. On August 4, he issued a decree appointing Ilham as Prime Minister. The same day, speaking in the Milli Majlis after the appointment was confirmed, Ilham downplayed his father's illness, emphasising instead the country's healthy economy.

"The Azerbaijani economy is on the rise and I will do everything to continue the course. I expect no serious changes in the government. As for the President's health, it is good. He planned to return a couple of days ago, but the doctors wanted to provide him with some additional treatment. However, I believe he will return to Azerbaijan soon," said Ilham.

Ilham moved into the Prime Minister's Office, began staffing positions around him and made all the necessary arrangements that one would expect if he was to remain in the position for sometime. Although the President was clearly very sick, consensus was that he would recover, even if he took on a less day-to-day role.

The British Prime Minister with the longest single term was Sir Robert Walpole, lasting 20 years and 314 days, also longer than the accumulated terms of any other Prime Minister. In Australia Sir Robert Gordon Menzies served as Prime Minister for a period of 17 years. In Canada Wilfrid Laurier was the longest serving continual Prime Minister with over 15 unbroken years of rule.

Ilham's Prime Ministership would last just 93 days — from August 4 to November 4. In October, suffering from failing health, Heydar Aliyev announced that he intended to step down as President. Above this, Ilham would be installed as the New Azerbaijan Party's candidate in the forthcoming Presidential Elections. Given the party's overwhelming success in Parliamentary Elections, and the Aliyev name, this made him an odds-on certainty to win the post.

Official results of the October 15, 2003, election gave victory to Ilham, who earned 76.84 per cent of the vote. By then the outgoing President was in the United States. He would never return to his beloved Azerbaijan alive.

The lion had roared his last.

Chapter Twenty-Three

Swiss Roll

I think it's fair to say that personal computers have become the most empowering tool we've ever created. They're tools of communication, they're tools of creativity, and they can be shaped by their user.
— Bill Gates, founder of Microsoft

Less than two months into his Presidency, Ilham faced an almost nightmarish array of difficulties between which he divided his time. There was criticism from some international organisations of the Presidential Election, an opposition intent on talking up this issue, and, meanwhile, a nation and society that required urgent attention.

Ilham's concerns were both the same, and different, to those of his father. Heydar Aliyev never sent an email. Ilham was well versed in the information age. His email accounts filled so quickly that he required assistance.

So, although both Presidents pursued an education agenda, Ilham's focus was through a prism of the information age, an era alien to his father. The Web was invented by English scientist Sir Tim Berners-Lee in 1989, when Heydar was already 66 years old. His generation was the last pre-Internet generation in human history.

On the other hand, President Ilham was IT savvy. He took much of his information from the Internet. He communicated extensively via email. The global Digital Revolution, especially the difference that this made to people's lives and to national economies, was something he believed in.

When Prime Minister, Ilham had scheduled a trip to Geneva late in 2003. Although his office had changed during the intervening period, he saw no reason to break this engagement.

The World Summit on the Information Society (WSIS) was to be held in two phases, the first hosted by the government of Switzerland from December 10 to 12, followed by a second meeting in Tunis nearly two years later.

The importance of the WSIS was clear — and the new President of Azerbaijan understood that his country needed far greater assimilation into the Digital Age. The Digital Revolution, fired by the engines of Information and Communication Technologies, had fundamentally changed the way people think, behave, communicate, work and earn their livelihood.

It has forged new ways to create knowledge, educate people and disseminate information, restructuring the way the world conducts economic and business practices, runs governments and engages politically. It has provided for the speedy delivery of humanitarian aid and healthcare, and a new vision for environmental protection. It has even created new avenues for entertainment and leisure. As access to information and knowledge is prerequisite to achieving the Millennium Development Goals — or MDGs — it has the capacity to improve living standards for millions of people around the world. Moreover, better communication between people helps resolve conflicts and attain world peace.

The Internet has ushered in the greatest period of wealth creation in history. How much the Digital Age had, thus far, penetrated into Azerbaijan was another question.

Internet penetration in Azerbaijan was good for the Caucasus at the time, but poor within the context of international league tables overall. Like her neighbours Azerbaijan needed other countries in order to have an Internet service. Georgia, for example, took its Internet access through fiber optic lines from neighbouring countries, whereby Azerbaijan's external Internet connection was provided by a satellite and fiber-optic link to Switzerland and others.

In terms of Internet penetration and development of local content, the Caucasus were better developed than Central Asia but less developed than Central Europe. Reliable estimates at the time were that 16 per cent of Azerbaijanis had 'regular' access to the Internet, a lower figure than Georgia but higher than Azerbaijan's other neighbours.

Yet Azerbaijan did have advantages, as the OpenNet Initiative reports:

> *During the Soviet-Era, Azerbaijan was a major centre for IT development, particularly in the area of process control systems. This legacy left the country with reasonably large and well-developed technical infrastructure, including several research institutes and a political leadership that was savvy about the importance of the ICT sector. Internet development is following the pattern typical of many developing countries, with access centred on the major cities, particularly the capital city Baku. Overall—supported by the government ICT strategy as well as the large Azeri Diaspora for whom the Internet is increasingly an important channel for maintaining contact with their homeland— Internet penetration is rising.*

One problem in utilising this advantage in Azerbaijan was cost. A 128k leased line, which is a typical connection used by a small business or household cost up to $200 per month in Baku and as much as $500 per month in rural areas. This sat in stark contrast to the West, where Internet connection could be obtained for as little as $10 per month. Even in Baku, Wi-Fi services were virtually unheard of. According to the organisation Reporters Without Borders (RWB), in 2002 there were 300,000 Internet users in Azerbaijan out of a population of 8.2 million (one million of those refugees and IDPs).

"President Ilham Aliyev was unhappy with the situation," says Ali Abbasov, Minister of Communications and Information Technology. "He felt that it was time for change, to alter the Internet demographics of the country." In time, the new Presidential administration would, through a variety of means, develop delivery of the Internet, work to spread services across the country and deregulate the telecoms system to introduce more market competition.

In 2002 RWB stated: 'The Internet has grown slower than in other Caucasus countries, mainly because of the communications ministry's monopoly of long-distance phone traffic through the state-owned firm Aztelekom.' However, in 2008-2009 the situation changed and the monopoly over the Internet ended.

Deregulation and the spread of the Internet would be pre-dated by a root and branch effort to bring IT into schools.

"It was shown that better education was closely associated with greater Internet and computer use. While education was at the heart of the President's agenda, he was personally involved in IT, pressing this issue forward," says Abbasov.

Results would be marked. From 2000 when Internet penetration was reported as low as 0.1 per cent and 12,000 users by the United Nations Department of Economic and Social Affairs, through the 300,000 users reported by RWB in 2002, by 2007 the UN Department of Economic and Social Affairs reported just under 10 per cent of the Azerbaijan population on line, some 829,000 users.

The concrete developments initiated by the President during his first year, and these startling results, could not obscure the fact that Azerbaijan lagged behind much of the world in penetration terms. Indeed, the WSIS had been consulted in an attempt to tackle a widely perceived crisis of the Information Age. United Nations Secretary General, Kofi Annan, had warned of the danger of excluding the world's poor from the information revolution, saying: "People lack many things: jobs, shelter, food, healthcare and drinkable water. Today, being cut off from basic telecommunications services is a hardship almost as acute as these other deprivations, and may indeed reduce the chances of finding remedies to them."

From 1990, when the Internet was in its early stages, access grew rapidly in the industrialised world. By 2002, although there were few users in West, Central and sub-Saharan Africa, for example, nearly half the population in North America, Australia, South Korea and Scandinavia, and about a third of the population in the rest of Europe, Malaysia and Japan, could use the Internet. While Internet penetration rates in Azerbaijan were on a sharp upward curve, it was clear that increased spread of computer and Internet use could raise productivity and boost education. But there remained a long way to go to achieve digital equality between Azerbaijan and the most Internet-connected countries of the world.

It was clear that the Digital Divide would not close by itself. But it was also clear that affirmative action could see the divide narrowed, indeed, it was also entirely possible that Azerbaijan could quickly become the Internet Hub for the Caucasus, and farther afield. Which led to Geneva.

Nearly 50 Heads of State and Vice Presidents, 82 Ministers and 26 Vice Ministers from 175 countries were due in Switzerland. They would mix with senior representatives from international organisations, NGOs, the private sector and civil society. Around 11,000 delegates from these countries attended the summit and related events.

Ilham was full of optimism that the Geneva conference was to look at ways of spreading the use of the Internet and other technologies across the world. But while there to show Azerbaijan's commitment to the Digital Age, he was already exploring ways domestically to transform the Internet in Azerbaijan.

Less than two months on from the Presidential Election which thrust him into power, and with a vast amount of pulls on his working day, Ilham had drawn an informal group around him that was exploring how the nation could cross the Digital Divide. As well as the Ministry of Communications and Information Technologies, the Ministry of Education, Ministry of Economic Development, Ministry of Finance and Ministry of Youth and Sports would all play a role, along with others, in ushering in a fresh, dynamic approach to the Web.

The President recognised that Internet penetration was hobbled because computer ownership was low, and 34 per cent of people asked, blamed the high cost of computer equipment and connectivity as the main reason for not being connected. The overall growth of the economy would help, but this was not good enough.

The Ministry of Communications and Information Technologies was charged with ensuring that telecommunications and the Internet were national development priorities, as both regulator and operator.

Ali Abbasov, who took on this portfolio in 2004, was charged by Aliyev with devolving and liberalising the Internet service provider network, in part to increase competition and building the non-profit project to provide connectivity to the educational and research community.

These were policies that the President took with him to Geneva, but he was going to learn, to participate and to absorb, as well as to throw Azerbaijan behind efforts that would benefit the world community.

In his speech to the gathering, Ilham said:

> *During the last decade, Information and Communication Technologies have become an integral part of our daily life. It is difficult to imagine today's world without the Internet, e-mail and many other features of the global cyberspace. Today we are talking about the new type of society — the Information Society, new style of governance — e-Governance. Decisions of this summit to the large extent refer to the young generation, since they are expected to create new realities of the information society. With this respect summit documents will be of great importance to Azerbaijan, a country where 70 per cent of the population is under the age of 35.*
>
> *The young generation of Azerbaijan is actively involved in a number of ICT projects implemented jointly with UNDP. On behalf of the government of Azerbaijan, I would like to stress that building the Information society is fully in line with our principles*

and therefore reconfirm our commitment to this idea. We are currently developing the State Programme 'e-Azerbaijan', including a number of projects ranging from e-Governance to e-Economy.

Economic and political stability, which exists in Azerbaijan for more than 10 years, is one of the major reasons of rapid development. The policy of economic and political reforms, aimed at integration into the international community resulted in rapid economic growth and further democratisation of our society. Annual growth is around 10 per cent for the last six years. Private sector share in GDP is more than 70 per cent. Azerbaijan for many years has held one of the leading places among former republics of the Soviet Union and countries of Central Europe in the amount of foreign investments per capita... Geopolitical situation of Azerbaijan makes our country a crossroad in regional transportation projects. Azerbaijan's role in the East-West and North-South transport corridor is important. Transport and energy resources flows are always accompanied by information flows. Necessity of their processing and transformation into products are challenges we are facing in the field of information and communication technologies.

We believe that our country is capable to act as a system integrator in the regional ICT Development, and ICT for Development in particular. This is a proposal we would like to make to all parties concerned. Azerbaijan not only participates, but also plays a crucial role in all the regional projects. Azerbaijan's participation in the regional cooperation will continue... Serious attention is paid in Azerbaijan to the creation and development of information and

> *knowledge market, IT-infrastructure and IT-services. Scientific potential, and technological achievements of Azerbaijan are sufficient for the creation of a knowledge-based society.*

Geneva was a busy time. In addition to the many WSIS meetings in which Ilham and his team participated, the Azerbaijan President's visit to Switzerland presented the first multi-national conference that he had attended since the election. There were a host of multi-lateral meetings with other leaders, and in between several hundred informal handshakes and words of encouragement from his peers from around the world. Among the official sit-downs scheduled were with the Presidents of Iran, Estonia, Romania, Kyrgyzstan, Macedonia, Turkey and Russia, the Prime Ministers of Bangladesh and Turkey, Richard Armitage, U.S. Deputy Secretary of State, and Ruud Lubbers, UN High Commissioner for Refugees.

It was an exhausting few days of conference sessions, meetings and quick meetand-greets. Ilham was experienced on the world stage, but on his global debut there were a lot of leaders with whom to become acquainted.

The Azerbaijan President, adopting a missionary-like zeal, breezed through these few days in Switzerland although squeezed between briefings, working breakfasts, WSIS sessions, meetings on the sidelines and official dinners, there were only a few hours each night for sleeping. It seemed not to matter, the new President used his debut within an international forum to emerge.

The WSIS meeting was a success for Azerbaijan. The Azerbaijani party learned a lot, forged many useful relationships and set in motion an immediate burst of development that the Internet and IT industry saw in the immediate years following Geneva. Indeed, as the OpenNet Initiative observes of Azerbaijan: "...Between 2004 and 2005 the number of Internet subscribers doubled..." and this figure would continue to spiral upwards.

The summit itself looked at ways of spreading the use of the Internet and other technologies across the world but at times was marred by disagreements over who decides how the Internet is run and over money. African countries were angry that richer nations had refused to provide funds to bankroll technology projects in the developing world. But the representatives, drawn from 175 countries, did agree a Declaration of Principles. The first paragraph said loftily:

> *We, the representatives of the peoples of the world, assembled in Geneva from 10-12 December 2003 for the first phase of the World Summit on the Information Society, declare our common desire and commitment to build a people-centred, inclusive and development-oriented Information Society, where everyone can create, access, utilise and share information and knowledge, enabling individuals, communities and peoples to achieve their full potential in promoting their sustainable development and improving their quality of life, premised on the purposes and principles of the Charter of the United Nations and respecting fully and upholding the Universal Declaration of Human Rights.*

Symbolically, Geneva represented something new for Azerbaijan. A new President, from a new generation, had emerged on the world stage and begun to define his modernist credentials in the most definitive way, by asserting his country's place in the 21st century Digital Economy.

But tragedy was to ensure that Geneva was far more of a definitive turning point than anyone had expected.

As the conference wound-down, the President of Azerbaijan had bilateral meetings scheduled with a variety of world leaders.

The following morning he was in a motorcade on the way to the airport, ahead of returning home, when he received a telephone call from the United States. An aide of the former President broke the news that the father of the nation was gone. Heydar Aliyev had passed away in the Cleveland Clinic in Ohio.

Everything was about to change. Again.

Chapter Twenty-Four

Father of the Nation

It is the will of God and Nature that these mortal bodies be laid aside, when the soul is to enter into real life; 'tis rather an embryo state, a preparation for living; a man is not completely born until he be dead. Why then should we grieve that a new child is born among the immortals?

— Benjamin Franklin, American statesman

More than a million mourners crowded on to the streets of Azerbaijan's capital, Baku, yesterday for the funeral of Heydar Aliyev, who ruled the country for three decades… In the largest public outpouring of grief in the former Soviet Union since the death of Stalin 50 years ago, they streamed down avenues strewn with carnations towards the Palace of the Republic where his body lay.

Tens of thousands had waited all night for a chance to pay their respects to their former leader, who was laid to rest in a coffin draped in red, blue and green, the national colours, and attended by a guard of honour… Thousands of mourners walked slowly past the coffin with tears streaming down their faces. One woman collapsed.

Sabad Aliyeva, a 68 years old pensioner who arrived in Baku at 5am, said: "He was a worthy son of all the Azerbaijani people. I don't believe such a person will ever be born again."

> *...the coffin was carried by eight Presidential guards to a gun carriage. The carriage was pulled slowly down the tree-lined Alley of Honourable Burial to a cemetery where the former leader was placed next to his wife, Zarifa, who died in 1985, and his older brother.*
>
> *Among the mourners at the funeral were a host of foreign dignitaries including the Russian President Vladimir Putin and Georgia's former leader, Eduard Shevardnadze. Mr Putin said Mr Aliyev was "an internationalist, a great friend of Russia and a patriot of Azerbaijan".*
>
> *Also attending was Recep Erdogan, the Prime Minister of Turkey, with which Azerbaijan has close ties. He said: "The Turkic world has lost an outstanding individual."*
>
> *The crowds were so large that police separated them into blocks, each tens of thousands strong.*

This was how Julius Strauss, a correspondent for Britain's *Daily Telegraph*, reported the extraordinary scenes on the streets of Baku on that bright, crisp winter day. The *New York Times* told its readers:

> *More than a million people filled the streets of Baku, the capital, for the funeral of Heydar Aliyev, whose name was associated with the governance of the oil-rich former Soviet republic for 30 years until he became too ill to continue in October. Joining the mourners were President Vladimir V. Putin of Russia and Eduard A. Shevardnadze, who was forced from the presidency of Georgia last month.*

Agence France-Presse added:

> *Heads of State joined massive crowds of ordinary people in Azerbaijan's capital for the funeral of Heydar Aliyev, the man who ruled the oil-rich republic with a rod of iron for more than three decades but was known by the affectionate nickname 'grandfather.'*

London's *Independent* informed its readers: 'The veteran Azerbaijani leader Heydar Aliyev made a career of adapting to changing conditions. Even his harshest critics grudgingly respected him as a master tactician who maintained order in a fractious ex-Soviet republic… 'The *BBC* called him: '…a colossus on the stage of Azerbaijani politics for more than 30 years.'

The throng on the streets of Baku made the feelings of ordinary Azerbaijanis plain. The population of Baku was a shade less than three million at the time. The one million plus reported by Julius Strauss represented over half the people living in the capital. As a national demographic, this mass of persons equates to 12.5 per cent of a national population of eight million. To give a broader international perspective, it is the equivalent of 38 million American citizens pouring onto the streets of Washington to mark the passing of a President, or 18 million Russians in Moscow, 16 million Japanese in Tokyo or 9.5 million Egyptians in Cairo.

While one would never seek a direct comparison with the great John F. Kennedy, an estimated one million people lined the streets to mourn and view the formal funeral procession on November 25, 1963, from the U.S. Capitol to St. Matthew's Cathedral, then to his final resting place at Arlington National Cemetery.

That Heydar could create such an emotional and sizeable turnout among his own people, however, is indicative of the standing in which he was held. Ultimately, this would have been more important to him than the opinions of obituary writers in New York and London.

The international media rolled out their obituaries, including the usual barbs, while in places begrudgingly recognising that he had achieved some remarkable feats.

While these publications and others repeated many of the West's opinions on the late President, some of them tired and patently overstated, the people of his country showed their feelings not by words, but through actions.

"They were extraordinary scenes. It was breathtaking," says Foreign Minister Elmar Mammadyarov. "Heydar Aliyev undoubtedly was a strong man and it was this which was focused upon in the international media. But it was that strength that had got Azerbaijan through the early and most difficult early years of the post-Soviet era, along with a war and occupation of 20 per cent of the country."

A Western-style democratic politician would never have lasted in the Caspian region. That is why none emerged in this region during this period. It was not possible for such a style of leadership to be maintained. Experiences elsewhere show as much. Georgia's political giant Eduard Shevardnadze lasted, but when he departed a measure of chaos followed. Armenia's Heads of State remained in power by placing the nation on a war footing, and propped up politically and financially by a neighbour, while the Presidents of Kazakhstan, Russia and Turkmenistan enjoyed few Western-styled democratic principles to speak of. Uzbekistan, Tajikistan or Kyrgyzstan were not held up as bastions of democracy in Washington, London or Paris either. Iran displeased the West with its skewed approach to elections, while the West failed miserably with its attempts to introduce these foreign concepts in Afghanistan and others.

By contrast, Heydar could be considered the 'Democrat of the Caucasus'. As early as October 1996, Azerbaijan Ambassador to the U.S., Hafiz Pashayev, told the Central Asia-Caucasus Initiative at Johns Hopkins University: "We have in the short space of five years held two Presidential elections and one for Parliament. Some critics complain that democracy in Azerbaijan does not match that of the West. But let me remind you that America did not achieve direct election of senators until 1913 and women did not receive the right to vote until 1920. And when the American constitution was not adopted until 11 years after independence, Azerbaijan's constitution was approved four years after independence."

It was an interesting comparison by Pashayev, and one which continues to hold true well over a decade on with further national elections completed.

Yet the democratic credentials of Heydar Aliyev, and his other achievements, were perhaps lost in the raw emotion of December 15, 2003.

"The funeral cortège, as it wound along the streets of Baku, was accompanied by a military band, playing sombre music, but my keenest memory of the day was to hear the wailing of women, crying out as they stood at the roadside," says Ali Hasanov, Deputy Prime Minister. "The former President's coffin moved slowly."

Traffic had ground to a halt in the normally busy Azerbaijan capital. Since the days of curfew at night, years before, the vast city had never been so silent. Now, at the moment of the official departure of the father of the modern nation, the normal sounds of a bustling city — car horns, construction work and the like — were strangely absent.

Bird song, so often drowned out by Baku's sprawling humanity, competed only with the outward emotion of the women who lined the route. Behind the body of his father, the nation's new President walked alone, looking almost impassive, but his face ashen, betraying his emotion.

Behind Ilham came an array of international leaders and the representatives of nearly 50 countries. Falling in behind them, the great and the good of Azerbaijani society and, further behind, a mass of humanity so great that they walked several kilometres behind the coffin.

The government worked meticulously during this period and proved that the system that he had created was supported by people. Ordinary Azerbaijanis showed great grief, a reflection of the veneration in which Heydar was held. Even though one million people had not been predicted, the funeral ran smoothly and remained dignified.

Says Ramiz Mehdiyev, Head of Administration of the President of the Republic of Azerbaijan: "It was expected that this would be a national event, a state funeral for a man who was effectively the father of the nation, and the streets thronged with grieving citizens."

Atakhan Pashayev, Chief of the National Archive Department, observes: "The mood was dark, of course, but it was a historical once-in-a-lifetime event. People wanted to observe and to be close to the man who had, in so many ways, shaped their lives and their nation. The sheer numbers speak volumes for what he meant to ordinary Azerbaijanis."

By early afternoon, the casket was moved by a military guard of honour to its final resting place, to be interred under a splendid black marble mausoleum. Amid a breathtaking sea of flowers, standing before the grave, Ilham led his country in a few moments of silence. With this, the official portion of the day was over.

Those close to Heydar Aliyev retreated to grieve in private. But there remained a general unwillingness among the crowd to melt away. The Presidential Office, in downtown Baku, quickly became a focus for mourners. For days afterwards those wishing to pay their private respects to Heydar filed quietly past the late President's office and left red roses and carnations on the steps of the building.

"This went on for days," says Mehdiyev. "One million people had attended the funeral, but it was a state occasion, an impersonal thing to many ordinary people. The Presidential Office became a focus, an impromptu shrine."

Over the ensuing week, an estimated 250,000 people brought flowers, spent a few minutes in prayer, or simply stood in silence, remembering the man.

As for the new President of Azerbaijan, private grief had to be momentary as the demands of country intervened. Despite this, conforming to Muslim traditions, he visited his father's grave regularly over a 40 day period, to pay him tribute and say prayers.

At the funeral were a host of leaders and representatives of many key allies. Even on the day of his father's funeral, Ilham would have a full diary of meetings. In Baku were Russian President Vladimir Putin, Turkish President Ahmet Necdet Sezer and Prime Minister Recep Tayyip Erdogan, the Ukrainian and Kazakhstan Presidents, Leonid Kuchma and Nursultan Nazarbayev.

Also present were Georgia's past and present Presidents Eduard Shevardnadze and Mikheil Saakashvili, along with a host of others.

An intrusion, maybe, but necessary meetings. In the potentially explosive Caucasus the death of Aliyev had arguably marked a watershed moment. The old guard were gone. As one commentator observed:

> *...for many Azerbaijanis, the departure of Heydar Aliyev, once one of the U.S.S.R.'s most powerful men and later Azerbaijan's strong-handed leader, who ruled the country for over three decades totally, is a turning point in the country's road to independence and the end of an era. In fact, the death of Aliyev, a patriarch of the region, is in a sense ending the 90s in Azerbaijan and in the Caucasus.*
>
> *With the Georgian patriarchal ex-President Eduard Shevardnadze ousted from office by a younger generation of leaders, Ilham Aliyev succeeding his father Heydar in Azerbaijan, and Russia ruled by the younger, more dynamic Vladimir Putin, the region faces a new political dynamic.*

For Ilham, that new political dynamic, coupled with a vast number of domestic and international challenges, would mean that there was little time to draw breath. After half a dozen meetings on December 15, the following day he was in the office.

According to those familiar with him, in doing so he was delivering a clear message. To his cabinet. To his government. To the wider world. Heydar Aliyev may be gone, but in Azerbaijan there was no let up.

It was business as usual.

Chapter Twenty-Five

Lessons from the Campaign Trail

The beginning is the most important part of the work.
— Plato, Ancient Greek Philosopher

"Every day of my working life, I speak about Nagorno-Karabakh, am involved in drafting papers on the issue, or discuss the issue with someone, either face-to-face, or on the telephone," says Ilham. "Nagorno-Karabakh is a constant."

It is September 3, 2009, and the Azerbaijan President is five years, ten months and four days into his tenure in the position. This period comprises 2,135 days, an unbroken stint in which this territory — Nagorno-Karabakh and the seven adjacent regions occupied represent some 20 per cent of the nation — have ranged high on the President's agenda.

On October 31, 2003, the date of Ilham's first inauguration, the issue was not new either. As Prime Minister, as a Member of Parliament, and as a more ordinary citizen when Vice President of SOCAR, it is an issue which burned into working days.

"It is normal for the President, ministers, government officials and ordinary Azerbaijanis, when interacting with foreigners, to discuss Nagorno-Karabakh and ensure that people all over the world understand the issue properly," says Ilham. "As President I have many opportunities to do this, but every Azerbaijani makes a difference."

To the neutral observer, if Azerbaijan had lost any war by 2003, its biggest defeat was not on a battlefield but in the field of public relations.

Armenia had woken up early to the court of world opinion, before the 1994 ceasefire in Nagorno-Karabakh, mobilising its silent forces, a vast diaspora around the world. The Armenian diaspora is widespread and undeniably successful. They include Dr Raymond Damadian, inventor of the MRI diagnosis machine, sports stars Andre Agassi and Alain Prost, musician Cher and singer Charles Aznavour.

The historical travails of Armenians mean that there are an estimated 11 million scattered round the world, of which an estimated 3.1 million live in Armenia. The largest pockets globally are, statistically, in Russia, United States, France, Turkey, Lebanon, Syria and Nagorno-Karabakh. Armenians abroad are numerous, well financed and incredibly well organised, punching well above their weight and influencing foreign governments. According to one 2007 *BBC* report:

> *Given that Armenians represent only about 1.5 million of America's 300 million population, what has won them such influence over the U.S. Congress — and perhaps the nation's foreign policy? Part of the answer lies in the organisation and determination of the Armenian-American lobby groups, says Dr Svante Cornell, of the Central Asia-Caucasus Institute at Johns Hopkins University.*
>
> *The Armenian National Committee of America (ANCA) and the Armenian Assembly of America (AAA) are among the most powerful. Another factor is that the Armenian-American community is largely concentrated in important states such as California, Michigan and Massachusetts, Dr Cornell said.*

> *"You have basically a number of places where the Armenian issue is very important in local politics — especially for anybody wanting to get elected in California," he said.*

The Armenians built their organisation, arranged their lobby and set the agenda, particularly successful in the United States, while Azerbaijan was passive and its politicians bickered between themselves on whom to blame for the Nagorno-Karabakh disaster. The result is a preponderance of pro-Armenian opinion in the Senate and House of Representatives, a political rout against Azerbaijan that overflows like a gigantic toilet into the print and television media, and has shaped international opinion.

A war which started in Nagorno-Karabakh is, today, played out on a battleground that is unfamiliar to ordinary Azerbaijanis and Armenians: Capitol Hill. Only the likes of Hafiz Pashayev, the eloquent, impressive and persuasive former Azerbaijan Ambassador in Washington, prevented an outright PR victory for Armenia. But one voice, however effective, could only do so much in the face of a well-financed and well-organised lobby.

Perhaps only in recent times has Baku been proactive, after granting their opponents head start. Public Relations was a concept that Heydar cared about. Ilham is from a generation that understands PR even more acutely. He believes that Azerbaijan has a persuasive and coherent stance, only that Azerbaijan never told its story coherently in Washington, or London, or Moscow, or Paris.

Only after 2001 was the Azerbaijan diaspora mobilised. Groups were formed among communities in about 40 nations, including Norway, Netherlands, Germany, Spain, Italy, Belgium, Bulgaria, the Czech Republic, Finland,

Estonia, Poland, United Arab Emirates, Egypt, Turkey and the U.S.. From Baku, the State Committee for Diaspora Affairs attempted to organise this movement.

"The diaspora are very important to Azerbaijan and we are increasingly able to rely upon Azerbaijanis abroad to promote the cause of Azerbaijan," says Ramiz Mehdiyev. "They represent a fantastic asset, being passionate about the causes that are important to their mother country."

During a 2007 diaspora conference, Ilham noted: "There is not much information about us in the world. A strong Armenian lobby is working against us. The representatives of diaspora organisations should actively take part in the political processes of their respective countries, be represented in legislative bodies, and take an important place in political life."

But even then, Armenia's base is strong. Its 1.5 million Armenian-Americans figure stronger than anything Azerbaijan could muster. The U.S. Azeri Network notes that there is:

> *An up to 400,000 strong Azerbaijani-American community, concentrating particularly in the states of California, New York, New Jersey and Texas, together with other Turkic communities, such as the half-million strong Turkish-American voter bloc, along with Iranian-Americans of Azerbaijani Turkic heritage...*

The numbers are against Azerbaijan, both in terms of votes and finance, but hopes are high that an impact can be made. "As the diaspora strengthens, the Azerbaijan state is starting to rely on it more," said Ilham in 2006, calling his diaspora a "stronghold."

Overcoming the odds, and a late start, the Azerbaijan government and its diaspora take what can be couched as the 'Human Web' option in getting their message across on Nagorno-Karabakh.

The long-standing theory is that there is a 'Human Web' and that nearly everyone in the world is connected to nearly everyone else through six relationships. This was popularised in the novel by John Guare and an experiment by academic Stanley Milgram, who asked people to pass a letter only to others they knew by name, aiming to get it to a named person they did not know in another city. The average number of times it was passed on, he said, was six — hence *six degrees of separation.*

Modern technological advances in communications and travel mean that friendship networks have grown larger and span greater distances, making this theory ever more plausible. Microsoft researchers studied the addresses of 30 billion instant messages sent during a single month in 2006, roughly half of the world's instant messaging traffic, coming up with the result that any two people on average are linked by seven or fewer acquaintances.

Six degrees of separation, or seven, makes the 'Human Web' a plausible theory. Harnessing that is another matter.

"I give speeches, bring up the Nagorno-Karabakh matter with my counterparts all over the world. Yet all Azerbaijanis, and the many friends of Azerbaijan, have a part to play in this, to explain this situation and inform the rest of the world," says Ilham. "A seismic change in international perception over the last few years is down to the truths of this occupation being explained."

While Baku was preoccupied in 2003 with the death of one former President and the election of another, Nagorno-Karabakh still remained at the top of the agenda.

In July, Armenian forces attacked an Azerbaijan military post and two Azerbaijani soldiers and five attackers died in the battle, according to the Defence Ministry in the Fizuli region, where a no-man's land separates Azerbaijan military installations and posts of Nagorno-Karabakh forces.

In December the same year, delegations from the Parliaments of Armenia and Azerbaijan met in the unlikely surroundings of Scotland. They eventually issued a statement stating both sides were "committed to finding a peaceful resolution" but the Georgia-brokered South Caucasus Parliamentary Initiative stalled, like so many diplomatic steps before. And after.

The trading of insults and deadly firefights was nothing new. Neither were the diplomatic initiatives that failed to spark. What was new was the clarity that the Azerbaijan President would show when speaking on the issue. One million Azerbaijanis were homeless. They want to go home.

"Azerbaijan has the full right to liberate its lands, using all possibilities," Ilham told reporters in January 2004. "We don't want war. We don't want our people to be martyred again."

For the first time — nearly six years ago now — Ilham noted that Azerbaijan's patience was not boundless. Speaking on the 14th anniversary of the Soviet crackdown in Baku, Ilham joined tens of thousands of people who laid carnations to commemorate the 134 people killed after Soviet tanks entered the city, and the victims of the Nagorno-Karabakh war.

"Today's independent, strong Azerbaijan is of great value to Azerbaijanis, and the people who have died to achieve this will not be forgotten," said Ilham, who went on to point out that economic indicators showed Azerbaijan to be heading in the right direction. He also made comment that the gradual strengthening of Azerbaijan's military would allow Azerbaijan "to achieve its goals."

"We will not grow comfortable with the situation that has been created," he said, referring to Nagorno-Karabakh, while voicing frustration at the Minsk Group of the Organisation for Security and Cooperation in Europe, for not bringing Armenia to the negotiating table.

The constant battle to hold the line and not allow the issue to become 'normal' at home, and constantly remind the international community may seem difficult. But it is a necessary task, one that the President of the country leads. In 2004, for example, Azerbaijan's national broadcasting council complained to the British Broadcasting Corporation that a crew visited the disputed region of Nagorno-Karabakh without the agreement of Azerbaijan's authorities.

Holding the line, reminding organisations such as the BBC as to whom international law says Nagorno-Karabakh belongs, remains a responsibility. If Cornwall were occupied, London would never accept American broadcaster NBC visiting its occupied territory at the behest of an internationally unrecognised, puppet Independent Cornwall Government.

The same year Nagorno-Karabakh's Armenia-backed administration organised municipal elections around the territory. Azerbaijan's Milli Majlis adopted a statement on June 22 condemning this, pointing out that any election had to be organised by a legitimate government, and questioning how an election could be possible without the votes of hundreds of thousands of displaced citizens who fled during the fighting of the late 1980s and early 1990s. Holding the line also cost Azerbaijan in political terms. The nation was set to host NATO military exercises in mid-September dubbed 'Cooperative Best Effort (CBE) 2004'.

Yet, however important this was to Azerbaijan, cementing its place as an ally of NATO and a legitimate player on the world stage, Baku repeatedly barred Armenia's participation. NATO was not best pleased, and several Armenian groups used the cancellation of 'Cooperative Best Effort 2004' to score a few PR points, yet standing on principle seemed to trump appeasing NATO based upon Azerbaijan's decision.

"It is hard sometimes to stand by one's principle, where it may be easier, or more convenient, to let it slide," says Ramiz Mehdiyev, who served both Aliyevs. "Yet being President is a job where the competing forces of pragmatism and principle are often at loggerheads."

Nagorno-Karabakh sits at the apex of this 'pragmatism against principle' dilemma for an Azerbaijan President. The temptation may always be there to set aside Nagorno-Karabakh in some circumstances and see Azerbaijan reach further into the political centre of the international community. Hosting NATO — with Armenian military forces allowed into Baku — would have been far more politically expedient and somewhat prestigious, for example, than denying the Armenians access and seeing NATO go elsewhere.

Not so, according to Mehdiyev, who says: "The President has been superbly coherent since 2003. His message has been consistent, giving the international community, and Armenia, a precise understanding of what must be achieved.

"Consistency of message is important. I have worked for two Presidents who have stated their policy and remained true to that throughout."

Mehdiyev adds that as both men, Heydar and Ilham, travelled around the country and concerned themselves with the million internally displaced persons, the consistency of Azerbaijan government policy was only ever underlined.

"The President is passionate about this," says Deputy Prime Minister Ali Hasanov. "Azerbaijan's Internally Displaced People (IDP) dominate thinking. I have seen how this issue affects him personally."

There is no globally recognised definition for IDPs as there is for refugees. However, a United Nations report, *Guiding Principles on Internal Displacement* uses the definition:

> *...internally displaced persons are persons or groups of persons who have been forced or obliged to flee or to leave their homes or places of habitual residence, in particular as a result of, or in order to, avoid the effects of armed conflict, situations of generalised violence, violations of human rights or natural or human-made disasters, and who have not crossed an internationally recognised State border.*

According to the Office of the United Nations High Commissioner for Refugees, at the beginning of 2010 there were an estimated 27 million IDPs around the world, the largest IDP populations being Sudan (six million IDPs), Colombia (two million) and Iraq (1.5 million). Azerbaijan's one million IDPs represent, along with Nagorno-Karabakh, the biggest burden that the President and government of Azerbaijan face. These figures represent 14 per cent of Sudan's population, less than five per cent of Colombia's and around eight per cent of Iraq's. Azerbaijan's million strong population of IDPs represents a shocking statistic.

"The people who were made homeless and driven from their lands represent a significant challenge," says Ilham. "But it is not an issue that one can become accustomed to. When you see what I see, and hear people's stories directly from them, it becomes an issue that overshadows everything."

"Everything" was a vast and continually evolving workload for the new President in 2004. The last few months of the previous year had been spent dealing with the post-election environment and then the passing of the former President. Planning would be something that enveloped the very sinews of all those in government. As Ilham knew from his days in SOCAR, things were about to change for Azerbaijan. Heydar Aliyev's hopes for the country were helped by the nation's mineral wealth, but the Contract of the Century, and the many deals which followed it, were not instant answers. The thousands of Azerbaijanis and foreign oilers now working in Azerbaijani territory would take time to weave their magic.

The Contract of the Century was, by this juncture, a decade old, made up of 23 oil contracts with 25 oil companies worth more than $50 billion. The deal was about to bear fruit.

It was expected that decades on, the country's marketed production of natural gas would rise considerably. Reaching some 30 billion cubic metres per year by 2015 and probably 50 billion cubic metres per year by 2020, Azerbaijan would become one of the world's major exporters of natural gas.

Azerbaijan's main challenge was the securing of export routes for oil and gas to help guarantee its independence. Construction of a one-million-barrels-per-day pipeline from Baku to the Turkish terminal of Ceyhan had progressed and would go on stream in 2005. A parallel pipeline was being built for the export of Azerbaijani natural gas, taking gas to Georgia, Turkey, Greece and other European markets.

These got underway in January 2004 as the final piece of financing for the Baku-Tbilisi-Ceyhan pipeline fell into place when a group of 15 commercial banks gathered in London to sign a $1 billion loan for the project. Led by BP, the pipeline would, for the first time, pump Caspian crude directly to a deepwater outlet on the Mediterranean, bypassing Russia and the congested Turkish straits. The loan was to be managed by ABN Amro, Citigroup, Mizuho and Societe Generale.

The $3 billion project was more than 50 per cent complete, and met schedules for an early 2005 opening.

Achieving these developments, and more, Azerbaijan now boasted the biggest number of international consortia in the Caspian region. By early 2004 the first and largest consortium, Azerbaijan International Operating Company (AIOC), was producing 155,000 bpd, up from 50,000 bpd in mid-1998, and was aiming to raise output to more than 400,000 bpd in 2005 and as high as one million bpd by 2010.

The Azerbaijan Ministry of Energy and Industry announced in 2004 that $3.4 billion would be invested by 2006 in the first phase of development of the Azeri-Chirag-Guneshli oil field, estimated to hold reserves of 5.4 billion barrels of oil and 100 billion cubic metres of natural gas. Ministry projections stated that by 2008 some 800,000 barrels a day, or 40 million tonnes a year, would be pumped out of the field, rising to one million barrels a day by the beginning of 2010.

But future millions of barrels of oil and billions of cubic metres of gas did not translate into immediate funds, and much remained to be done.

Ilham had campaigned around the themes of jobs, education, renewed health services and new infrastructure. It was a campaign that resonated with people, as much of the opposition confined itself to an anything-but-Aliyev platform. The Aliyev brand may not have had the lustre it enjoyed in the balmy post-1994 days when Heydar took power as a saviour, but a platform with ideas was better than simple muck raking.

Broadly, the former President had stretched Azerbaijan into a direction in which it was making sustained progress. Ilham had his own ideas and agenda. Something else was different.

"The common thread between the Presidents was an attention to detail," says Natig Aliyev, Minister of Industry and Energy in Azerbaijan. "If you tell President Ilham Aliyev something once, he retains it and, weeks later, he brings up any deviation if the same thing is explained again. He is a nuts-and-bolts man."

By the first few months of 2004 the new President had taken stock and began to roll out a government shaped in his own image. One of the cornerstones was the State Programme for Socio-Economic Development of the Regions, which aimed to support rural infrastructure development. Agriculture had traditionally played a central role in Azerbaijan's economy and remained the second largest sector. In the early 1990s, rural Azerbaijan had well developed infrastructure. However, after the state and collective farms collapsed — once responsible for operating agricultural supply chains and maintaining infrastructure in rural areas — this quickly disintegrated.

"During the election campaign, wherever I travelled in rural areas, I heard the same thing," says Ilham. "People told me

'Give us the means to do the job, and agriculture will be of even greater value to Azerbaijan'."

Propelled into the Presidential hot-seat, this was one of the lessons that were assimilated into government policy. There was a compelling economic argument that any investment on the part of the government could be repaid many times over, in addition to creating many jobs. The State Programme for Socio-Economic Development of the Regions reversed this decline, contributing to improved living standards of about four million people living and working in the sector.

"Jobs were at the heart of the programme I campaigned on," says Ilham. "Jobs are fundamental — and we needed more. I wanted to create an economy that eventually brought us full employment."

In macroeconomics, full employment is a state of the national economy, where all or nearly all persons willing and able to work at the prevailing wages and working conditions are able to do so. Most neoclassical economists consider 'full' employment as being over zero per cent. Eminent economist John Maynard Keynes believed that up to a tenth of the population could remain in idleness. British economist William Beveridge suggested full employment was a fact when unemployment rate was at three per cent, while others hypothesised at between two and seven per cent. But Azerbaijan was nowhere near such levels and unemployment was rife throughout the Caucasus region following the collapse of Moscow's command economy.

"The election campaign taught me something else that remains fundamental to my job, even today," says Ilham. "Unemployment affects people's psychological condition and, on a more basic level, the very fabric of Azerbaijani society. It is a cancer."

Youth unemployment was particularly troubling, hovering at something approaching a quarter in Baku during 2003. That year Ilham promised 600,000 new jobs, a figure achieved by 2006.

According to official statistics, Azerbaijan's unemployment rate in 2010 was 5.6 per cent, down from 9.7 per cent when Ilham assumed the Presidency in 2003. Even John Maynard Keynes would be impressed.

Former U.S. President Bill Clinton has commented: "I do not believe we can repair the basic fabric of society until people who are willing to work have work. Work organises life. It gives structure and discipline to life." It was that structure and discipline — a sense of purpose — that the government in Baku was giving its people, particularly among youth.

The 2003 campaign would provide many lessons that the new President would carry into government, but the repercussions of the campaign itself would rumble on into 2004. The government got on with its agenda.

2004 would be a seminal year.

Chapter Twenty-Six

Seminal Year

I have news for the forces of greed and the defenders of the status quo: your time has come — and gone. It's time for change…
— Bill Clinton, U.S. statesman

By 2005, about a year into the post-Heydar Aliyev era, you could begin to see the change in substance and style.

It was a change that could be measured. According to the National Bank, Azerbaijan's money supply grew 15.8 per cent in 2005, while the State Statistics Committee announced that GDP was up by over one fifth on the previous year, which was in itself a good year, 2004 showing a 10.2 per cent increase over 2003. According to *Market Europe*:

> *Azerbaijan is a rising star on the world economic stage — a rising star, that is, if international financial sources are to be believed… The Commonwealth of Independent States statistics committee reported that Azerbaijan's GDP had grown 21.8 per cent during the first three quarters of 2005. This was noted as a 'record high' in the history of the commonwealth, which was formed in 1991.*
>
> *The story reported that GDP was likely to end 2005 having grown between 18 per cent and 19 per cent. AzerNews also reported predictions that GDP*

growth would be between 26 per cent and 27 per cent in 2006. The International Monetary Fund (IMF) was named as the source for these predictions. The Azerbaijan government was even more optimistic.

In 2005, industrial output rose by over 30 per cent, while the previously moribund agricultural sector, which had posted contractions in previous times, leapt by over seven per cent, in no short measure down to the State Programme for Socio-Economic Development of the Regions.

After independence, Heydar Aliyev took a strategic decision to send to Parliament a new law on the privatisation of property. Passed in 1996, this bill apportioned land as personal property.

Under Communist rule, collective farms grew only state-prescribed crops and farmers received a monthly income that bore no relation to how much they produced or how hard they worked. After this system collapsed, in countries such as Kazakhstan and Uzbekistan, land was rented or leased to farmers. In Azerbaijan, farmers work land now belonging to them, land that will be passed on from generation to generation in the same families, giving them a deeper intrinsic stake in their lands, and a long term view of its cultivation. The downside of sweeping, untargeted privatisation of property was that it created many farmers without farming tradition and with insufficient knowledge of private farming, or how to produce food for the new private sector. This needed to be addressed with urgency. Although there was not a crisis, handing the agrarian industry over to inexperienced hands had proven to be disastrous when attempted elsewhere in the world.

There are horrifying examples when agriculture falls into the hands of people who know little, or nothing, about the industry. Disaster usually follows.

Preventing such a scenario in Azerbaijan was helped through expertise and fiscal input. USAID, the Food and Agriculture Organisation of the United Nations and International Fund for Agricultural Development all contributed to this process, among others. But forging a modern agricultural sector was a process that needed to be driven from Baku.

It was a period of enormous upheaval. Ilham was spending a few days each month travelling in the regions, sitting with members of the public, and personally gathering many of the ideas that were later put into practice through policy.

Deputy Prime Minister Ali Hasanov agrees, adding: "The President returns to Baku from trips with his own ideas, forged from sitting with ordinary people and understanding what they need. Then his ministers are expected to do something about it. He gives his commitment that something will be done, and then follows the progress that a ministry makes in fulfilling that commitment.

"When his word is given to people, he takes delivery seriously."

During the period from 2003 to 2005, two years after becoming President, Ilham made some 31 official visits to the regions in Azerbaijan.

The State Agency on Agricultural Credits, under the Ministry of Agriculture, which disbursed loans to provide farmers and entrepreneurs with credits within a variety of Rural Development Projects, was one of many initiatives emanating from Baku. The World Bank initiated a privatisation support initiative which helped 23,000 Azerbaijani farmers. USAID's Azerbaijan Rural Enterprise Competitiveness Programme made a difference, and a

European Union Agricultural and Rural Development Support Programme also had an impact.

"A lot has changed in these years since independence," says Chingiz Huseynov, a farmer in Salyan. "Not everyone may vote for Ilham Aliyev, but even those who don't support him will begrudgingly admit that he knows farming and understands farmers. This has helped us."

Things had begun to change, as Azerbaijan's economic indicators showed, but undoubtedly the highlight of the year related to the ubiquitous Azerbaijan-led pipe project that was scything across the region, focal point of the emerging east-west energy corridor. In May 2005, during a ceremony at the Sangachal Oil Terminal, near the Azerbaijani capital Baku, the Presidents from Azerbaijan, Kazakhstan, Georgia and Turkey inaugurated the first section of the 1,768 kilometre Baku-Tbilisi-Ceyhan pipeline, that would bring Caspian oil directly to Western markets.

This pipeline had been launched as one of the most important projects for Azerbaijan and Georgia. The construction of this pipeline played the role of a cornerstone for the energy security of Azerbaijan, diversification of oil exports and sustainable development.

Hailed by foreign correspondents as a "much-needed alternative to Middle East energy resources," the $3.2 billion project was of key importance to the present and future of Azerbaijan. The *Chicago Sun-Times* reported Vafa Guluzade, a former foreign affairs adviser to the President in Baku as saying: "This global project will completely change the economic situation in Azerbaijan, and in the political sense it will influence the rest of the Caucasus and Central Asia." The report continued:

> *Until now, Caspian states sent almost all their oil through Russian pipelines to reach world markets. The new route will neutralise any Russian attempts to use economic levers to bring former Soviet republics back under its wing, Guluzade said. Experts say oil from the new pipeline will provide only short-term relief to a world that is consuming more crude every year. The Caspian oil should supply 168 million to 210 million gallons per day, on a par with Iran.*

At the May event, Ilham told the media: "The construction of an oil pipeline linking Azerbaijan to Turkey's Mediterranean port of Ceyhan has helped increase Azerbaijan's independence and has strengthened its role in the region". He added that the pipeline "completely changed the situation in the Caucasus-Black Sea region. Azerbaijan's economic development will grow even more successfully and Azerbaijan's role in the region and the world will strengthen."

U.S. President George W. Bush sent a greeting hailing the "great strides" that Azerbaijan had made, adding that: "The United States will continue to work in partnership with Azerbaijan to promote world energy security, and to achieve a peaceful, prosperous and democratic future for the people of Azerbaijan and the region."

Kazakhstan President, Nursultan Nazarbayev, was in Baku as his nation was now preparing to link into the Aliyev-led pipeline system. An intergovernmental agreement was in the offing to set up an Aktau-Baku trans-Caspian oil transportation system, that would link into the Baku-Tbilisi-Ceyhan (BTC) project.

A sub-sea Aktau-Baku system would require the construction of a 700 kilometre pipeline, a new terminal close to Atyrau, an unloading system in Baku and connection to the BTC pipe, encompassing an investment up to $3 billion. When work began in 2007, the Aktau-Baku pipeline was targeted to be completed in 2011, then taking crude from Kazakhstan's Kashagan and Tengiz reservoirs to the Sengacal Terminal in Baku and then on to the Heydar Aliyev Terminal in Turkey.

"In his unique position, having served within the national oil company, and now as Head of State, Ilham Aliyev was equipped to forge the pipeline," says Natig Aliyev. "The East-West Energy Corridor may not have happened without him."

All was not entirely rosy for the project, however. In November 2005 the Turkish portion of the pipeline was pushed back several months due to delays, meaning that the first shipment might not happen until spring 2006. Turkish state-owned pipeline company Botas, which was responsible for completing the Turkish section, had still not finished building pump stations during that period.

As they waited for BTC to start up in earnest, BP and the pipeline consortium had ramped up production in Azerbaijan, output rising to 380,000 bpd, of which around 240,000 barrels were from the central Azerbaijan field and the balance drawn from Chirag.

According to official figures at the time, the west Azerbaijan field would soon begin production, driving overall production to 500,000 bpd by the end of 2006, with east Azeri set to come on stream in early 2007. BP said that it would reach peak output of one million barrels by 2008-09.

Yet while Turkey was taking time, Azerbaijan's partners in Georgia were going forward well across its 249 kilometres.

In October, Ilham flew to Tbilisi for ceremonies marking the opening of the pipeline there. A ceremony took place in the small town of Gardabani, southeast of the Georgian capital, nearly five months after the Azerbaijani section was opened. Gardabani is a town well known to ordinary Azerbaijanis, for although being in Georgian territory the area has a majority Azerbaijan population.

"We are glad to see that Azerbaijan is developing in a way that suits Georgia. Azerbaijan is becoming a rich country, a country where social infrastructures are developing, a country where the economy is developing, and a country where there are structures that help improve the people," said Georgian President Mikheil Saakashvili. "I am glad to see that Azerbaijan has a leader who not only represents a great hope for his people and whose achievements are obvious, but who is also a man very close to us."

The gripers were much in evidence. The *CEE Bankwatch Network* issued a 45-page report detailing violations of environmental safety. The Georgian Young Lawyers Association accused the BTC consortium of violating the country's labour legislation. Saakashvili acknowledged that his government would have done "certain things differently" if it had been in power during the initial phase of the BTC project. But he nonetheless reiterated his support for the pipeline, understandably so when, with the addition of an Aliyev-led natural gas pipeline stretching between Baku, Tbilisi and Turkey's eastern Anatolian city of Erzurum, Georgia would be energy independent.

"This gas pipeline means real economic and energy independence for Georgia. This is why today is a historic day for us. Of course, we must be patient. But the main thing is that our region has ceased to be a dead end. Our region is becoming important, and our country can now choose among several energy alternatives," said Saakashvili.

According to the *Economist*, BTC's eventual million barrels a day capacity would be around 1.3 per cent of global supply. Carrying an interview with David Woodward, BP Azerbaijan Associate President, the June 11, 2005, issue of the *Economist* stated:

> *The oil off the coast of Azerbaijan, says Mr Woodward is "an oil-man's dream." The water is relatively shallow, and the drilling conditions good. The trouble has been finding a way to get it to market. America lobbied hard for the BTC; the route avoids both Iran and Russia and it will help to reduce global dependence on Middle Eastern supplies. The fillip it brings to Azerbaijan, and to a lesser extent to Georgia, will help to shore up the shaky finances of two ex-Soviet countries... In the unstable Caucasus, the BTC's completion, albeit after a decade of wrangling, is a triumph. Each time the government of one of the participating countries has changed, says Mr Woodward, the new one had to be re-educated...*
>
> *The hope is that, as the oil travels south-west, stability will flow the other way along with the revenues. But there are big risks. Armenia still occupies part of Azerbaijan, and there are separatist enclaves in Georgia and restless Kurds in Turkey. Mr Woodward says that other targets will be easier for terrorists to strike, and more difficult to rebuild than the pipeline, which is buried at least one metre under ground and will be guarded by horseback patrols. Earthquake risk has been mitigated, says Mr*

Woodward, by laying the pipe obliquely across the fault zone.

Saakashvili's unrestrained enthusiasm for BTC was replicated in Baku, where the windfall that the pipeline provided will remain for generations. "If Heydar Aliyev was the grandfather of the BTC project, then Ilham Aliyev was its father," says Natig Aliyev, Minister of Industry and Energy. "As Vice President of SOCAR he had run with the concept. Within government he had nurtured BTC. As President he had followed through and brought that vision to its conclusion."

"BTC was a tremendously personal thing to him, as a tool that would have a marked difference on the prospects of Azerbaijan now and in the future. It also represented one of the key legacies of Heydar Aliyev."

Kickbacks blight the oil industry in transition and post-war economies. Fighting that was hard and required political will, the latter to a backdrop in some states where oil money was being used to appease corrupt elites in order for governments to remain in power.

Anti-bribery measures were introduced and Ilham created what is arguably the most transparent administration in the former Soviet Union. Concerns that Azerbaijan's windfall would be squandered through corruption rather than pumped into alleviating poverty were met head on. The State Oil Fund of Azerbaijan (SOFAZ), brainchild of Heydar, came into being at the end of 2000 and has its accounts audited every quarter by Ernst & Young. In 2007 the organisation won the UN Public Service Award for Transparency.

"SOFAZ is a symbol of fiscal prudence and openness. Azerbaijan has demonstrated to the world that it has been very prudent from the very beginning," says SOFAZ

Executive Director Shahmar Movsumov.

SOFAZ is loosely based on the successful Norwegian Oil Fund, a Sovereign Wealth Fund. SWF's have a growing presence in global financial markets with total assets estimated at about $3.8 trillion today. The Norwegian Oil Fund is widely considered to be a template for best practices and international standards.

"SOFAZ began as a rainy day fund designed to cater for future generations turned into a provider of funds for projects judged to be of strategic importance," says Movsumov. "President Ilham Aliyev intends that SOFAZ will take an instrumental role in developing the non-oil sector. Today, SOFAZ spends money on key projects such as power and water supply, social infrastructure, healthcare and education, for the benefit of the nation."

Ernst & Young is one of the Big Four global auditors, along with PricewaterhouseCoopers, Deloitte and KPMG, a global organisation of member firms in more than 140 countries. Ernst & Young signs off on SOFAZ's accounts, a guarantee of transparency, a service that the company also provides for the likes of Lockheed Martin, 3i, the Royal Mail, FedEx, Porsche, Time Warner, Hilton Hotels Corporation, Apple, AT&T and American Airlines.

"Transparency is the key to SOFAZ," says Movsumov. "Our mandate is to ensure that my great-grandchildren, and their great-grandchildren, feel the benefit of today's oil revenues."

More immediate, in addition to modern infrastructure, are the needs of providing full-time accommodation and basic facilities to IDPs made homeless during the war with Armenia. Millions have been invested in re-housing IDPs, and SOFAZ was at the heart of the success when the re-housing project was finally completed in 2009.

SOFAZ also served as the vehicle which financed a 25 per cent stake in the Baku-Tbilisi-Ceyhan pipeline. SOFAZ provided $200 million in equity financing for BTC and repayed hundreds of millions of dollars to international lenders. In undertaking this role, SOFAZ acquired 70 per cent of the shares in AzBTC Ltd that had been held by SOCAR.

In 2005 there was around $1 billion under SOFAZ control, most of which was drawn from 'profit oil' from the BP-operated Azeri-Chirag-Guneshli field. Overseas assets were 55 per cent held in Dollars, 35 per cent in Euros and 10 per cent in Sterling and other international currencies.

Yet the heritage fund was set to grow sharply. From 2006 the government charged a 70 per cent levy on SOCAR revenues above $40 per barrel, with the proceeds going into the fund. With fluctuating oil prices on an upward curve, this would prove to be a windfall.

Yet the real bonanza would begin over ensuing years, when Azeri-Chirag-Guneshli returns grow past the one million barrels per day mark.

Predicting oil revenues over the next 20 years, SOFAZ used a conservative oil price of $30. This would give the government $70 billion up to 2024. At a $40 price, Azerbaijan's take would increase to $130 billion. At $50 a barrel it would exceed $150 billion.

SOFAZ assets totaled $14.9 billion on January 1, 2010. Some 84.27 per cent of assets were placed in securities with an 'AAA' rating as graded by international rating agencies such as Moody's and Standard & Poors.

"The President takes the lead with SOFAZ," says Movsumov. "There has never, ever, been any question as to his intentions, underpinned by his desire for better transparency."

According to the *Revenue Watch Institute,* a non-profit policy institute and grant making organisation funded by, among others, the Bill and Melinda Gates Foundation:

> *Azerbaijan was among the first countries to endorse the Extractive Industries Transparency Initiative. An NGO coalition to improve EI transparency was formed in 2004, and it quickly became a part of the global Publish What You Pay (PWYP) coalition. The government has taken another important step toward transparency by publishing annual reports from the State Oil Fund of Azerbaijan (SOFAZ).*

The successes and failures of 2005 had been played out to a troubling situation at home. The 2003 Presidential Election had left behind a polarised political scene. The opposition was hurting and increasingly determined to ensure that, as they saw it, the 2005 elections for the Milli Majlis could not be stolen.

The government, as they saw it, would attempt to keep a lid on what was becoming an emotional and fractious situation. Throw in an international media that was baying for fresh headlines, and a combustible scene was set.

The Milli Majlis elections of 2005 would prove the most challenging of Azerbaijan's short democratic history.

Chapter Twenty-Seven

Anything-But-Aliyev

A great revolution in just one single individual will help achieve a change in the destiny of a society and, further, will enable a change in the destiny of humankind.
— Daisaku Ikeda, Japanese peace activist

Pacifist floral imagery is nothing new. Perhaps the first non-violent banded uprising was the Carnation Revolution of Portugal. This was a left-leaning military coup in April 1974 that transformed the Portuguese government from an authoritarian dictatorship into a democracy.

Samuel Huntington, summarising the mix of primary causes for the 'third wave' of democratisation that began in 1974, listed a new but not decisive factor that had been absent in the preceding two waves: "Changes in the policies of external actors… a major shift in U.S. policies towards the promotion of human rights and democracy in other countries…"

It was 15 years later, and in Prague, when the next branded movement occurred. Czechoslovakia's Velvet Revolution in 1989 saw the overthrow of the Communist government and remains viewed as one of the most important of the revolutions that occurred that year. By 2003, Georgia set the ball rolling with its Rose Revolution. Political oppositions and the media jumped on the bandwagon. Any self-respecting movement had to have a brand behind it. The Lebanese went for a Cedar Revolution and Kuwait's suffrage movement opted for the Blue Revolution. In a world dominated by brands, Coke, McDonalds, Ford, *et al,* social movements would co-opt brands of their own. George W. Bush jumped on the bandwagon and called the Iraqi democratisation process a Purple Revolution.

In January 2005 Ukraine went through an Orange Revolution, while three months later Kyrgyzstan had a Tulip Revolution. In these two events, nongovernmental organisations and student activists played a critical role, but there remained a suspicion that foreign forces also played a part. Britain's *Guardian* wrote that a consortium of USAID, National Endowment for Democracy, International Republican Institute, National Democratic Institute for International Affairs and Freedom House had a hand in some of these events. Both the *Washington Post* and *New York Times* have published articles along the same lines.

As the dust settled on the revolutions in Ukraine and Kyrgyzstan, the media licked its lips with anticipation and looked towards Azerbaijan. The 2003 Presidential Election left an opposition that was riled. It was a situation that was stoked by foreign journalists and, while the legitimate opposition planned its next step, a small section of society lost faith with the ballot box and planned something else altogether. The scene was set for Ilham's rollercoaster year, economic and political triumphs, a tumultuous election season, and foreign media baying for blood. In Baku, the government went about its normal business although there was a whiff of tension in the air.

"We hoped that the Parliamentary Elections would run smoothly, but there was no opportunity to focus on the November elections," says Ilham. "I had a mandate. It was my job to ensure that I continued to fulfill the promises I had made in 2003."

"The President's days are intense. There are enormous demands on him," says Ali Hasanov, Head of the Socio-Political Department at the Presidential Administration. "The country faces so many great issues that big decisions are made on a daily basis, decisions that are made which will affect people's lives. He has never lost sight of that."

In April a memorandum of understanding was signed between Iran, Azerbaijan and Russia to set up a company to design, build and operate a new railway in Iran from Qazvin, via Rasht, to Astara on the Azerbaijan border. This would create a new rail link from Russia via Iran to the Arabian Sea. Elsewhere, Ilham began a campaign to tackle red tape, a programme that would eventually see Azerbaijan named as one of the most improved places to do business in the world.

During a conference at Gulistan Palace, the President stated that all obstacles for private sector growth in Azerbaijan should be eliminated, saying: "Entrepreneurial activity in this country is still interfered with by red tape. This is inappropriate if we are to hold a place in the global economy. This holds true for the government."

The BTC pipeline filled many newspaper inches, yet growing political tensions were also apparent and the crescendo of politicking for the election in November began early.

This started with terrible tragedy. There was an outpouring of grief on March 2 when Elmar Huseynov, founder and editor of magazine *Monitor* was shot in the lobby of his Baku apartment building. The opposition blamed the government. The government blamed the opposition.

"I was, and am still not, prepared to see Azerbaijan go in that direction," says Ilham. "Politics can be very polarising,

but I don't want us to ever be a nation where such killings are part of political life. Our society will never accept this." At the time, he called Huseynov's death a "serious provocation against the state" and warned the political class not to use this to foment unrest. The murder triggered a series of anti-government events organised by the opposition.
The only common denominator was raw anger and frustration. Attempting to keep hold of the situation, on March 3, Ilham issued an official Presidential Statement which read:

> *I have given necessary instructions to heads of law enforcement bodies. As you know, now there is an investigation, and we all wait for its results.*
>
> *Today I have held a meeting of the Security Council in which the given question was discussed. Preliminary results of the investigation have been reported... This is the first such incident in the modern history of Azerbaijan. Until now, journalists have never been exposed to such violence... I consider that this will have a big, negative impact on the democratic development of Azerbaijan. We already know that we must do our utmost to ensure that upcoming elections pass in fair, transparent conditions and that the will of Azerbaijan's people is followed.*
>
> *This murder is a provocation, a misdeed, and certainly a cause for extreme concern. On a more basic level, a young man is killed and his family is left without its head...*

Former U.S. Secretary of State Madeleine Albright, visiting Baku, stated that: "Election day is important, but the months leading up to the elections are also crucial." It was to be a difficult, demanding year, for the President and all the Azerbaijani people, those drawn from all areas of the political spectrum.

"Such a drawn out election cycle was not good for Azerbaijan," says Etibar Mammadov, leader of the opposition National Independence Party of Azerbaijan. "I don't agree that we need this. There is work to do and, even if we do not agree with the government, we as citizens want to see the government working on our behalf, not spending the best part of a year engaged in electioneering."

The distraction of an opposition already campaigning, eight months before the polls opened, was the first of several unedifying features of 2005. Too many people still remained unemployed and below the poverty line, yet Ilham, and those who worked for him, were gradually dragged into a protracted campaign.

"My job is to lead the country. I love that job and continue to do so," says Ilham. "Politics less so."

Yet domestic politics were increasingly on the agenda. The opposition claimed, and the international media were happy to report, that Azerbaijan had a reflexive post-Soviet suspicion of opposition and a belief that only overwhelming election victories count. In the wake of 2003 the world was watching.

Headlines reporting that a foreign government was doing its best, attempting to build a democratic tradition from scratch, do not sell newspapers or make news bulletins watchable. What does are tasty stories of oppression and ham-fisted officials involved in ballot box stuffing. The truth, perhaps, was somewhere in the middle. But that did not matter.

"How hard it must be, for a culture that had been living under Soviet dominance for 71 years, to emerge into a full fledged democracy in a mere 14 years. Old ways are difficult to abandon, and trusting in the new precepts of democracy requires a lot of courage, since it is, for most, a tentative step into the unknown," wrote Bob Lawrence on *U.S. Newswire*. "However, the people on the street, in the mosques, and in the polling stations, uniformly expressed their hopefulness for a future under democratic laws and actions."

Ilham had a major role to play in this. There were obvious temptations for any man in his position. His party's majority in the Milli Majlis supported his agenda. A hostile parliament would be a significant drag factor. Yet the bigger picture was that skewing the election in favour of the New Azerbaijan Party was not a good idea, and would kill the tentative roots of a democratic future.

The President told the cabinet, and indeed many people within the administration, that there was no need to go beyond political persuasion. He and the party were riding high in the polls, the opposition squabbled between themselves and there was no clear agenda from them. There was no prospect of the New Azerbaijan Party losing its majority in the Milli Majlis.

Like 2003, the Anything-But-Aliyev agenda was emerging as the paramount policy initiative. At least at this time, the public at large were nowhere near being in the same place as their opposition.

As Lawrence had reported, Azerbaijanis had suffered 71 years under the Soviet yoke. But they were not political fools. They had quickly developed a feel for professional politicians and the techniques of retail politics.

Siraj Kazimov, whose father was one of those who gave his life to the cause of freedom in January 1990, says: "Too many people in politics treat ordinary people like they are stupid. It is a carry-over from Soviet days when our leaders thought they knew best for us, so we were not consulted. If politicians from all sides want to win support, they need to show an agenda and they need to speak with the electorate like they are not stupid.

"The President will go around saying 'we will do this', 'we will do that'. Then these things would be done. The opposition mostly campaigns on bland, meaningless generic slogans."

"Things are getting better in Azerbaijan," says Jafarov Mirsamad, a taxi driver. "The opposition says things could be better if it was done their way, but do not tell us what way that is. It is frustrating and offers no clear alternative."

The Anything-But-Aliyev approach would do more to ensure continuity in the corridors of power than anything the administration could itself do. While Ilham admits that he and the government must "and will" do better, the opposition also managed to repeatedly shoot itself in the foot.

One high profile example of this concerned the opposition's bugbear. They complained of media bias. Yet when the Council of Europe (CoE) drafted a code of ethics, which was signed by government-leaning media outlets, the opposition declined to participate. The code demanded that signatories "endeavour to cover the election campaign in a fair, balanced and impartial manner" and the CoE promised to call on those signatories who backed away from their commitments. Yet opposition newspapers refused to sign, denouncing what they described as a smear campaign against opposition leaders on Azerbaijani television.

The opposition's misstep did not endear them to the people at large. Having inherited some of his father's astute political savvy, Ilham knew this. From a long way out the New

Azerbaijan Party was coasting to a success, leaving its leader to, in some ways, further Azerbaijan's democratic base.

"There was a lot of international interest in the Milli Majlis election. It was an important election, a key step on the road to democratisation," says Ilham.

A May 2005 Presidential Decree meant that opposition candidates gained rights under the law, while the procedure for public rallies was simplified and guaranteed a more level playing field when it came to public media access. The opposition remained unhappy that they were not guaranteed the same rights in the private media, which the OSCE stated was biased towards the government. This liberalisation was followed by another initiative on October 25.

"My intention was to move further forward and strengthen the system where we were able," says Ilham. "At the time this decree won plaudits, but for me it was simply a logical expression of the direction we were going."

In a *Washington Times* Op-Ed piece, Ambassador Hafiz Pashayev wrote:

> *We are the first to recognise that independence, stability and prosperity depend on successful democratic reform. President Ilham Aliyev wants an orderly transition, as our last few years of unprecedented economic growth would be jeopardised by political instability. Towards this end and to conduct elections according to international standards, the President issued an Executive Order outlining steps to be taken:*
>
> *(1) Allowing all political parties to organise rallies free from violence and intimidation. (2) Welcoming domestic and international election observers.*

> *(3) Providing access to media, thus ensuring fair coverage. (4) And ensuring central and regional authorities create the necessary conditions for exit polls.*
>
> *Among many provisions of the Order already carried out are those that concern participation in the political arena by opposition parties. There has been dialogue between ruling and opposition parties, all opposition parties may freely conduct rallies and demonstrations and, thus far, all opposition activists — including those who called for overthrow of the government in October 2003-have been allowed to become candidates if they wish.*
>
> *During his visit to Azerbaijan at the end of August, Sen. Richard Lugar, Indiana Republican, said: "The opposition leaders underlined that the registration process of the MP candidates went well, which is a step forward compared to the previous elections." President Aliyev went further by warning all regional election officials not to interfere in the old Soviet fashion, when ballot-stuffing was common.*

On October 25, a second Presidential Decree went further, directing the Central Election Commission to draw up plans for applying indelible ink to voters' fingers, in order to prevent multiple-voting, while also requesting parliament to lift a ban on election monitoring by non-governmental organisations (NGOs) that receive more than 30 per cent of their funding from foreign sources.

During a televised meeting that day with government officials and election commission heads, the President openly stated that the inking was in response to inefficiencies within the system in place. Calling this measure "exceptional and temporary," he added that: "We should not have a real need for this (the ink system) because of the availability of voter cards. But I cannot be satisfied with this because, according to some reports, one voter received several.

"Therefore we have to consider the possibility of marking fingers with indelible ink on election day so that there will be no doubts about whether transparent elections have been held," he added.

A day later, Ilham told U.S. Vice President Dick Cheney that: "Every condition has been created for the transparent and fair conduct of the election in the country," while the Central Election Commission formally announced that it will ink voters' fingers and provide each of the 5,000 electoral precincts with an ultraviolet lamp and two pens to apply the ink.

Council of Europe Secretary General Terry Davis stated that the proposed measures would enhance observation of the elections and help promote the "one person one vote" principle, stating: "If I were entitled to vote on November 6, I would feel reassured to have my finger — and everybody else's finger — inked. I would know that nobody else had voted twice, and that is my basic right."

Azerbaijan's largest opposition bloc, Azadlig (Freedom), which united the Musavat Party, Popular Front Party of Azerbaijan and the Democratic Party of Azerbaijan, welcomed the decree.

During an election broadcast on state television, Musavat Party Chairman Isa Gambar stated that the decree: "should be assessed positively" and urged the opposition media not to present the President's decision as a "retreat" or "defeat". Gambar also called on the President to use the opportunity to start a dialogue with the opposition to resolve outstanding differences. Also appearing on national television, the same day, Popular Front Party Chairman Ali Karimli congratulated: "every citizen fighting for a free election" on the Presidential Decree. "We do not think this was your defeat. This is our land, our country."

But there was a note of caution from Democratic Party First Deputy Chairman Sardar Jalaloglu who stated: "The Presidential Decree from May 11, 2005, was positively evaluated by the international community, but has not been properly implemented."

To most observers, Ilham's biggest task was to rein in "old style" election officials and over-zealous police. Throughout, the campaign provided both positives and negatives for the present and future of democracy in Azerbaijan. Several large opposition rallies were permitted in Baku and some other cities, while a number of unauthorised rallies were suppressed.

Unarguably the most sensational event of the campaign was a failed coup attempt by Rasul Guliyev, formerly the head of an oil refinery, who had been investigated for misappropriation of funds. He was also leader of the Azerbaijan Democratic Party, and had been residing in the United States for several years.

Guliyev tried to return to Baku on October 17, having been permitted by the Central Electoral Commission to register as a candidate. However, in line with the law the Prosecutor General's Office announced that he would not enjoy immunity from arrest from the long standing embezzlement charges that remained on file. Guliyev's aborted return led to a moment of pure political theatre, when it was announced that several officials had been arrested and charged of conspiracy with Guliyev to "create confrontation, stage riots and seize power by force."

Weapons, ammunition and explosive devices and substances were subsequently unearthed in different parts of Baku. Among those detained were Economic Development Minister Farhad Aliyev, Health Minister Ali Insanov, Head of the President's Administrative Department Akif Muradverdiyev, former Finance Minister Fikrat Yusifov and head of the Academy of Sciences Eldar Salayev.
Aside from all these charges, the above-mentioned people were also charged with corruption. They were subsequently found guilty of misappropriation of state funds.
On October 25, *The Washington Post* reported:

> *The recent scandal, which is still developing, involves arrests of Ali Insanov, the notoriously corrupt former Minister of Health, and Farhad Aliyev, the ex-Minister of Economic Development. Farhad and his brother Rafiq, the owner of the largest private petroleum company (no relation to President Ilham Aliyev), are accused of funding Rasul Guliyev, opposition leader who was recently arrested in Ukraine and returned to London. Azerbaijan issued international warrants against Mr Guliyev on charges of embezzlement and sedition.*

It was all very dramatic. The colourful piece was mirrored in reporting elsewhere in the world. Yet pertinently it added:

> *Alexei Malashenko, the leading Caucasus affairs expert at the Carnegie Endowment Moscow Centre pointed out that President Aliyev and his party are significantly more popular (with 65 and 40 per cent respectively) than all the leaders of the Azadlig*

coalition combined and their parties, who poll 10 to 15 per cent.

"Yes, I knew that the party was popular, and that New Azerbaijan would coast to a resolute success, as we were the ones with the ideas and the track record," says Ilham. "But we were not in the business of sitting back and expecting the electorate's support. No-one has a divine right to power. That was the thinking we had suffered in the Soviet Era."

The New Azerbaijan Party stayed on course by presenting an agenda that was essentially an extension of the same ideas and policies that has been successful in the Presidential Election two years earlier. Ilham, whose poll ratings hovered between 62 and 72 per cent throughout, campaigned on continuity.

The largest opposition alliance comprised of a plethora of non-governmental organisations and four major parties, the Social Democratic Party of Azerbaijan, Party of National Independence, Liberal Party of Azerbaijan and National Movement. Musavat, headed by the defeated 2003 Presidential Election candidate Isa Gambar, was also set to provide effective opposition, while Hajiaga Nuriyev, leader of the minority Islamic Party, was barred from standing.

Referring to his own election success of 2003 Ilham had pointed out to the World Leaders Forum at Columbia University that there was "...political disarray within the opposition party." And for the most part this had not changed.

Yet while the ruling party could perhaps afford to be laconic given its poll numbers, when focus shifted from the claims and counter-claims of politicians in Baku, there were the briefest glimpses of what the election was really about. It was not about preening Milli Majlis politicians, or the rabble rousing elements of the opposition in downtown Baku, but the people at large. Azerbaijan may have still been learning the democratic traditions, but its politicians had already taken up at least one of the bad habits of their counterparts in Washington, London, Bonn and other global capitals — talking to themselves. So much effort was going in to protests on the streets, and trading insults on the hustings, that there was surprisingly limited domestic reportage on the problems that ordinary Azerbaijanis still encountered. The transition from Soviet Union to independent Azerbaijan was hard, and still had many victims who were desperate for help.

An army of 1,500 observers was already arriving in the nation to take part in election monitoring — a figure the President termed "unprecedented". Some 663 were from the Organisation for Security and Cooperation in Europe and 52 from the Council of Europe, while dozens of other groups sent delegations.

To this backdrop, coupled with two far-reaching and unique Presidential Decrees, the international community continued to voice concerns. A pre-election mission from the Parliamentary Assembly of the Council of Europe took the government to task for failing to reform election commissions so that representation was more equally held between opposition representatives and government, or pro-government representatives.

"I cannot say that everything is perfect," said PACE co-rapporteur Andreas Gross on the BBC. "But recent steps have been taken in the right direction." On the day of the election, Isa Gambar, leader of the Musavat Party stated: "I know that in any case, today is the beginning of a drastic democratic transformation."

President George W. Bush sent congratulations to his Azerbaijani counterpart stating: "I welcome your commitment to a free and fair election, which is essential to sustaining a strong partnership between our two countries. I look forward to working with you after these elections."

The opposition had campaigned its Anything-But-Aliyev agenda and made election fraud the central plank of its campaign. Ali Karimli told the opposition's final rally: "We will disappoint those who want to steal our victory!"

On November 6, 2005, the seminal election took place. There were 2,062 candidates across the nation. Some 17 per cent were opposition candidates compared with 21 per cent for the New Azerbaijan Party. Over 50 per cent were independents or undeclared. New Azerbaijan faced two main opposition forces — the New Policy bloc, founded by a number of intellectuals, the National Independence Party and Azadlig.

The Central Election Commission reported 62 per cent of votes cast for New Azerbaijan, three per cent for the Equality Party, one per cent for the APFP, two per cent to independent candidates and two per cent each to two other small parties. This result was initially some surprise to a Mitofsky International and Edison Media Research poll effort, which had used exit polls to estimate that New Azerbaijan would have from 56 to 75 seats in the 125-member assembly, with the Azadlig bloc getting 12 seats.

This was reasonably accurate, with New Azerbaijan claiming 58-seats. The second biggest bloc was among independent Members of Parliament, who numbered 40. With a majority of those leaning toward the Ilham-led New Azerbaijan, this equated to a comfortable majority.

The CEC reported on the night of the election that there were few voting irregularities and the next day announced turnout was reported at 46.8 per cent of the 4.6 million registered voters. A harsh preliminary assessment was provided by the International Election Observation Mission. It reported that the progressive elements of the election (such as candidate registration) had been undermined by government interference in campaigning, media bias favouring pro-government candidates and significant deficiencies in tabulating results.

On November 6, Ilham appeared on television to state that his government would study the criticism of Western election observers and take steps to correct shortcomings but that violations in weekend legislative polls had occurred only in a small number of districts.

"The opinion of the OSCE and other international organisations will be taken into account, their comments will be studied and serious measures will be taken," said Ilham Aliyev. He said that violations had been registered in seven or eight of the country's 125 districts and that he had instructed prosecutors to investigate. In the rest, he said, "the results don't awaken any doubts."

A day later, CEC announced new elections would be held in four districts and that some recounts would take place in other districts, but on November 23 submitted election results to the Constitutional Court for certification.

On November 30, 2005, a comprehensive report provided to the United States Congress stated:

> *Some observers argue that President Aliyev is committed to democratisation, as evidenced by his May and October decrees and his postelection dismissals of several regional and district leaders on charges of*

> *interfering in the race. They view Aliyev's pre-election purge of his administration as increasing his appeal among the electorate that he backs reforms, and as boosting votes for the ruling and other pro-government parties. At the same time, these observers assert that the small number of seats the opposition parties won demonstrates that these parties have failed to gain people's trust…*
>
> *…The main opposition parties continue to pledge to "remain within the law" in protesting the election, and officials in Baku have given approval for several opposition rallies. Along with honest efforts to address electoral regularities, such cooperation could nurture civil society and greater respect for the sitting government and the rule of law.*
>
> *A violent police crackdown on peaceful demonstrators on November 24 has raised concerns among many observers that political instability may increase.*
>
> *While raising concerns about the election, most international organisations and countries have not endorsed calls by some Azerbaijani oppositionists for a new election, but rather have urged investigating irregularities (and possibly holding some new constituency contests) and punishing guilty officials.*

Yet the tide was not with the opposition. On November 9, *The Washington Post* reported: '…Opposition hopes for a 'colour revolution' that will oust Mr Aliyev probably won't succeed, if only because the President, unlike his counterparts in Georgia and Ukraine, has the support of most of the country', while the same day the *International Herald Tribune* added: 'That the ruling New Azerbaijan

Party won in the parliamentary elections in Azerbaijan on Sunday was no surprise. The good news is that the election was far less fraudulent than the last, even though the OSCE reported that the voting fell short of international standards.'

But while the New Azerbaijan Party staged a rally to celebrate its victory in parliamentary elections and pro-government demonstrators went onto the streets, the international media was still alluding to rose, cedar, blue, purple, orange and tulip revolutions. Whether this emboldened the opposition one can never know. But it was clear from even the most adverse reports that Ilham and his party had won overwhelming support from the electorate.

There was no mandate for a change of government. There was no widespread fraud that had come anywhere near changing an election result. There were kinks for sure, that the international community had the right to highlight, but apart from opposition voices in Azerbaijan no evidence of anything more.

A relatively small number of opposition activists — at a peak 20,000 people from a population of eight million — kept the protests alive. While most were peaceful, any such movement anywhere in the world attracts rabble, and they made their presence evident.

"In any country in the world, if peaceful protest morphs into violence, the authorities have a duty to act," says Ilham. "Anything less is a disservice to ordinary law abiding people. I don't see why Azerbaijan should be held to a different standard than is applied to Western countries."

The President enjoys a tangible benefit through incumbency, the same as the occupant of Chigi Palace, the White House, Downing Street, the Kremlin or Palácio da Alvorada, when facing an election. In Azerbaijan — still seeding a Civil Society — it may hold true that incumbency is a big advantage.

Yet the lack of an agenda beyond Anything-But-Aliyev did not help, along with the opposition's frequent reference to events in Ukraine and Kyrgyzstan, a point pressed home by media outlets.

By the beginning of December the rallies petered out and life went on. Opposition leaders retired to their party offices to lick their wounds and consider what next.

The same analytical process was going on in the Presidential Palace. A second sweeping victory at the ballot box, one with far wider acceptance, was about to embolden a renewed agenda. Ilham's second national electoral success would open the floodgates for change.

Leyla (centre) and Arzu Aliyeva with their grandfather, Heydar Aliyev. Ilham admits that the arrival of his children altered his perspective on life.

Ilham Aliyev and Mehriban Aliyeva visit a school.

Heydar and Ilham Aliyev with French President Jacques Chirac.

Heydar and Ilham Aliyev participate in an old Azerbaijani tradition of marking faces with the first oil from a new field.

According to foreign news agencies upwards of one million people flooded on to the streets of Baku for the funeral of Heydar Aliyev.

After an election campaign that took him to all parts of the country, Ilham Aliyev was sworn in as President of Azerbaijan in 2003.

Azerbaijan's first couple arrive in Downing Street ahead of a meeting with British Prime Minister Gordon Brown.

Chapter Twenty-Eight

"...the year to do it."

All the world's a stage, And all the men and women merely players; They have their exits and their entrances; And one man in his time plays many parts.
— monologue from William Shakespeare's As You Like It

Given that all polling evidence predicted as much, that the ruling party of Azerbaijan won the country's Parliamentary Elections, was no surprise. What was, was the direction that this second electoral mandate would ultimately send Azerbaijan and its President. Abroad, at least, 2003 had not been perceived well. But the Milli Majlis election had been a second ringing endorsement of the President and his agenda.

Barack Obama won the White House with 52.9 per cent of the popular vote. Nicolas Sarkozy won the French Presidency with 53.06 per cent. Tony Blair's New Labour, at its 1997 zenith, claimed 63.4 per cent of the national vote. In South Africa's first multi-racial elections, in which full enfranchisement was granted and led by the giant that is Nelson Mandela as its Presidential nominee, the ANC won 62 per cent of the vote.

That is not to compare any of these leaders. In the much-maligned 2003 election Ilham had claimed 76.8 per cent of the vote. But in 2005, Parliamentary Elections that were as much a second referendum of the President and somewhat commended for their greater transparency by the international community, 63.9 per cent of the vote went to the New Azerbaijan Party. In an era when the most wildly popular politicians — surely an oxymoron — can only hope to claim two thirds of a vote, this represented a firm endorsement from the people.

That second affirmation, at least to foreign observers, changed a great deal and emboldened a stronger agenda. Azerbaijan began making a break with its past. Broader political freedoms, greater transparency, a stricter application of the rule of law and a strong push on poverty and jobs noticeably followed. While a minority still pressed for a Ukraine-style Orange Revolution, Ilham, emboldened, marched forward with his programme.

For whatever reason, there was a growth in Ilham the President around this time. His moral authority was greater and one could see a greater reach in his aspirations. It was no coincidence that after the 2005 elections the government threw itself harder into economic development.

Ali Hasanov, Deputy Prime Minister and Chairman of State Committee for Refugees and IDPs, disagrees saying: "He remained the same. Arguably some viewed the President differently. But he was always ambitious. He wakes up every morning aware that there are people out there living in poverty and he finds that completely unacceptable."

"All the world's a stage" is the phrase that begins a famous monologue from William Shakespeare's *As You Like It*, spoken by a melancholy Jaques. The speech compares the world to a stage and life to a play, and catalogues the seven stages of a man's life, sometimes referred to as the seven ages of man: infant, schoolboy, lover, soldier, justice, pantaloon and second childhood. It is one of Shakespeare's most frequently-quoted passages.

"*And then the justice,*" writes Shakespeare, musing over a period in life when a man becomes a wise judge, full of quotes and whose life experiences allow him to advise people. He compares people's misfortunes with his own and tells them how to solve them.

Whatever your viewpoint, 2003 had been a rough-and-tumble election year. The Milli Majlis elections represented a political coming of age for Ilham in political terms. The legitimate complaints of the opposition were somewhat inconsequential to the overall, and the more wild-post election claims discredited them. In the final analysis, ordinary people had rejected the opposition and a strong majority had lent their support to the President and his party. The second of these elections had served to further legitimise the President.

Those close to the Azerbaijan President insist that he remained the same. Outside observers claim that he now walked taller. But whatever the view, there was no denying that the former university lecturer, small businessman, oil company executive, Parliamentarian and, briefly, Prime Minister, was now in the era of his life defined by Shakespeare as his '*justice*'.

Having swept Parliamentary Elections and the representation in the Milli Majlis having resulted in what he would have desired, Ilham Aliyev now faced the prospect of delivery. He had been demonised by political rivals. It was time to prove them wrong in practical terms.

"You would have to be a monster to recede into a comfort zone in Baku and forget what you saw and heard," says Ilham. "It is basic human nature to wish to alleviate the problems you encounter, and I encountered them often, not just in election year."

The national and geopolitical situation means that Ilham is not a citizen who can get in his car and drive anywhere he likes. But he tries — and often succeeds — to maintain a degree of personal autonomy.

"I can go anywhere I want to, with five minutes notice for my security team," says Ilham. "Several times each week, at some point in the day, I try to drop by and see what is going on, visit developments, speak to real people."

Election campaign or not, the President gets out of his capital and heads into the country. He takes with him a cabal of ministers and officials.

"We go out, ask the people what they need, and deal with what should be done to improve their lives," says Ilham.

Deputy Prime Minister Ali Hasanov was along for the ride during many of these official visits.

"President Aliyev is no-nonsense," he says. "I remember one particular trip where he heard from people that medical services were unsatisfactory. His reaction was to directly promise action." The minister was then instructed to gather information and report back on what could be done to correct the situation.

"The ministry had a week to come back with a firm proposal," says Hasanov. "The President then ordered us to proceed and asked to be updated as to the progress. Several weeks later he enquired again. The community involved was no more than a few hundred people, yet the President followed this project through to its absolute conclusion.

"And from my side, and through the experiences of my colleagues in cabinet, I can tell you that this is a scenario that is replicated hundreds of times."

Adds Natig Aliyev, who has held the key portfolio of Minister of Industry and Energy since 2005: "He does not take well to people making excuses. In this cabinet you have to get the job done."

If the success of November 2005 had emboldened Azerbaijan's President it was just as well. There remained much to be done. The world was watching. The *International Herald Tribune* observed:

> *...A decisive move towards progress and reforms in Azerbaijan will send a positive message through the Middle East and Central Asia, regions where the United States and Europe are struggling to promote democracy. Azerbaijan could serve as a model for change in Iran and beyond.*
>
> *...The Azeri elite is oriented westward; EU and NATO memberships are long-term objectives. It is in the interest of Europe and America to work closely with Azerbaijan in coming years to cement democratic and market reforms throughout the South Caucasus and to gain momentum for change in Central Asia...*

The year began with a gesture which even the opposition could not deride, when the publishing debts for more than 150 pro-government and opposition newspapers were written off in a move hailed by media advocates and a trans-Atlantic security group. Hundreds of thousands of dollars owed to the main state-owned printing press were written off by an order which cited the "material-technical and financial situation of the newspapers, with the purpose of providing help for the development of the free and independent press."

From many sides there were comments that the move was a positive step for freedom of speech in Azerbaijan, while Maurizio Pavesi, head of the Organisation for Security and

Cooperation in Europe's office in Baku, praised the move and said more should be done to "tackle the remaining constraints on media freedom in Azerbaijan."

It was to be a year when foreign policy dominated, yet the domestic results that were already looking positive were the result of foundations laid by Heydar Aliyev, and the fresh brush of Ilham Aliyev. During the first quarter of 2005 industrial growth and industrial output was up, inflation was under control and foreign reserves were rising. The President's Office was showered with positive data.

"You learn not to get overconfident," says Ali Abbasov, Minister of Communications and Information Technology. "But the two Presidents had laid a base and put in motion economic and social development that would become the envy of many of our neighbours. This took time to set root, of course. Rebuilding a nation is a generational project."

Observers report that Ilham pores over plans to build Azerbaijan. He took the difficult decisions and suffered the pangs of guilt when things went wrong, or did not work fast enough. Every day he sets out to achieve positives.

With April came a foreign policy focal point. An official visit to Washington is an opportunity to interact with the world's only remaining superpower in its lair. The city may, according to some observers, have begun to lose some of its lustre under the Bush Administration, but it remained the world's diplomatic centre. It hosts 176 foreign embassies, the headquarters of the World Bank, the International Monetary Fund (IMF), the Organisation of American States (OAS) and is headquarters to corporations and institutions such as trade unions, lobbying groups and professional associations.

Many leaders come to Washington cap-in-hand. Many arrive at the White House for a talking to. Others are humiliated by a nuanced diplomatic snub. It is a place where foreign politicians can sometimes find their reputations enhanced or rubbished.

The Oval Office and its occupant sit at the very apex of global politics and is not afraid to use such inherent power. Yet for all its dangers the Official Visit is also a tool that re-enforces a relationship with America that, for many countries, is one of the most important they have. A grip-and-grin with the President of the United States is merely the public focal point. Behind the scenes, a foreign Head of State and the team accompanying him will sometimes undertake hundreds of meetings at all levels across the city.

In 2005, Azerbaijan sat at a crux of a plethora of geopolitical challenges in which the U.S. was involved, including the War on Terror and energy issues that Washington took seriously. Azerbaijan had its own agenda. *U.S. News* reported:

> *The President of Azerbaijan, Ilham Aliyev, had a lot to discuss with President Bush. Not only does the small Muslim nation occupy a strategic location between Russia and Iran at a time when tension between the United States and Iran is high, but it is also on the verge of a huge oil boom. This summer, a 1,000-mile pipeline originating in Azerbaijan will begin pumping oil across three countries to a Turkish port on the Mediterranean Sea.*

When elaborating upon Azerbaijan-U.S. relations, three fundamental issues are often mentioned: energy security, regional security and democratic reforms. For a post-Soviet country like Azerbaijan, to establish relations with the U.S. meant freedom from traditional dependency.

In the 1990s, with participation of the major U.S. oil companies, the 'Contract of the Century' was signed and relations with the U.S. reached unprecedented levels.

After the construction of the BTC pipeline, for the first time in the history of the U.S. an oil agreement was signed in the White House. This was signed by the then Vice President of SOCAR, Ilham. Azerbaijan, as a country blessed with energy resources, built efficient cooperation with American firms and sold itself as a reliable partner. Indeed, all the provisions on the contract were met and, unusually, no amendments were made to the original version of the agreement, signed in 1994.

In the political arena, Azerbaijan was one of the first Muslim countries to join the coalition against terrorism after 9/11 and sent troops to both Iraq and Afghanistan.

Yet despite this, the perfunctory approach of American policymakers towards the South Caucasus and an inability to view Azerbaijan as a regional leader, causes occasional friction. NGOs funded by the U.S. government, and Congressmen heavily supported by an aggressive Armenian lobby, highlight perceived mistakes in Azerbaijan. Azerbaijan, a reliable partner, leader in the region, and a country that exhibits a very positive attitude towards the U.S. faces double standards from Washington.

And Ilham portrayed the importance of his nation to the U.S., and indeed the rest of the world, when he stated on national television: "If you look at the map and see where we are situated, you'll see, wherever you look from Baku, hostility, wars, conflicts, existing, and potential. In these circumstances, Azerbaijan is an island of stability and development..."

It was repeatedly noted that Baku had sent troops to Iraq, Afghanistan and Kosovo and that the country's leader had gone on record stating his nation would "do its best to stand shoulder-to-shoulder" with the U.S. on security.

As Azerbaijani officials fanned out across the city for their own meetings, Ilham's diary took him to a variety of meetings, including with Vice President Dick Cheney and the equally hawkish Defence Secretary Donald Rumsfeld. He spoke at a public forum sponsored by the prestigious Council on Foreign Relations, an open question-and-answer meeting during which he discussed oil, economic development and democracy with an audience of reporters and others.

High on his agenda was Section 907, the controversial Freedom Support Act which banned any kind of direct United States aid to the Azerbaijani government, an act strongly pursued by the Armenian lobby. In 2001, the Senate had adopted a amendment that would provide the American President with powers to waiver Section 907, and he had done so since. Yet Section 907 remains an anomaly between two friendly nations.

It was at the Council on Foreign Relations that he delivered the biggest headlines of the visit. Bush was stoking up tensions in Iran's direction. Having named the country as part of his 'Axis of Evil', America was becoming increasingly nervous over Tehran's nuclear programme. When pressed, Ilham was adamant.

"Azerbaijan will not be engaged in any kind of potential operation against Iran and our officials in the past, including myself, have made this very clear," he told the influential policy institute. "Therefore I think it is time to stop speculating on this issue." He noted that bilateral agreements with Iran forbade either country from staging aggression against the other from their respective territories, adding: "At this time it is best to concentrate on a peaceful resolution."

Azerbaijan's fraternal policy towards Iran stemmed from the national interests of the country. Greater Azerbaijan was divided between the Russian and Persian Empires in 1828, when a huge portion of Azerbaijan was merged into Iran. Currently, 35 million ethnic Azerbaijanis reside in Iran, constituting the country's second biggest ethnic group.

The South Caucasus represents an important region for the security of Iran's northern borders and analysts state that Iran remains wary of unification of Azerbaijani lands. This is perhaps why Tehran did not oppose Armenian occupation of Azerbaijani territories, indeed, built gas pipelines and roads and became one of Armenia's most important trade partners.

The Azerbaijan President's office had announced that the Aliyev-Bush meeting would touch on "problems related to democratic developments", "security in the Caucasus" and a range of other topics. After the official photo call, the two Presidents had a private meeting. Bush later told reporters that their discussion was "really interesting." Bush also stated that he and Ilham Aliyev were "candid."

Candid is a word often used, in diplo-speak, for "tense." Bush was known for being forthright. Ilham also had a reputation for offering straight talk.

"For all his training as a diplomat in Moscow, and being the son of a consummate politician, the President does not readily stand behind diplomatic language," says Ali Hasanov, Deputy Prime Minister and Chairman of State Committee for Refugees and IDPs. "He observes the norms and protocols, yet when opportunity allows he is the most clear and concise political figure I have ever met."

The three-day visit, by all accounts, was a tremendous success. It was an opportunity to press the U.S. government in particular, but also to highlight that most eponymous of Presidential subjects — Nagorno-Karabakh. However, despite the successes of the visit, Section 907 and the Jackson-Vanik amendment still remained in force.

Two months before his successes in the U.S., Ilham had been in Paris for the first major effort that year to break the impasse with Armenia. French President Jacques Chirac expressed hope that talks between the leaders of Armenia and Azerbaijan could lay the groundwork for a peace accord in a long-standing conflict. Chirac held separate 45-minute meetings with Ilham and then Armenian President Robert Kocharyan, talks which he stated would form "a new perspective for peace."

Mediators stated that they were more hopeful than they had been in years that a settlement was close, while the U.S. State Department Spokesman said he was hopeful about the talks, calling them the most important meetings on the enclave in five years. The official, who spoke on condition of anonymity because of the sensitivity of the negotiations, said both Presidents understood that 2006 could be a crucial year.

The Château de Rambouillet is a castle in the town of Rambouillet, southwest of Paris. It is the summer residence of the Presidents of the French Republic, and has played a role in French and international history.

Prior to the liberation of Paris, General Charles de Gaulle set up his headquarters in the castle. In November 1975 it was venue for the first 'G6' summit, organised by Valéry Giscard d'Estaing for the heads of the world's leading industrialised countries; Gerald Ford of the U.S., Britain's Harold Wilson, Italy's Aldo Moro, Japan's Takeo Miki and Helmut Schmidt of West Germany. The château continued to be used as a venue for bilateral summits. In February 1999 it was host to negotiations on Kosovo and, indeed, the two leaders met with all signs that Azerbaijan and Armenia were on the cusp of a ground-breaking deal. The *International Herald Tribune* stated:

> *An official at the U.S. State Department said the talks were a crucial moment. "We're at the stage where the Presidents have to turn the corner from negotiations to decisions," said the official, who is involved in the negotiations. He added, "2006 is the year to do it."*
>
> *He spoke on the condition of anonymity because of the sensitivity of the talks. "There are no elections in either country this year and there is a readiness in the international community to aid stability in the southern Caucasus," he said. "Russia's holding of the presidency of the Group of 8 industrialised nations this year is another factor that makes conditions favourable," he said.*
>
> *In six months of consultations involving the two sides, mediators have drawn up a draft document that they hope could be the basis for an agreement on core principles. The document, less than a page long, is a concise description of an agreed approach to the major problems in the conflict, including the status of Nagorno-Karabakh, troop withdrawals and the deployment of an international peacekeeping force. The main sticking point remains the status of Karabakh…*

But while the former home of Napoleon may have had a hand in forging global agreements and leading towards peace in some of the most terrible of conflicts, it takes goodwill to achieve anything. Armenia was widely blamed for coming to the table with an unmovable and publicly aired "Red Line" position. Providing interviews with a variety of international media outlets, the most vocal of the country's officials, Hamlet Gasparian, a spokesman for the Foreign Ministry, pre-empted talks with a demand for self-determination for the remaining ethnic Armenian population of the ethnically cleansed territory. The talks ultimately collapsed and the *China Daily* reported:

> *The Presidents of Armenia and Azerbaijan failed to reach agreement after two days of intense talks on how to end the bloody conflict over the enclave of Nagorno-Karabakh.*
>
> *"Despite intensive discussions, the positions of the parties on some difficult principles remained as they have been for some months," U.S., French and Russian mediators said in a statement on Saturday.*
>
> *But international mediators said Armenian President Robert Kocharyan and Azerbaijani President Ilham Aliyev made little progress during their one-on-one, closed-door negotiations at a chateau in Rambouillet, south of Paris, a favoured site for international peace talks.*
>
> *The sticking points were the future status of Nagorno-Karabakh and whether Armenian forces would withdraw from the border town of Kelbajar, said a source close to the discussion.*
>
> *The mediators will consider the question of more talks when they meet in early March in Washington. The mediators said the two Presidents "highly appreciate the ongoing process" of talks and had instructed their foreign ministers to explore further prospects for a settlement in the future.*

"It led to nothing," says Ilham sadly, shaking his head. "Too often this has been the case."

In May 2005 there was yet another missed opportunity. Europe's leaders gathered in Paris for a NATO Summit. Azerbaijan offered face-to-face talks on the sidelines of the summit. Kocharyan refused.

During the event, Ilham spoke at the NATO Parliamentary Assembly and called Karabakh "a black hole of Europe". It was an unusually pessimistic address. Chirac, recognising his Azerbaijani counterpart's frustration, issued a statement which urged Ilham to push for a peaceful settlement over Nagorno-Karabakh.

"There is no alternative to a peaceful, negotiated settlement," said Chirac, while expressing support for the Minsk Group that had, ahead of the NATO event, urged compromise and asked the leaders to meet in Paris.

In the event it was the Organisation for Security and Cooperation in Europe which prodded Yerevan back to the negotiating table. On the sidelines of a Black Sea summit in Bucharest, Romania, the two Presidents met again. However the result of these talks harked back to Château de Rambouillet and ended with nothing to show for a lot of preparation. lham again reiterated that talks with Armenia over the occupied territories of Azerbaijan were going nowhere and vowed to restore sovereignty.

"These negotiations are taking place in different frameworks but these talks are ineffective because we can't obtain a result," he said, accusing Armenia of dragging out the negotiating process. "Azerbaijan will restore its territorial integrity, either through peaceful or military means."

Today Ilham gives off a resigned air when questioned on the matter "We will do everything within our power to resolve this matter, within international law," he says. "But

if these avenues prove fruitless, international law also gives Azerbaijan the right to restore its territorial integrity."
Pressed further on the issue, the Azerbaijan President states his belief that his country will be free of occupation within his tenure in office.

Internationally, at least, 2005 can be categorised as a failure. The ticking time-bomb of peace or war over Nagorno-Karabakh remained, the few bright hopes ultimately coming to naught. Opportunities were wasted and, in more contemporary times, meetings in Kazan and Sochi have also failed to yield a breakthrough. In July 2011, Armenian President Serzh Sargsyan showed his real stance during a public address when he stated "We have taken Karabakh…"

Yet 2005 will probably be remembered more as one of triumph. A concept that spanned two generations of the same family finally came into being. "This was one of *those* moments that define a country," says Ilham.

On July 13, 2006, Turkish President Ahmet Necdet Sezer, Georgian President Mikheil Saakashvili, Turkish Prime Minister Recep Tayyip Erdogan and British Petroleum Chief Executive Officer John Browne joined Ilham in a symbolic event to assemble the last pieces of the Baku-Tbilisi-Ceyhan (BTC) pipeline at an opening ceremony at the Heydar Aliyev Terminal near Turkey's southern city of Adana.

Recognised as the second longest oil pipeline in the world after the Druzhba pipeline, the first exchange of ideas on the construction of the Baku-Tbilisi-Ceyhan pipeline came in March 1993 in Ankara. A dozen years later BTC was finally completed. The first oil which loaded at the Heydar Aliyev Terminal went onto a tanker named *British Hawthorn*, which sailed with about 600,000 barrels of Azerbaijani crude oil. ExxonMobil had purchased this first consignment.

"BTC had been a long time in coming, but was worth the wait," says Natig Aliyev. "I would mention that since his return to Baku, a decade before he became President, Ilham Aliyev worked on BTC from the days when it was still being sketched, somewhat optimistically, on maps."

Adds Khoshbakht Yusifzade, Vice President at SOCAR: "When President Ilham Aliyev was Vice President of SOCAR, he and I used to arrive at the office in the morning having dreamt about pipes and come up with a few ideas. At times it was an obsession!"

The sight of *British Hawthorn* taking on crude oil, drawn from deep under the Caspian, was the end of a journey that took Azerbaijani oil along a 46-inch pipeline which went in the ground in Baku and then came out the other end, some 1,760 kilometres away. One report stated that this was: "a pipeline that cuts across several national borders, and the interests of some of the world's great powers." Indeed it was, but the $4 billion BTC was a strategic achievement that changed a great deal for the country, quadrupling oil exports.

In 1901, 51 per cent of the world's output in crude oil came from Azerbaijan. Events, and the oil industry, went on to pass the nation by during the Soviet era. BTC changed all that. The pipeline had been built to pump more than a million barrels of oil a day from offshore platforms all the way to waiting tanker ships in the Mediterranean Sea. With oil reaching record prices of more than $70 a barrel at the time, that was a lot of money for Azerbaijan. By 2010, according to estimates, the pipeline would help generate revenues for the state several times beyond current GNP and a 10-fold increase in state revenues.

"The role of the Baku-Tbilisi-Ceyhan Pipeline in strengthening the independence of Azerbaijan is indisputable and very important," said Ilham in an address to the nation. "Azerbaijan has been independent for 15 years and during this time we have shown the world that we can be a successful independent state. We have based policy on national interests and aimed for quick integration in the world community. Azerbaijan's position in the world is getting stronger and there is stability inside the country. Azerbaijan will continue to be independent."

Noting that the launch of the BTC Pipeline coincided with the 88th anniversary of the Democratic Republic of Azerbaijan he added: "The BTC will ensure Azerbaijan's development for a long period and strengthen our economic potential. Azerbaijan is a country with a fast and dynamically developing economy. Azerbaijan has wonderful potential and without doubt our country will gain much benefit from the BTC."

Ending the broadcast, he promised: "Each citizen will feel positive changes in their everyday life."

"*And then the justice,*" wrote Shakespeare.

It was a period when Azerbaijan's increasing maturity was becoming clear in economic terms. A slew of good results began with the State Statistics Committee's announcement that Azerbaijan had boosted oil output by 43 per cent in 2005, and gas production by 15 per cent. Interfax reported that the Azerbaijan International Operating Company (AIOC), which developed the Azeri-Chirag-Guneshli fields, produced 13.2 million tonnes of oil, up 100 per cent from 2004. Gas production in Azerbaijan rose 14.7 per cent to 5.66 billion cubic metres in the period, as AIOC raised associated gas production 83.93 per cent to 1.7 billion cubic metres.

Yes these statistics, however good, were not just indicative of an economy well handled. Across the world nations increase output, but then drop the ball through poor economic management and outright corruption. What was indicative were the succession of positive figures for 2005, which rolled out to January 2006, making pleasant reading for the country's leader.

Industrial output was up 33.5 per cent from the previous year, while the Finance Ministry announced that the state budget deficit was a lower than forecast 0.7 per cent of GDP. State revenue was 43.5 per cent higher than in 2004, and spending was up 42.5 per cent. Capital expenditure grew 80 per cent, while foreign currency reserves grew 30 per cent. The CIS Interstate Statistical Committee also chipped in, crediting Azerbaijan with the highest year-on-year industrial growth among CIS countries in 2005. Perhaps bolstered by such positive progress, and certainly with a confident swagger, towards the end of the year Baku informed the International Olympic Committee that it intended to bid for hosting rights to the 2016 Summer Olympics. Other bidders for 2016 included Madrid, Rome and Rio de Janeiro, one U.S. city and probably Prague and Doha.

Times had changed. While some could equate Shakespeare's *justice* with the nation's President, it was, perhaps, Azerbaijan that was reaching maturity. Just 15 years on from independence the country was ready to emerge on the world stage.

Chapter Twenty-Nine

Yerevan

In order to rally people, governments need enemies. They want us to be afraid, to hate, so we will rally behind them. And if they do not have a real enemy, they will invent one in order to mobilise us.
— Thich Nhat Hanh, Vietnamese scholar

"Let them try," chuckles David Saghatelyan. Dressed in a smart pin-striped suit, confidently speaking Queen's English, while clutching a top-of-the-range Nokia mobile. Next to him sits a Gucci briefcase. On his head he wears a smart pair of Mont Blanc sunglasses. The urbane Saghatelyan is dressed far smarter than most customers of the pleasant coffee shop in which we are sitting, a stone's throw from Yerevan's city centre.

It's July. The weather is balmy and clear, the wind fresh, and the cafeteria, on a tree lined boulevard off Republic Square, is a pleasant way to wile away the afternoon.

His English skills, Saghatelyan explains, are the result of working abroad, in Dubai, London and New York. He sold Information Technology systems and was doing well, but the call of home became stronger than the desire for wealth. Business is not as good in Armenia as in still booming Dubai, but it has compensations. As he explains this, he looks indicatively at his silent Armenian girlfriend sitting alongside. She's wearing a sweet diamond ring.

The strange thing about Saghatelyan is that there is nothing strange about this boastful conversation, despite him being well-travelled and, seemingly, well read.

"We kicked Azerbaijan twice, we will kick them again if they try anything, as their army is full of cowards. Karabakh is ours now, no matter what anyone says. If Azerbaijan tries to take it back I would join the army and fight for it myself."

He goes on to reel off the reasons why Nagorno-Karabakh belongs to Armenia. What is odd is that, despite Saghatelyan's education and well-travelled demeanour, his pro-war list is repeated parrot fashion, the same way we have heard from people everywhere in Armenia. Saghatelyan also states the oft repeated conviction that Armenia's armed forces will crush those of Azerbaijan's by virtue of their just cause. It is a common thread to conversations.

"Our fighting men believe, the Azeris don't, they know they are wrong. So our army will fight harder," says Saghatelyan with complete conviction. "They can buy as many tanks as they like. It will not matter."

There is, it seems, no room for discussion on the merits of war and peace. Nestled in the picturesque Ararat Valley, Yerevan, the capital of Armenia, is surrounded by mountains on three sides. To the south of the city, home to over one million people, are the mountains, while the city itself descends to the banks of the river Hrazdan, which is a tributary of the Arax river. The Hrazdan divides Yerevan in two within a sometimes stunningly picturesque canyon.

Yerevan has been the capital of Armenia since the First Republic in 1918, the most logical choice for a capital of the young republic at the time. But on November 9, 1920, the Bolshevik 11th Red Army occupied Yerevan during the Russian Civil War. Nationalist forces freed the city in February 1921, but Soviet forces prevailed again on April

2, 1921. The day after April Fools Day would be no joke. In a pattern seen throughout the region, victory for the Bolsheviks marked the beginning of a yoke of oppression that would stretch out for nearly seven long, miserable decades.

As a satellite republic ruled by Moscow, Yerevan became the capital of the newly formed Armenian Soviet Socialist Republic. Unlike some other capital cities in the region, the Soviet-Era was actually good to Yerevan in many ways. The tired somewhat underdeveloped city was transformed into a Soviet industrial metropolis.

On September 21, 1991, Yerevan became the capital of the Republic of Armenia. The early years of independence were tough and one of the biggest problems to affect citizens was maintaining supplies of gas and electricity. Regular electricity supplies began only in 1996, while Armenia courted controversy when it built a nuclear complex at Metsamor, in an area with considerable history of seismic activity, presenting the possibility — perhaps inevitability — of an ecological disaster.

"This was not the fault of our government, it was a result of the Azerbaijan embargo," says Susanna Gevorgyan, Executive Manager of SIMA Tours, on nearby Teryan Street. "But the embargo will change nothing."

According to the U.S. Department of State in February 2009:

> *Although a ceasefire has held since 1994, the 20 year old conflict with Azerbaijan over Nagorno-Karabakh has not been resolved, in spite of intensive efforts by the OSCE Minsk group to reach a settlement. The consequent closure of both the Azerbaijani and Turkish borders resulting from the war has prevented Armenia*

> *from realising its economic potential, because of Armenia's dependence on outside supplies of energy and most raw materials. Land routes through Azerbaijan and Turkey are closed, though air connections to Turkey exist; land routes through Georgia and Iran are inadequate or unreliable. In 1992-93, GDP fell nearly 60 per cent from its 1989 level.*

Armenia's economy suffered greatly from the closure of borders with Azerbaijan and Turkey resulting from the occupation of the territories of Azerbaijan. Only routes through Georgia and Iran remained open for trade. The prospect of a deeper crisis was offset, somewhat, by direct foreign investment and aid from the Armenian diaspora abroad.

The large Armenian diaspora comprises of around eight million people, close to five million more than the population of Armenia itself. According to one World Bank Report:

> *Roberts (2004) suggests that private transfers to Armenia (which remain outside of the official charity channels) amounted recently to $900 million a year, which is about 30 per cent of Armenia's official GDP.*

Yet despite this helping hand to the economy Armenia suffered from high unemployment and a staggering level of poverty (at one point as high as an estimated 55 per cent of citizens earning less than $25 a month in 2001), while an estimated one-sixth of Armenia's workers had left the country seeking employment abroad.

The government blames "embargo circumstances" and not once has it taken responsibility for the ills that befall ordinary Armenians. For sure there were challenges. In 1988 an earthquake destroyed or damaged 30 per cent of industrial capacity, while the 1998 Russian financial crisis dealt a blow to exports and expatriate remittances. In 1999 economic growth was cut by half following a terrorist attack that resulted in the deaths of the Prime Minister and Speaker of Parliament. But for the most part, governments in Yerevan relentlessly blamed the blockade for all the ills people faced. For a generation this has been the message.

Undoubtedly primary factors to Armenia's faltering economy are the Nagorno-Karabakh dispute, Armenia's armed intrusion into the region, and the subsequent blockade. But mismanagement of the economy (coupled with the need to pour funds into building the Armenian armed forces because of the situation) was also a primary factor.

Yet Armenian leaders have been lucky. Citing Nagorno-Karabakh as the *cause celebre* of the nation and setting up Azerbaijan as a common enemy, politicians had framed their neighbour for all Armenia's ills. It is a persuasive argument that appealed to the lowest common dominator of nationalism. But it also worked.

"Those Azeris lost Nagorno-Karabakh, which was not theirs, so they try to starve us. Only it will not work," says the bellboy at the Armenia Marriott hotel, which looks out majestically on to Republic Square.

Serj is 28. He says that since leaving school he has had three jobs, but been unemployed most of the time. His monthly salary is around $100. With this he supports his parents and two brothers and one sister. All his siblings are unemployed despite being in their 20s.

He invites me to visit his home near the State University Guest House. His father, a veteran of the Nagorno-Karabakh campaign, lost a leg in combat, although he studiously avoids saying where. Or how.

Through the only employed member of the family, who was acting as translator, he says: "I would lose the other leg. Karabakh belongs to Armenia, every piece of evidence in history says so. The others (he never refers to Azerbaijan by name) stole it."

On the way back to the Marriott it becomes evident that the economy is, in some ways, booming. The several dozen street side girlie-bars we pass are closed. They only come alive after dark.

"I wouldn't go there," advises Serj. "They charge you $5 for a beer and it costs $50 for anything more than a dance."

The same afternoon the wily and undoubtedly noble Levon Ter-Petrossian makes himself available. He ranges large in any history of modern Armenia. The same U.S. Department of State report summarised the nation's recent political sagas saying:

> *Armenians voted overwhelmingly for independence in a September 1991 referendum, followed by a Presidential Election in October 1991 that gave 83 per cent of the vote to Levon Ter-Petrossian. Ter-Petrossian had been elected head of government in 1990, when the Armenian National Movement defeated the Communist Party. Ter-Petrossian was re-elected in 1996 in a disputed election. Following public demonstrations against Ter-Petrossian's policies on the predominantly ethnic Armenian enclave of Nagorno-Karabakh that is located within Azerbaijan, the President resigned under pressure in January 1998 and was replaced by Prime Minister Robert*

Kocharyan, who was subsequently elected President in March 1998.

Ter-Petrossian is, one could say, a pragmatist. His softening position towards Nagorno-Karabakh was a disaster for him politically, costing him his job in 1998. But he perhaps understood that the people had suffered enough for a piece of land that, according to international law, was not the property of Armenia, and that had little tangible value in itself. Perhaps he had even foreseen that the past, present and future nationalist governments were setting a tone that would harden the people and set the country on an inexorable course towards war.

A pragmatist maybe, a politician certainly. In an interview he replied to many questions but gave not a single answer. He does not have a poker face however. His smile tightens when either of the Presidents Aliyev are mentioned, although an aide is more forthcoming and, as we are ushered out, drops in to conversation that the former Armenian President believes that there must be a "proper resolution".

Quite what this means to Ter-Petrossian's electoral prospects is debatable. Popular in himself, the suspicion remains among many Armenians that his earlier bout with pragmatism could be repeated if he reaches office again. Therefore many remain suspicious of him.

"Armenians will never forgive a leader who cedes one inch of Karabakh, under any circumstances," says Alexander Bakhtamyan.

Bakhtamyan is taking a break in a coffee shop close to his Ministry of Transport office on Nalbandyan Street. He gestures to the Monte Cristo, a notoriously gay-friendly nightclub with a reputation for "liberalism" after midnight, adding that Armenians are tolerant, easy going people, who will allow for most things. But he repeats that Karabakh is a red line.

"No leader will dare. Karabakh is in the heart of every Armenian," says Bakhtamyan. "Not now. Not ever. The people will not bear any intrusion from Azerbaijan. Let them try."

It is a familiar theme. Svetlana agrees. She is from Ukraine, a nation whose economy is as bleak as that of Armenia. She is an economic refugee working in Omega, on Teryan Street. Omega is a strip joint and Svetlana is a dancer. She and a handful of Ukranians, along with some athletic Armenian girls, take it in turns to strip on a pole. A singer, said to have represented Armenia in the Eurovision Song Contest a couple of years ago, entertains us with some ballads.

"We are busy every night. The money is good," says Svetlana. "There are lots of places like this in Yerevan, but this is the busiest, where the money is."

A girl from Armenia's second city, Gyumri, won't give her real name but dances under the pseudonym Katie. She agrees to talk only in return for a $20 private dance in a side room. While writhing on a pole she offers that her family thinks she works in a shop, but that she sends hundreds of dollars home to support her mother and keep her siblings in school. Her father is dead. He had cancer. But the dilapidated health service could not help. Refocusing on the matter at hand, yet building on this story, she makes a pitch that goes beyond dancing.

One common thread connects Katie, and Alexander, and Serj and David. Their stories are one of some hardship, some of loss. Their situations are common because they are a result of economic hardship, some caused by the government's own incompetence and corruption. Some because of the loss of trade with Turkey and Azerbaijan, Armenia's neighbours and natural commercial partners.

Their conversations share a common theme also. The nationalist agenda has been relentlessly imbibed into an unbending national consciousness. As a result they will almost gladly suffer economic woes, although most have never visited Nagorno-Karabakh. Several, while assuring me they would spill blood for the cause, could not tell me the name of the capital of the region, or name the rivers Kura and Araxes, which are so important to the geography of Nagorno-Karabakh.

Yet this poster child of Armenian nationalism hangs heavy over Yerevan. The occasional spring thaw in relations between Azerbaijan and Armenia has inevitably been followed quickly by an enduring winter freeze.

Settlement of the long running Nagorno-Karabakh conflict is the most significant obstacle to stability and regional economic prosperity in the South Caucasus. In a better economy, David Saghatelyan could probably be with his fiancee without having to give up the potential to make money he found elsewhere in the world. Serj could look forward to some stability in his employment. Girls like Katie would not be forced to give their bodies to strangers in order to put their siblings through school.

Yet an end to that obstacle remains elusive. Following the 1994 ceasefire, both Azerbaijan and Armenia have been saddled with burgeoning defence budgets, while there have been a growing number of ceasefire violations. By 2009, there are ominous signs that time for a peace agreement is running out.

In Baku, the President makes noises that Azerbaijan will look at options. The days of tub-thumping are over. It's a peace deal or — eventually — war. The much hyped

OSCE Minsk Group seemingly takes one step forward and two back, but is trying. Yet the Armenian President Serzh Sargsyan stays on the sidelines.

"Sargsyan is a good man," says the English manager of one of the city's less oppressive casinos, of which there are hundreds, both legal and illegal. "But he has no options. If he gives a signal that Armenia will even look at options over Nagorno-Karabakh his opposition will call foul and the people here are so fed with nationalism that Sargsyan will go the way of Ter-Petrossian."

Walking out of the Armenia Marriott one is struck by the picturesque Republic Square. The reddish brick buildings give off a glow in the sunlight. Sitting in the high end coffee shop adjacent to the hotel, one is among Yerevan's glitterati. The waiter points out a Gucci-clad Armenian singer. Several well-to-do couples sip espressos and watch the world go by. A couple of portly red-faced businessmen enjoy the sunshine, sporting status length-cigars, distinctively Cuban.

But walk 100 metres from Republic Square in any direction and Yerevan's facade drops. Roads are potholed, rubbish is piled everywhere and pedestrians navigate deep chasms in the pavement. It is a city unkempt and poorly maintained. Buildings are grimy, as are the beggars. Of course there is not a city, or an economy, in the former Soviet Union without its problems.

But Armenia's many issues have barely been addressed. The relentless portrayal of Azerbaijani phantoms as the cause is as unedifying, as it is patently untrue. The politics of nationalism has prostituted the nation to financial reliance on its diaspora and handouts from the Russians and international community. The government's relentless drum-beat of nationalism has created a situation where they have nowhere to go when it comes to compromise, and they have created a society that seems comfortable with the inevitability of war.

From that position, war will inevitably follow.

Chapter Thirty

Silk Road

Truth, like gold, is to be obtained not by its growth, but by washing away from it all that is not gold.
— Leo Nikolaevich Tolstoy, Russian thinker

Wherever it is found, oil has the potential to lift populations from penury. But at what cost and for how long? Other natural windfalls have, throughout history, harmed their beneficiaries. Gold and silver from the New World made Spain rich in the 16th century, but distorted its economy and ultimately weakened it. Peru enjoyed a boom in guano (used for fertiliser) in the mid-19th century, and later Brazil had a rubber boom. These made a few people rich but left no useful legacy — only some gaudy buildings, including an opera house in the Amazon jungle.

Gold Rush sites in California and Alaska turned into ghost towns when the mining stopped. The trouble with booms is that they typically bring neither sustained economic growth nor cultural improvements. The riches they create are spent with abandon, disrupting normal behaviour, fomenting unrealistic expectations and inspiring envy. Booms always, always, come to an end.

"It is striking how many countries have not used their natural resource wealth wisely," says Nobel Laureate Joseph E. Stiglitz. "And as a result, the abundance of wealth has not enhanced growth."

Countries with a rich natural resource endowment are more likely than others to suffer from lower than average economic growth, non-democratic forms of government and civil conflict. This occurs because the income from these resources is often misappropriated by corrupt leaders and officials instead of being used to support growth and development. Moreover, such wealth often fuels internal grievances that cause conflict and civil war. This pattern is widely referred to as the "natural resource curse", where this supposed bounty creates stagnation and conflict, rather than economic growth and development.

"We are aware of the so-called 'natural resource curse'," says Ilham. "People talk of this a lot. But there are examples where nations have prospered and used their natural wealth to propagate a bright future.

"The number of people living under the poverty line in Azerbaijan has been slashed through job creation and sustainable, permanent improvements to our economy. Poverty has fallen dramatically and will be reduced further. Elsewhere, every economic indicator shows that the government's policies are forging the fundamentals of the nation's economy, shaping and modernising Azerbaijan with an eye on the long term future."

The fate of many oil exporters is to have sold the bulk of this one-off inheritance cheaply, and live post-peak production years cramped for income and wondering where the promise of long-term inheritance went. The State Oil Fund of Azerbaijan (SOFAZ) was one key attempt to offset this and ensure a long-term benefit for future generations, including those born after the oil-producing era.

Industry experts highlight the cases of Britain and Indonesia, two oil-exporters who have turned net importers without an oil fund or, indeed, an oil legacy that can really be measured. Britain exported oil for a quarter century, but while the nation enjoyed relatively high global prices of the early 1980's, the bulk of Britain's exported oil was sold into a weak price environment up until 2002.

Hotelling's Rule is a widely accepted explanation of non-renewable resource management, produced by Harold Hotelling and first published in the *Journal of Political Economy* in 1931. Hotelling defined net price path as a function of time, the Rule including rent in the time of fully extracting a nation's non-renewable natural resource.

Today, the status quo viewpoint is that oil producers will always be price-takers. Others argue that collective consensus shaped 20th century oversupply, combined with a growing cost-disparity between OPEC oil supply and non-OPEC oil supply. This view is supported by those who decry the fact that oil is priced daily by somewhat odd market conditions.

How oil producing nations prepare for their post-oil futures is a matter of considerable debate today. Some do better than others. A few do nothing. It was Abraham Lincoln who said: "Give me six hours to chop down a tree and I will spend the first four sharpening the axe." It was an allusion to the importance of education, preparing youth for the future.

With advice from international organisations on how to mitigate some common pitfalls of fast oil wealth, Ilham turned his attention to what critics alleged was a mismanaged educational system. It was certainly not great, although there had been significant improvement.

"I am computer literate, so are my ministers, and those who work in the Presidential Administration," says Ilham. "This is how we, as a government, communicate with the rest of the world. There is no question that computers and the Internet are intrinsic to modern life and today's global economy."

A modern education steeped in computer literacy was, therefore, high on the agenda being, as Ilham puts it, "more important than bridges and roads."

The government rolled out dozens of new initiatives, but arguably the headline grabber was one of the world's biggest scholarship programmes, a fund that would offer 5,000 Azerbaijani students the opportunity for further education. The fund, announced in April 2007, remains Azerbaijan's most ambitious educational reform, open to students once they graduate from secondary school.

Students at a bachelors, masters or Ph.D. level are sent to study abroad for the next eight years, with the caveat that they return to work in Azerbaijan for the public sector for a short period. After this they are free to remain, or join the private sector.

In October 2006, Ilham signed a decree establishing the programme officially. For the first year, the government allocated $2.5 million to cover administrative costs and tuition expenses of students. This would be set to grow markedly over subsequent years. A number of problems quickly emerged, highlighted by a lack of public awareness. The programme required pre-departure training and orientation, allowed only a small list of eligible universities and had unclear procedural rules for the application process as well as vague eligibility criteria.

The government tackled these issues quickly and in cabinet this became recognised as one of the President's hot button issues, which he viewed as a fundamental. What finally emerged was one of the most ambitious scholarship programmes anywhere in the world.

This programme was a very public expression of determination on Ilham's part. During the 2003 and 2005 elections he promised to create 600,000 new jobs. Several thousand McJobs would be of little use. The scholarship programme aimed to create a new generation of school leavers who were employable within a progressive economy.

According to the Central Asia-Caucasus Institute by this time, under his leadership, the government had already built more than 170 new schools, refurbished another 630 secondary schools and launched a process of computerisation of schools. The government's stated policy was to provide one computer for every three students nationwide, while class places as a whole were growing with hundreds more primary and secondary schools budgeted and on the drawing board.

"Azerbaijan's market economy was not getting what it needed from education," said Baku-based freelance journalist Fariz Ismailzade, quoted in a newspaper interview. "People are not equipped to apply for a job. They don't even know how to write a CV."

Ismailzade later had a role to play in the rebirth of Azerbaijan's education as Director of Training at another of the country's fresh scholastic initiatives, the Azerbaijan Diplomatic Academy. Azerbaijan had emerged on the world stage, an injection of globalisation that saw the country roll out 32 embassies in two years — more than doubling the country's 2004 tally of 24 embassies. Yet this left Azerbaijan with a shortage of diplomats. This resulted in the creation of a new academy to groom diplomats under the nation's most revered international diplomat, Azerbaijan's Ambassador in Washington, Hafiz Pashayev.

The Azerbaijan Diplomatic Academy was the country's first training centre for diplomats, boasting professors from

Georgetown University and the Virginia-based George C. Marshall Foundation. The Academy later introduced Azerbaijan's first professional master's programme.

Amid the growth of education, the economy continued to expand. Azerbaijan's trade surplus in 2006 was $1.1 billion, 650 per cent up on 2005. Another statistic showed that Azerbaijan had been the subject of investment totalling $42 billion between 1995 and the first half of 2007, according to Economic Development Ministry figures. Foreign investment accounted for 70 per cent of this, and the ministry forecast another $40 billion of investment from all sources between 2008 and 2011.

The government held bilateral negotiations with the United States, the European Union, Taiwan, South Korea and Japan in 2007 within a framework of accession to the World Trade Organisation, under a WTO commission. Azerbaijan had applied for entry into the WTO in 1997.

While WTO processes were underway, the nation embarked upon a boom, amid a global financial crisis called the most serious since the Great Depression by leading economists, with its global effects characterised by the failure of key businesses, declines in consumer wealth estimated in the trillions of dollars, substantial financial commitments incurred by governments, and a significant decline in economic activity. As late as December 2007, *The Korea Times* reported:

> *With undeniable advantages in rich natural resources and clear signs of an economic upturn, the former Soviet-bloc country is giving chances to local contractors to satisfy their greater appetite for more orders by offering tax incentives and administrative support.*

> *South Korean builders have won $260 million worth in contracts from road to plant projects in the country so far this year, according to data from the Ministry of Construction and Transportation. Before that, for the past 10 years, only one contract was received by Korea there.*
>
> *"The local players who have rich experience in constructing bridges, hotels, pipelines for delivering natural gas and other residential complexes are shifting their eyes to countries which have much oil but are still underdeveloped," an official from the ministry said.*
>
> *"Talk of more orders is now underway," the official added without elaborating.*

More work was being created. Unarguably the showpiece infrastructure initiative of 2007 came when Georgia, Azerbaijan and Turkey agreed details of a project to lay a rail line that would stretch from Turkey to Azerbaijan, via Georgia. The line will eventually link Kars in Turkey to Baku, and pass through the Georgian town of Akhalkalaki and Georgia's capital Tbilisi. The project involved renovating a 160 kilometre line from Marabda to Akhalkalaki, laying a new 20 kilometre line from Akhalkalaki to the Turkish border, and building a facility in Akhalkalaki for transfer to European-gauge tracks.

"I believe that this will become one of the key developments in the regional economy, an artery that will create many opportunities for the three countries, and especially the people and communities that sit along the route," says Ilham. "Azerbaijan has led this project."

Azerbaijan and Turkey would lend Georgia $220 million, which Georgian Railways would repay with incomes from the new railway. The project is valued at over $1 billion, according to Georgia's Minister of Regional Development and Infrastructure, Ramaz Nikolaishvili. The cornerstone-laying ceremony of the Baku-Tbilisi-Kars Railway was held in November the same year, while SOFAZ allocated the first instalment of $50 million out of a planned $200 million budget for construction. Azerbaijan also financed a $200 million loan to Georgia's Marabda-Karsi Railroad Company for 25 years at a one per cent interest rate annually, the money to be spent on construction of a 29 kilometre railroad in Georgia, a station on the Turkish-Georgian border and the restoration of old rail tracks.

The railroad was expected to open in late 2011, able to transport one million passengers and 6.5 million tonnes of freight at the first stage, with capacity eventually reaching three million passengers and over 15 million tonnes of freight.

Georgia's President Saakashvili presented the BTK railroad as a "geopolitical revolution" while the implementation of the East-West energy corridor, coupled with BTK, was hailed as a step in the considerable political evolution of the South Caucasus. Turkish President Abdullah Gul, on a visit to Azerbaijan, went as far as to propose a special economic zone between Azerbaijan, Georgia and Turkey.

Azerbaijani Minister of Foreign Affairs Elmar Mammadyarov went further. He stated that the BTK railroad would "create conditions for the revival of the historical Silk Road and develop the Europe-Caucasus-Asia corridor, deepening the region's integration into Europe."

The Silk Road was the most well-known trading route of ancient Chinese civilisation. Trade in silk grew under the Han Dynasty and caravans from the empire's interior would carry silk to the western edges of the region. Chan Ch'ien was the first known Chinese traveller to make contact with the Central Asian tribes and it was he who came up with the idea to expand the silk trade and therefore forge alliances with Central Asian nomads. Because of this idea, the Silk Road was born.

The route grew with the rise of the Roman Empire because the Chinese initially gave silk to the Roman-Asian governments as gifts and it eventually spanned a 7,000 mile route crossing China, Central Asia, Northern India and the Parthian and Roman Empires. It connected the Yellow River Valley to the Mediterranean Sea and passed through places such as the Chinese cities of Kansu and Sinkiang and present-day countries Iran, Iraq and Syria.

Mammadyarov's ambitious statement acknowledged the fact that Azerbaijan had successfully positioned itself — through its east-west energy corridor, the BTK railroad and BTC pipeline, along with its neutral, geopolitical stance — at the heart of a post-Soviet Euro-Asian new world order.

The allusion to a new Silk Road is not without its merit. One which perhaps had identifiable features, other than economic, that would be worthy of consideration. The Silk Road provided a conduit for culture, religion, politics and major technological advances, including a diffusion of modern technologies like movable type printing, gunpowder, the astrolabe and the compass. A new Silk Road would provide cross-cultural, multi-religious, energy-connections and new economic links between two parts of the world that needed to forge a closer relationship.

Azerbaijan's place in a new Silk Road, or indeed in the new world order, was being firmed through the economy's assured economic performance. During the first two thirds of 2009 industrial output in the Commonwealth of Independent States (CIS) grew highest in Azerbaijan at 32.7 per cent, according to the CIS Interstate Statistics Committee, followed by Ukraine with 10.9 per cent, Tajikistan 8.2 per cent, Belarus 7.7 per cent and Russia seven per cent, while Armenia sat on 1.7 per cent.

The latter's economy remained battered though the global financial crisis, coupled with its exclusion from the economies of its neighbours in Turkey and Azerbaijan due to the Nagorno-Karabakh conflict.

While ordinary Armenians suffered, the nation's political leaders had squandered several opportunities to emerge from the morass. The UN Security Council had condemned the Armenian invasion and occupation, making its position clear and unambiguous through four resolutions 822, 853, 874 and 884. Ultimately, the Security Council condemned the seizure and occupation of the Kalbajar, Aghdam, Fizuli, Zangilan districts and all other occupied areas in Azerbaijan and demanded the immediate cessation of all armed hostilities, along with the unilateral withdrawal of occupying forces from all those districts and areas. But that had not happened. Several chances of permanent peace had been lost just in 2006, most notably following the collapse of talks near Paris at the beginning of the year.

That led to something that Azerbaijan, and indeed Armenia, could do without. For Azerbaijan's part, money would be invested in the Armed Forces when, in the final analysis, the extra spending could have gone into Nagorno-Karabakh for schools, hospitals and fresh infrastructure, if it was not illegally occupied by Armenia.

While military spending could not be removed altogether from the Azerbaijan budget, in 2007 it reached 10 figures for the first time, largely as a result of the need to pursue a 'back up plan' should diplomacy continue to fail.

"In the past several years, we have increased our military expenditure several times. In the 2007 budget, these expenditures stand at one billion dollars… I have instructed that military expenditure be increased," said Ilham at a meeting with representatives of IDPs from Nagorno-Karabakh. "Although one billion is a very big amount, and I can say that we are in the lead among CIS countries, it's because we live in a state of war, our land has been occupied, which is why we must fund this sector."

The continuing occupation and resulting state of war meant that more money than otherwise would be the case went into Azerbaijan's military budget. There were purchases of combat aircraft such as the MiG-29, rocket artillery and battle tanks. The Ministry of Defence Industry of Azerbaijan now directs a growing domestic defence production capability, cooperating with the defence sectors of Ukraine, Belarus and Pakistan.

For example, Azerbaijani defence industries and Turkish companies, produce 40mm revolver grenade launchers, 107mm and 122mm Multiple Launch Rocket Systems, Cobra 4x4 vehicles and joint modernisation of Armoured Personnel Carriers in Baku.

Azerbaijan also produces its own armoured personnel carriers and infantry fighting vehicles, while an advanced capability to build military aircraft and helicopters is probably within half a decade.

These expenditures are at odds with the country's political stance when it comes to defence. For example, Azerbaijan is a signatory to the Minsk Accord, the Nuclear Non-Proliferation Treaty, the Comprehensive Test Ban Treaty and is a member of the International Atomic Energy Agency. According to Foreign Minister Elmar Mammadyarov, Azerbaijan does not have and is not going to have nuclear weapons. "There is no nuclear weapon in Azerbaijan and it is not planned," he says.

Yet Nagorno-Karabakh has forced the country to plough otherwise unnecessary funds into conventional forces, funds that could be well spent anywhere.

For example, the University of Cambridge has an annual budget of around £600 million, Harvard University's operating budget in 2008 was $1.6 billion. The University of Chicago has 13,700 students, 4,000 of them undergraduates and an annual budget of around $1 billion.

Imagine in Azerbaijan a seat of learning, one that grows to be the educational centrepiece of the region. Thousands of Azerbaijanis are joined in receiving the highest quality of education by the leading students of their generation from Kazakhstan, Turkmenistan, Turkey, Georgia, Afghanistan, Russia and Iraq, even Armenia. It is considered the Harvard of the East, and represents to the Caucasus the same venerable seat of learning as Oxford or Cambridge in Britain. It is a dream with merit, yet whenever nations are at loggerheads the resulting military build-up only serves to suck out money from budgets that would be better directed to areas such as education and health.

Armenia's failure to respond to the UN's urgings over Nagorno-Karabakh has cost both countries, and indeed the region. According to World Bank figures for 2008, Azerbaijan's military budget exceeded the entire combined GDP of nations such as Saint Vincent and the Grenadines, Vanuatu, Grenada, East Timor and Guinea-Bissau. According to the same source, Armenian GDP for 2008 was just $18.7 billion, while the IMF expected its GDP to fall 15 per cent in 2009. Armenia's government spending for 2009 was approved by Parliament setting spending at $2.6 billion for the year, including foreign aid and a significant deficit.

In 2011 Azerbaijan's defence spending will account for about 20 per cent of the government's total expenditures, roughly $20 billion. This represents nearly a twofold increase in defence outlays over 2010.

All these figures do not add up. For Armenia. Or Azerbaijan. Or even the world. Summarising some key details from Chapter Five of the Stockholm International Peace Research Institute's 2009 Year Book, world military expenditure in 2008 was estimated to have reached $1.464 trillion, a four per cent increase in real terms since 2007 and a 45 per cent increase over the 10-year period since 1999, some 2.4 per cent of world GDP and $217 for each person in the world.

"We don't want to increase spending in this area," says Ilham. "I prefer schools to tanks and fighter aircraft, of course, but the fact remains that some 20 per cent of Azerbaijan's territory is occupied."

An increasingly modern and capable military also meant that Azerbaijan was prepared to play an international role where required. The nation played a part in Iraq, Afghanistan and Kosovo, leading to an expectation that joining NATO was on the agenda. Not so says the country's President. In 2007 he told German television channel *Deutsche Welle* that his country needs to continue its interaction with NATO "as partners". "Azerbaijan takes part in NATO's peacekeeping operations around the world. We are reliable partners," said Ilham. "We feel equally comfortable cooperating with Russia, the European Union and the United States."

After the failed, hoped-for settlement on Nagorno-Karabakh in 2006, prospects for averting a war dimmed further in July 2007 when the breakaway region staged Armenia-backed 'Presidential' Elections. A man named Bako Saakian became the least internationally recognised "President" in the world.

In the wake of this, in November, Minister of Defence Safar Abiyev offered one of the bleakest assessments of the situation as it stood. Visiting Kazakhstan for a meeting of Defence Ministers of ex-Soviet republics he stated: "As long as Azerbaijani territory is occupied by Armenia, the chance of war is close to 100 per cent."

Such words stand at odds with everything modern Azerbaijan stands for. Today Azerbaijan has 73 diplomatic representative offices abroad and holds membership in 38 international organisations, while holding observer status in the Non-Aligned Movement and World Trade Organisation. Diplomats who have served in the U.S. and UN state that Ilham believes whole-heartedly in the UN as a medium for global diplomacy. As a nation with territory under occupation, and with one million IDPs, Azerbaijan had consistently engaged with the world body.

The UN is the centre of world diplomacy. Ilham has resolutely attempted to use the world body, along with other diplomatic avenues, in order to free Azerbaijani territory. This has not yet happened, but the UN Charter underscores that argument.

Ilham adds: "The Azerbaijani position is flexible and pragmatic, we want a solution. Diplomacy is our first language."

Chapter Thirty-One

Thirteen Seconds

Olympism is not a system — it is a state of mind.
This state of mind has emerged from a double cult;
that of effort and that of Eurythmy — a taste of excess
and a taste of measure combined.
— Pierre de Coubertin, French Olympian

It took only 13 seconds for the world's top-ranked judoka at 73 kilograms to win Azerbaijan's first gold medal at the Beijing Olympic Games in 2008. At 19 years old Elnur Mammadli defeated South Korea's Wang Ki-chun with an *ippon*, a throw that ends a match instantly. *Ippon* means 'one full point' in Japanese and is the highest score a fighter can achieve. Mammadli pinned his opponent's legs for an *ippon*, and automatic victory, avenging his defeat to Wang in the World Championship final a year earlier. Winner of a Gold medal at the European Judo Championships in 2006, and a Silver at the World's a year later, Mammadli became Azerbaijan's first Olympic judo champion.

The Azerbaijani team had returned from the 29th Summer Olympic Games a few days after Mammadli's success. There was a special welcoming ceremony that included his parents, relatives and friends, along with relatives of silver medalists in Greco-Roman wrestling, Rovshan Bayramov and Vitali Rahimov. Representatives of various ministries, federations and sports organisations participated at the event, staged at Heydar Aliyev International Airport.

The 29th Summer Olympic Games had encompassed 10,000 athletes from 204 countries competing for 302 gold medals. Sportsmen of 87 countries managed to win medals. China took the first place with 51 gold, 21 silver and 28 bronze, while in terms of medal quantity the USA beat all countries with 110 medals. Russia was ranked the third both in quality and quantity.

Azerbaijan had sent a team comprising of 44 sportsmen and women, winning one gold, two silver and four bronze medals, in its fourth Olympics since independence. Azerbaijan first participated at the Olympics as an independent nation in 1996, and has sent athletes to compete in every games since. Azerbaijani athletes competed as part of the Soviet Union at the Olympics from 1952 to 1988, and after the dissolution of the Soviet Union, Azerbaijan was part of a Unified Team in 1992.

By 2008, Azerbaijan's athletes had consistently scored two medals more than the previous games, at every games since Atlanta in 1996. The team scored a single medal in Atlanta, two gold and one bronze in Sydney, one gold and four bronze in Athens and then seven medals in Beijing. During the Beijing games, Azerbaijan had notched medals in wrestling, boxing and judo.

Olympic champion Mammadli told the reporters that he had gone to China with only Gold on his mind, adding: "Our judo team failed in the last three Summer Olympics Games. I wanted to break this chain. I hope that this may be considered a victory for all Azerbaijani people, not only me."

Mammadli noted that he would still be only 23 years old by the time of the London games in 2012 and that he planned to strike gold in the British Capital.

In the post-Beijing environment there was much back-slapping among officials. Azerbaijan sat well down the medals table, but when extrapolating results in China against population, the reading of these results was better, among a theoretical table showing medals per million of population (score calculated as three points for a gold medal, two points for silver and one for bronze). If success was calculated in this way, Jamaica topped this ranking, Slovenia was second and Bahrain third. Azerbaijan would be placed 19th of the 204 countries represented at the games, while of the sporting big-guns China was 45th, the United States was 31st and Russia 26th.

There was more to ruminate upon beyond the all-important medals table. In sports where medals weren't awarded Azerbaijani athletes and teams had done significantly better. Beijing had been a triumph.

"We have come a long way in a short time," says Minister of Sports and Youth Azad Rahimov, while gold medalist Mammadli adds: "The NOC, under President Aliyev, has done a great deal for sportsmen and sportswomen in Azerbaijan. Across the board we have seen improvement, at all levels."

Sport is an integral part of life of Azerbaijan. Many different kinds of games and competitions, which have been played for generations, remain part of the fabric of life in Azerbaijan. There are rich traditions of horsemanship, wrestling and different types of athletics, along with chess and other intellectual games. Many Azerbaijani sportsmen have written eminent pages into the history of the world sport, even if most of them are remembered as being from the Soviet Union.

In addition to co-opting Azerbaijani sporting talent into its national teams, the Soviet Union left another sporting legacy; decay.

The history of sport in Azerbaijan comes from very ancient periods. Historical sources show that centuries ago Azerbaijani knights were skilful swordsmen, lancers, archers, and so on. In later times athletes used to demonstrate their strength and agility, competing in an event that saw them lifting heavy stones and racing over short distances.

The beginning of the 20th century can be considered as a new era for sport development in Azerbaijan. In Baku, an economically developing city, various kinds of sport became popular; gymnastics, swimming and athletics. Football started to gain interest.

Swimming was one area in which Azerbaijan excelled and, indeed, became well known. In 1912, Baku swimmer Leonid Romachenko swam 48 kilometres in the Caspian Sea in 24 hours 20 minutes. Romachenko went on to cross La-Manche and beat the records of the previous English swimmer Burgess. In the 1920's 'sport communities' started to be established and competitions took place. It is interesting that boxing started to evolve in Azerbaijan at the beginning of the last century and the first championship was conducted in 1920 in Baku. A year later national championships in football were held. In 1925 a national Greco-Roman wrestling championship was staged, as were competitions in weight lifting.

In the Soviet Union, the dependence of sport on the political system had always been explicit, where this institution was regarded as an extension of the state politically and ideologically. The Soviet sport programme always had specific sociopolitical objectives affixed to it as evidenced by a party resolution appearing for the first time in 1925:

> *Physical culture must be considered not only from the point of view of physical training but should also be*

> *utilised as a means to rally the broad working masses around various Party, government and trade union organisations through which the masses of workers and peasants are drawn into social and political life... Physical culture must play an integral part in the general political and cultural training of the masses.*

Some sources conservatively estimate that by the mid-1990s $2.2 billion was spent annually in fulfilling an axiom attributed to Lenin that "a nation cannot be strong, unless it is strong in sports." The United States and Soviet Union both believed in the political nature of sport and a link between physical culture and national defence and in the struggle between them. Sport was one of the favourite arenas for the demonstration of the prowess of the 'New Soviet Man' and the 'All-American Boy'.

'Homo Sovieticus', as 'New Soviet Man' was dubbed by his enemies, drew from a vast array of formerly independent states, particularly in sporting terms. After 1952 some 46 Azerbaijani sportsmen and women competed at nine Olympic Games for the former U.S.S.R., claiming 10 gold, 11 silver and seven bronze medals. Freestyle wrestler R. Mammadyarov was the first, claiming a bronze medal in the Helsinki games in 1952. In the last games at Barcelona before true independence, Azerbaijan was represented within the Commonwealth of Independent States by five Azerbaijanis. Nazim Huseynov claimed gold in judo and Valeri Belenki won gold in gymnastics.

But while this was an admirable performance, the corroded former Soviet system left behind in its wake a social system that was in tatters, an economy in ruins and sporting infrastructure that was on the verge of collapse.

Facilities were run down and there was no support for athletes. For a nation with such a proud sporting history, Azerbaijan found its sporting fabric in crisis. Something had to be done.

In 1992, the Azerbaijan National Olympic Committee (NOC) was established. According to the International Olympic Committee, based in Switzerland, '…The National Olympic Committees propagate the fundamental principles of Olympism at a national level within the framework of sports activity…'

NOCs are mandated to be committed to the development of athletes and support the development of sport for all programmes and high performance sport in their countries, participating in the training of sports administrators by organising educational programmes, also ensuring that athletes attend the Olympic Games. There are currently 205 NOCs, ranging from Albania to Zimbabwe.

"My father enjoyed sports and during his period at the heart of the Azerbaijan S.S.R. had set in place many of the facilities, such as gymnastics arenas, football stadiums and facilities," says Ilham. "But over the last years of the Soviet Union investment dropped off in terms of both athletes themselves and sporting infrastructure."

The Elchibey administration had, understandably, other things on its mind amid the chaos of that period. When the Heydar Aliyev Presidency began that long standing athletic heritage was at an extremely low ebb.

The nation's elite athletes had received no central funding for years, requiring that they left their training programmes and took employment. Mid-level athletes were being asked to train in diabolical, run-down facilities that had a negative impact rather than positive. Just as bad was the next generation of athletes, stifled from development through a total lack of support. There was no equipment, facilities were closed, no coaching or trainers, and the economic conditions of the day meant that there was little scope for people to put any more than the most cursory effort into sport.

Taking power in a nation that was fundamentally shattered from top to bottom, Heydar had an enormous task ahead of him, and had a bigger picture to contend with. While he had shifted his political compass from Communist to democrat, he remained convinced that youth needed to be shaped, moulded and occupied by physical education and sports. Heydar Aliyev believed that it was the duty of the state to provide the means to pursue a physical agenda and to support young people's natural desire to play sports and remain fit.

Under the Soviet regime, the empire had just one, centralised, organisation dedicated to young people — the *Komsomol* — a governmental entity whose activities naturally conformed to Communist ideology. Likewise, there was only one organisation for the administration of sport — the Committee of Sports. With the collapse of the Soviet Union and its ideology, these ceased to exist, leaving behind a huge void. During the same period that Ilham was called home by his father and appointed Vice President of SOCAR, he was also elected President of the nation's National Olympic Committee (NOC).

"In many ways this was just as demanding a role as SOCAR," says Ilham. "Sport in this country was at a low ebb. We had the traditions and the sporting heritage, but that had been allowed to dissipate through years of official neglect. This is what we had to reverse."

Ilham's NOC and the Ministry of Youth and Sports sat at the crux of what happened next. In July 1994, three short months after a ceasefire between Azerbaijan and Armenia, the first new Ministry established by Presidential Decree was the Ministry of Youth and Sports. With limited budgets, the government embarked upon a top to bottom exercise, from the construction of Azerbaijan's Olympic Complexes to the provision of small scale facilities in communities all across the country.

Olympic Complexes in Baku, Nakhchivan, Sheki, Ganja, Guba, Lankaran and Barda acted as hubs for elite sportsmen, yet the scale of Azerbaijani sport was as wide as it was deep. Within several years official statistics reported the country had 8,940 sport grounds, facilities and fitness areas.

"This was especially important because of the refugees around the country," says Ilham. "The misery and hopelessness that this caused hung over the country, and some 30 per cent of them were under 25 years old. We needed to provide them with some means of alleviating their misery."

In 1997 Heydar Aliyev wrote: "The world should know that of all the countries on earth, Azerbaijan has the highest ratio of refugees per capita. No other country in the world has such a great proportion of refugees. Out of Azerbaijan's total population of eight million people, one million are refugees. Nearly one out of every eight people living in Azerbaijan is a refugee."

The Ministry of Youth and Sports, the State Committee for Refugees and other ministries whose remit was the plight of the displaced. The NOC also has a significant impact upon the lives of many displaced Azerbaijanis, many of whom then resided in tent camps.

"Across the nation, this was our renaissance period in sporting terms," says 2008 Gold medalist Mammadli.

"By the late 1990s the rudiments of a national sporting architecture were coming into place. A lot was achieved, and particularly notable was the renaissance of sport in schools."

In the streets of Baku, other cities and settlements, boys play football and other games like in any other country. Physical training and physical sports are widely popular in Azerbaijan. There are physical training committees in all universities and colleges.

According to the Mayo Clinic in the U.S.: 'Childhood obesity is a serious medical condition that affects children and adolescents. It occurs when a child is well above the normal weight for his or her age and height. Childhood obesity is particularly troubling because the extra pounds often start kids on the path to health problems that were once confined to adults, such as diabetes, high blood pressure and high cholesterol.'

Over the last three decades the prevalence of obesity in adolescents spiralled in the west. Yet schools can play a critical role in increasing physical activity by offering quality, daily physical education and other opportunities for recreation. Physical education not only gives children an opportunity to be active but it teaches them the skills they need to be active throughout their lifetime.

Investing in quality physical education in all schools, for all grades, is a logical and important step towards improving the health of the next generation. The various ministries recognised that increasing obesity and rising healthcare costs threaten the national competitive advantage and national security. Unfortunately, in 1993 the collapsing Azerbaijani schools system could barely offer daily physical education in grades K-12. The Ministry of Education recommended a minimum weekly standard for elementary and middle schools.

"One of the most important issues we have tackled in more recent years is that physical education should be taught by certified physical education teachers," says Ilham. "That is the least we can do for our children. From the 1990s, as head of the NOC, I ensured that we worked exceedingly hard to work with the Ministry and individual schools to help evolve the national programme."

The Azerbaijan NOC also supplied funding for programmes that encourage physical education. Physical training classes were included prominently in the curricula of the secondary schools. All universities and schools had a sports curriculum and schools were increasingly encouraged to participate in a wide range of seasonal sporting competitions in regional, national and international events.

"All around you could see a sea change in the culture of Azerbaijani youth," says Azerbaijan's national football team captain Rashad Sadigov. "Not just in schools, but on playing fields, bits of flat ground, there were kids playing football. In the newspapers there were more pages with results from club sports competitions. Things were moving forward."

In 1995, just 165 Azerbaijani sportsmen took part in different World and European competitions. The following year this number increased to 412.

Then came the Atlanta Olympic Games. Worldwide, it was a games best remembered for Muhammad Ali lighting the Olympic torch during the opening ceremony. Michael Johnson won gold in both the 200 metres and 400 metres. Carl Lewis won his fourth long jump gold medal at the age of 35 and Andre Agassi won the tennis. One of 14 countries making their Olympic debut in Atlanta, the nation erupted with nationalistic fervour, especially when Namig Abdullayev won silver in Men's Freestyle Wrestling (he went one better in Sydney four years later). Abdullayev's was the country's only medal.

"It was a beginning, but also one that infused the nation with hope that Azerbaijan could emerge as a true sporting nation," says Ilham. "This has been the case, for our performance has improved at every Olympic Games. But more importantly than this, our top class athletes inspire the generations that follow them to take up sports."

These days, in Azerbaijan there are more than 80 different youth sports organisations independent of the government, membership is growing and the achievements of Abdullayev and the likes of world weightlifting champion Nizami Pashayev demonstrate sport can be a profession as well as a lifestyle.

The nation's sports stars take a stipend from the government and those successful at the highest level are awarded with apartments and pensions. But perhaps the most interesting aspect of the government-sport axis is how deep this goes. Ilham became head of the NOC when serving as Vice President of SOCAR. He did not relinquish this position when appointed Prime Minister, or when elected President in 2003.

"In my view, the head of the NOC commands a position that allows him to have enormous influence on the sporting scene in his or her nation, which is why I have remained there," says Ilham. "Sport is of vital importance to a nation on so many levels. When we see Azerbaijani sportsmen and women competing, and winning, at the highest level, it is of tremendous value to the country."

He was talking about the likes of Farid Mansurov, Olympic gold medal in wrestling and 2009 World Champion, Zemfira Meftakhetdinova, winner of an Olympic gold medal for skeet shooting, freestyle wrestler Namig Abdullayev, another Olympic champion, boxing star Vugar Alekperov, twice-European judo champion Elchin Ismailov, sprinting record holder Ramil Guliyev, multiple weightlifting champion Nizami Pashayev, World Taekwondo champion Niyametdin Pashayev and Teimour Radjabov, the youngest grand master in World Chess.

It took just 13 seconds for Elnur Mammadli to win Azerbaijan's first gold medal at the Beijing Olympic Games in 2008. But to get him there, to the pinnacle of international sport, representing an increasingly sports-orientated nation, had taken 13 years.

Chapter Thirty-Two

'It's the economy, stupid'

A politician thinks of the next election.
A statesman, of the next generation.
— James Freeman, American statesman

In 2008, among others, there were Presidential Elections in Georgia, Serbia, the Czech Republic, Pakistan and Cyprus. There were seminal votes in Russia, Lebanon, Cuba and South Africa. The Presidential Election in the United States was one of those which made history, returning the country's first African American President. Boris Tadic (Bosnia), Vaclav Klaus (Serbia), Asif Ali Zardari (Pakistan), Dmitry Medvedev (Russia) and Jacob Zuma (South Africa) were among those who won elections in that year.

It was also a poll year in Azerbaijan. Ilham had been elected as President in November 2003. His five year term was nearly over. Towards the middle part of the year attention began to turn towards a contest that would inevitably be a lively one.

Times, it seemed, were changing, nearly half a decade on from the 2003 poll. In January 2008 the Council of the European Union had issued a declaration praising the work done towards protection of human rights and freedom in Azerbaijan. A few months later, Azerbaijan's government reported that it was preparing to report to the UN Human Rights Council under its Universal Periodic Review Mechanism. This would cover the Constitution, protection of human rights and implementation of obligations under the various international bodies and global agreements of which Azerbaijan was a signatory. Those preparing the report were the Presidential Administration, the Ministries of Internal Affairs, National Security, Justice, Defence, Education, Youth and Sports, Culture and Tourism, Economic Development, the Public Prosecutor, State Committee on Affairs of Refugees and IDPs, other state structures and the heads of some NGOs operating in the field of human rights.

"There was some positive motion, yes," says Rasim Musabayov, a Member of Parliament and a political analyst with the Open Society Institute, part of the Soros Foundation Network, which funds volunteer socio-political activity. Soros foundations are autonomous institutions established to initiate and support open society activities.

Musabayov worked as an adviser to the President of Azerbaijan during the early 1990s and is today considered an independent political analyst. He has seen politics in Azerbaijan from both sides of the fence, as part of government and opposition. Most observers consider him "constructive opposition," lacking the vitriol of the anti-Aliyev parties, but not being considered pro-Aliyev either.

"But the positive motion in Azerbaijan was not quick enough. I take the line that it could be worse, as we have seen in some countries around Azerbaijan, but it could be better."

Pressed on Ilham himself, Musabayov remains circumspect and non-committal. The Open Society Institute does not do attack-dog politics and its statements offer only the most tentative of praise.

"I think that we can draw positives, but there are negatives," he says. "The Open Society Institute enjoys a dialogue with the government and other key bodies within Azerbaijan's Civil Society."

Consensus both before and after the 2008 election was that Azerbaijan had travelled some distance along the road towards democracy. Between the 1789 success of George Washington and the 2008 victory of Barack Obama there had been 56 Presidential Elections in the United States. There were other national polls. In its current sitting, this is called the 112th United States Congress.

In Britain modern historians generally apply the title of First Prime Minister to Sir Robert Walpole, who led the country for 21 years from 1721 to 1742. Since his first electoral mandate, in 1722, there are considered to have been 68 national elections, up to and including Tony Blair's 2005 success.

Prior to the 2008 Azerbaijan Presidential Election there had been four Presidential polls, three Milli Majlis elections and one nationwide referendum. Of course, Azerbaijan had many informational and organisational advantages over, for example, those who were charged with Sir Robert Peel's election of 1841 or Woodrow Wilson's in 1916. There were many international models to use as a template. Yet six national elections and no democratic experience or knowledge left the country on a steep learning curve.

"Government and opposition were learning, but politicians become polarised easily, so it is the case that the nation itself must build a Civil Society," says Professor Eldar Ismayilov, Director of 'For the Sake of Civil Society', which declares itself an 'independent assistance and consulting centre'.

There are many definitions of Civil Society, but the The London School of Economics Centre's definition says:

> *Civil Society refers to the arena of uncoerced collective action around shared interests, purposes and values. In theory, its institutional forms are distinct from those of the state, family and market, though in practice, the boundaries between state, civil society, family and market are often complex, blurred and negotiated. Civil Society commonly embraces a diversity of spaces, actors and institutional forms, varying in their degree of formality, autonomy and power. Civil Societies are often populated by organisations such as registered charities, development non-governmental organisations, community groups, women's organisations, faith-based organisations, professional associations, trade unions, self-help groups, social movements, business associations, coalitions and advocacy groups.*

Organisations such as the 'Open Society Institute' and 'For the Sake of Civil Society' represent the beginnings of an Open Society and the number of these was growing year-on-year. But in a nation that for seven decades had been used to a Civil Society comprising of the Communist Party, and the Communist Party only, a myriad of voices, many of them competing, was a dramatic development.

"It took some years, but the Civil Society set down its roots and ordinary people learned to accept the many voices they now encountered," says Professor Musa Qasimli of Baku University. "The one voice of the past had become many. At the beginning it was confusing."

As spring gave way to summer, attention turned to the impending election. In this, Ilham was not an easy man to work for. Those concerned with his campaign in the New Azerbaijan Party state that he is a natural retail politician.

He's a candidate who focuses on local events and meeting individual voters, and his power of recollection is strong, so in that way he is an ideal candidate. Following Ilham on a bog-standard working day, on a public appearance just outside Baku, it is clear that he does not mind old-fashioned shaking hands and kissing babies. But he is also interested in the fine print of his job.

He also appears to be a policy wonk. The intricacies of policy and how it works in action is of interest to him. But on the other hand, he enjoys campaigning, the grip-and-grin side of politics.

New Azerbaijan Party hierarchy may have had a willing candidate on their hands, but his personal decisions were often not in the best interests of his own candidature. In August, three months before election day, Ilham ordered officials to remove his portraits from the streets. On August 6, *The Associated Press* reported:

> *President Ilham Aliyev told his cabinet on Tuesday that he doesn't like to see his picture in the streets, according to the official state media. "They must be removed," he reportedly said. "They shouldn't be here in the run-up to the vote and afterwards. I don't need them."*

If the retail politician was undercut by an apparent dislike of aggrandisement, then he left his New Azerbaijan Party plenty of scope when it came to the economy.

'It's the economy, stupid' was a phrase that became famous when coined during Bill Clinton's successful 1992 Presidential campaign against George H.W. Bush. Bush had been considered a shoe-in to retain the White House because of foreign policy developments, highlighted by a successful Gulf War campaign. James Carville, senior Clinton campaign strategist believed that the public would see beyond this and eventually view Clinton a better choice because Bush had not adequately addressed the economy. In order to keep the campaign on message, Carville hung a sign in Clinton's Little Rock, Arkansas campaign headquarters that, among other things, said 'The economy, stupid'. Although the sign was an internal campaign message, the phrase became something of a slogan. Clinton's campaign used the recession to successfully unseat Bush.

In Azerbaijan's case, Ilham was the incumbent and the economy was *his* issue.

"You can debate how we run elections and, indeed, we can only get more accustomed and knowledgeable at running national polls," says Ilham. "But there is a tendency to become myopic about politics and ordinary people have other concerns."

Says Etibar Mammadov, leader of the National Independence Party: "Politicians in Baku have to remember that the shortcomings of elections are not the only issue. They wish to hear us debate jobs and the economy, how government is approached and the future of Azerbaijan."

After the October 15 election, the Organisation for Cooperation and Security in Europe, the Parliamentary Assembly of the Council of Europe and the European Parliament would report that the poll did not have robust competition and vibrant political discourse and, in their judgement, did not reflect all the principles they would like to have seen.

By contrast, the United States welcomed "progress" and State Department spokesman Sean McCormack told reporters: "We congratulate the Azerbaijani people on having this election and instituting some improvements in the way this election occurred over previous elections." Asked if the voting result bothered Washington, McCormack said: "Well, like I said, there's more to be done, but it was an improvement. The assessment of the monitors on the ground was that it was an improvement over past elections."

Yet the Organisation for Cooperation and Security in Europe, the Parliamentary Assembly of the Council of Europe and the European Parliament all reported that 2008 was significantly better than 2003.

Omphaloskepsis, the contemplation of one's navel, is well known in the usually jocular phrase directed towards excessive introspection, self-absorption and concentration on a single issue.

Opponents of the status quo in Azerbaijan, particularly the Musavat Party, arguably the main opposition to New Azerbaijan, seemed to be gripped by omphaloskepsis and announced it would boycott elections. There was a suspicion that the boycott was a good means of avoiding a drubbing on polling day.

It was left to Igbal Aghazade of Azerbaijan Umud (Hope), Fazil Mustafayev of Great Creation, Gudrat Hasanguliyev of Whole Azerbaijan Popular Front and independent candidate Gulamhuseyn Alibayli to provide opposition. Hasanguliyev, Mustafayev, Fuad Aliyev and Alibayli had once belonged to the boycotting party but had left to form their own organisations.

Campaigning began in mid-September when candidates were limited to an intense four-week campaigning period. The media was perceived as having strong favourability towards the sitting President, yet there was an air of positivity around Azerbaijan as the country was hit by a tsunami of good economic news.

There was a strong feel-good factor during the summer. If reporting the increasingly positive economic news of this period meant that the media was biased, then it was. But there was a lot of talk among ordinary people about the direction the country was going.

'It's the economy, stupid' applied well to the 2008 Azerbaijan Presidential Election. The navel gazing by Baku-based politicians stood at odds with the feel of a general public buoyed by an economy going in the right direction.

In 1664 William Petty, an adviser to England's Charles II, compiled the first known national accounts. He made four entries. On the expense side, food, housing, clothes and all other necessaries were estimated at £40 million. National income was split among three sources: £8 million from land, £7 million from other personal estates and £25 million from labour income.

Four and a half centuries on, The World Bank represents a vital source of financial and technical assistance to developing countries around the world. With 186 member countries, the bank produces an annual report that assesses the business environment in nations across the world.

Doing Business looks at all sets of indicators, ranks economies on their overall ease of doing business, and analyses reforms to business regulation — identifying which countries are improving the most. The indicators are used to analyse economic outcomes and identify what reforms have worked, where and why.

Doing Business 2009 was to provide unprecedented international commercial kudos to Azerbaijan, and the undoing of those at home who campaigned against Ilham's economic handling.

This named Azerbaijan as the world's top reformer in 2007/08, with improvements on seven out of ten indicators of regulatory reform. Extensive changes moved it far up the ranks, from 97 to 33 in the overall ease of doing business. Some 181 countries were surveyed for the report.

When it came to simplifying business regulations, Azerbaijan went further than any other economy and catapulted 64 places in the global rankings to 33, the biggest jump ever recorded. The report said Azerbaijan undertook reforms in seven of the 10 areas studied by the report, including making it easier to start a business, contract enforcement and property registration, easing tax administration burdens and employment restrictions, plus strengthening investor protections and credit information. Reforms led to jobs.

"This was not a surprise," says Ilham. "Azerbaijan approaches business with forward-thinking. Our one-stop shop approach, a single window regulation system, was created in 2008, which reduces costs and paperwork associated with new businesses. This new system cuts business registration time from weeks — and even months — down to a matter of days. Azerbaijan is open for business."

The World Bank credited this new system for the 40 per cent surge in new business registrations in the first half of 2008. It was a statistic borne out in jobs, which were being created through the arrival of many of the world's biggest names. Bill Gates' Microsoft Corporation was one of those, announcing plans to create a regional information centre in Azerbaijan.

In the wake of the World Bank, the CIS chipped in with its own regional economic indicators, stating that Azerbaijan posted GDP growth of 16.5 per cent in the first half of 2008, a leader in regional tables in terms of capital investments (up 31.9 per cent), per capita income (up 34.2 per cent) and other indicators. The CIS Interstate Statistics Committee ranked Belarus second in the region, with GDP growth of 10.4 per cent. Later the CIS Interstate Statistics Committee released further information that Azerbaijan had the fastest growing industrial output among the countries of the Commonwealth of Independent States, with 14.3 per cent.

These successes were underlined at a conference of CIS countries entitled *Financial Markets of CIS countries: development and integration*, when Elman Rustamov, Chairman of Central Bank of Azerbaijan Republic, then National Bank of Azerbaijan, informed his counterparts that during 2008, state budget increased ninefold, state investments 33-fold, strategic currency reserves 11-fold, exports eightfold and revenues from non-oil sector doubled.

In other areas there were further developments. News broke that Azerbaijan may join the World Trade Organisation as early as 2010 if conditions were favourable. During the same period it was reported that the assets of the State Oil Fund of the Azerbaijan (SOFAZ) had crossed $10 billion for the first time, a four-fold increase since the beginning of that year. In addition, Azerbaijan's strategic currency reserves, which include funds at the National Bank, SOFAZ and the Finance Ministry, had reached $20 billion, it was reported, citing Finance Minister Samir Sharifov.

Azerbaijan would boost oil production by about 16 per cent in 2008 to 50 million tonnes, and to 60 million tonnes in 2009, allowing the government to forecast investment in the country's economy between 2009 and 2012, from all sources, would reach $43.22 billion.

It was earlier reported that total investment in the Azerbaijan economy between 1995 and 2008 reached $50 billion, of which $44 billion had been brought in over the preceding five years. Industry and Energy Minister Natig

Aliyev had gone on record estimating that rising estimates of hydrocarbon reserves in the Azeri-Chirag-Guneshli field and rising oil prices would bring an increased $400 billion in oil export revenue between 2008 and 2024.

All these were very nice, but as President George H.W. Bush found out in 1993, people vote according to their personal circumstances. For the most part, economic fear trumps everything else when a citizen is standing alone in the voting booth and making a final decision where to place that all important 'X'.

How World Bank reports, CIS Interstate Statistics Committee league tables, World Trade Organisation membership and SOFAZ assets relate to an ordinary voter in Ganja, Sumgayit, Mingachevir and Khirdalan depends upon the government and its handling of the economy as it relates to ordinary people.

Ilham had announced in February, well before the election campaign, that per capita GDP was expected to reach $4,500 against $3,700 in 2007 and stated that the economy had increased by 96 per cent during that period. But how would that translate to the thought of a voter in the city of Shirvan, on the Kura River, come election day?

As far as the New Azerbaijan Party was concerned, campaigning for the incumbent featured 650,000 new jobs and there was much emphasis that minimum pensions and salaries in Azerbaijan had risen eight-fold and four-fold respectively over the previous five years. State Social Protection Fund payments to the population had increased 4.6 times.

During the campaign there were a lot of accusations traded, but it seemed that the electorate did not care for mud-slinging. They wanted ideas. This, perhaps, obvious belief mirrored the views of many of the non-political people that one encounters in Azerbaijan, and indeed even the politicos.

Professor Eldar Ismayilov of 'For the Sake of Civil Society' states: "There are claims that Azerbaijan will take time to build a Civil Society, and the somewhat dubious idea that the country will take time to learn democratic principles properly. But one area in which we are very much in sync with the most developed democracies is polarisation, rabble-rousing and a growing tendency by our politicians to reach towards the lowest common denominator.

"I would hope for a level of maturity."

Chapter Thirty-Three

War and Diplomacy

Every gun that is made, every warship launched, every rocket fired, signifies, in the final sense, a theft from those who hunger and are not fed, those who are cold and are not clothed. The world in arms is not spending money alone. It is spending the sweat of its labourers, the genius of its scientists, the hopes of its children.

— Dwight D. Eisenhower, American statesman

Former Armenian President Levon Ter-Petrossian had been forced to step down in February 1998 after advocating compromise over Nagorno-Karabakh. In October 2007 he was back on the agenda when, in announcing his candidacy for the following year's Presidential Election, he accused President Robert Kocharyan of running "an institutionalised Mafia-style regime". He attacked rampant corruption and claimed that Kocharyan and his coterie had stolen "at least three to four billion dollars."

Kocharyan had reached his term limit. Born in Stepanakert, and a former Prime Minister of a Nagorno-Karabakh administration that was illegal under international law, Kocharyan had been an unlikely (possibly even unwilling) player in efforts to end the impasse over the territory.

The election was held on February 19, 2008, when the Republican Party of Armenia's Serzh Sargsyan won in the first round, according to official results, with 52.82 per cent of the votes. Ter-Petrossian, claiming victory, accused the government of rigging the election, although OSCE and Western monitors said that the election was largely free and fair.

Sargsyan was born in 1954, like his predecessor in Stepanakert (modern day Khankendi). His record gave little room for hope that he would show a degree of pragmatism. A former chairman of the so called Nagorno-Karabakh Republic Self-Defence Forces Committee, he was elected to the Supreme Council of Armenia in 1990 and went on to organise some militia operations during the Nagorno-Karabakh War. On his way to the Presidency, he served within the Armenian government as Minister of Defence, then in the state security department and Minister of National Security in 1996. Riding on his compatriot's coat tails, he served as Kocharyan's Chief of Staff and later served as Defence Minister and Prime Minister.

On New Year's Eve 2008, the President of Azerbaijan had issued an address to the people of his country. The statement tackled an array of issues and, as is inevitable, he touched on Nagorno-Karabakh.

"If the Armenians of Nagorno-Karabakh want to self-determine, they should do that within the framework of Azerbaijan's territorial integrity. If they don't want that, they should leave Nagorno-Karabakh and create their second state elsewhere… Nagorno-Karabakh will never be granted independence, the leadership and the people of Azerbaijan will never agree to that," he commented. "We are reinforcing our army because we must be ready to free our lands of occupiers at any moment and by any means… The strengthening of the army will remain a top priority."

Six weeks later, the people of Armenia spoke at the ballot box and their decision leaned towards the status quo. Sargsyan seemed a political clone of Kocharyan.

If Ilham was personally disappointed he did not show it in public, and returned to diplomatic avenues, instructing his nation's representatives in New York to renew their efforts. The United Nations General Assembly is one of the five principal organs of the United Nations, and importantly it is one where all member nations have equal representation. Voting in the General Assembly on important questions — such as recommendations on peace and security — is by two-thirds majority of those present and voting, while other questions are decided by majority vote. Although General Assembly resolutions are not binding, they do represent the will of the international community and therefore the world's prevailing thought on a given subject.

As Agshin Mehdiyev, Azerbaijan's Ambassador Extraordinary and Plenipotentiary and Permanent Representative to the UN, observes: "Under President Aliyev we are a nation that believes in diplomacy. He engenders a policy where Azerbaijan has stood on the side of peace and justice on every major question that has faced the world, and insists that our stances are framed towards the greater good, even, at times, when our own strategic interest is not best served. Our voting record shows this."

On March 14, the General Assembly weighed in. A statement from United Nations' headquarters in New York stated:

> *Seriously concerned that the armed conflict in and around the Nagorno-Karabakh region of Azerbaijan continued to endanger international peace and security, the General Assembly today reaffirmed Azerbaijan's territorial integrity, expressing support for that country's internationally recognised borders and demanding the*

> *immediate withdrawal of all Armenian forces from all occupied territories there.*
>
> *By a recorded vote of 39 in favour to seven against, with 100 abstentions, the Assembly also reaffirmed the inalienable right of the Azerbaijani population to return to their homes, and reaffirmed that no State should recognise as lawful the situation resulting from the occupation of Azerbaijan's territories, or render assistance in maintaining that situation.*
>
> *At the same time, the Assembly recognised the need to provide secure and equal conditions of life for Armenian and Azerbaijani communities in the Nagorno-Karabakh region, which would allow an effective democratic system of self-governance to be built up in the region within Azerbaijan.*

Introducing the draft resolution, the representative of Azerbaijan said he did not accept the argument that the text was unilateral and untimely. It had been prepared in accordance with international law and was impartial. It had been prompted by unfolding circumstances, both regionally and internationally, which had heightened concerns over the status of the settlement process. It was, therefore, apropos and timely.

Meanwhile, he said, Azerbaijan was gravely concerned and alarmed at the lack of clear proposals from France, the Russian Federation and the United States, the cochairs of the Organisation for Security and Cooperation in Europe (OSCE) Minsk Group, under whose auspices talks had begun in 1992.

The co-chairs had expressed in words their support for the objective of liberation for all the occupied territories and the return of the Azerbaijani population to Nagorno-Karabakh, but by their deeds, they were trying to belittle that common endeavour.

The co-chairs had no right to deviate from the principle of territorial integrity for the sake of their "notorious neutrality", stressed Mehdiyev. Neutrality was not a position; it was the lack of one. There could be no neutrality when the norms of international law were violated. Neutrality under such conditions meant total disregard for those norms. Four Security Council resolutions adopted in 1993 demanded the immediate withdrawal of the occupying forces from Azerbaijan, while the General Assembly's dispatch of a fact-finding mission to the territories in early 2005 had confirmed Armenian settlement there.

Several delegates, speaking in explanation of their position before the vote, expressed support for the text and for Azerbaijan's stance. They included the representative of Pakistan, who spoke on behalf of the Organisation of the Islamic Conference (OIC), noting that the group had repeatedly called for the immediate, complete and unconditional withdrawal of Armenian forces from all the occupied territories, and for the peaceful resolution of the conflict on the basis of respect of territorial integrity and the inviolability of internationally recognised borders. OIC was deeply distressed by the plight of more than one million Azerbaijani displaced persons and refugees, and called for the creation of conditions for their safe return home.

Also speaking before the vote, the representative of the United States noted that the Minsk Group co-chairs had jointly proposed to the two sides the previous November a set of basic principles for the peaceful settlement of the conflict. The proposal comprised of a balanced package of principles currently under negotiation. Today's resolution did not consider the proposal in its balanced entirety.

Because of that selective approach, the three co-chairs must oppose that unilateral text, which threatened to undermine the peace process.

However, he reaffirmed the negotiators' support for the territorial integrity of Azerbaijan, and thus did not recognise the independence of Nagorno-Karabakh. But, in light of serious clashes along the Line of Contact, which had occasioned loss of life, both sides had to refrain from unilateral and excessive actions, whether at the negotiation table or in the field.

Calling the resolution a "wasted attempt" to predetermine the outcome of the peace talks, Armenia's representative said that was not how responsible members of the international community conducted the difficult but rewarding mission of bringing peace and stability to peoples and regions. The co-chairs had found that the text did not aid peace talks. So had Armenia. Refugees and territories had been created by an Azerbaijan that had "unleashed a savage war against people it claims to be its own citizens." Only when the initial cause was resolved would the fate of all the territories and refugees concerned be put right.

Taking action on the draft resolution, the Assembly adopted the text by a recorded vote of 39 in favour to seven against. Only Angola, Armenia, France, India, the Russian Federation, United States and Vanuatu declared themselves against, with 100 abstentions.

In favour were Afghanistan, Azerbaijan, Bahrain, Bangladesh, Brunei Darussalam, Cambodia, Colombia, Comoros, Djibouti, Gambia, Georgia, Indonesia, Iraq, Jordan, Kuwait, Libya, Malaysia, Maldives, Moldova, Morocco, Myanmar, Niger, Nigeria, Oman, Pakistan, Qatar, Saudi Arabia, Senegal, Serbia, Sierra Leone, Somalia,

Sudan, Turkey, Tuvalu, Uganda, Ukraine, United Arab Emirates, Uzbekistan and Yemen.

Whether Sargsyan and his government, who fought the resolution, were left quaking in Yerevan over this diplomatic bloody nose was a question only they could answer. But certainly, in Baku, there was happiness that the world body had reaffirmed that Armenia was plain wrong.

"Not only on a daily basis, but sometimes twice or three times a day, we circulate letters, addressing the President of the Security Council, or Secretary General, where we inform them of ongoing hostilities in the region. We ask the President or Secretary General to circulate this to all members, in the six United Nations languages," says Elmar Mammadyarov, Minister of Foreign Affairs. "This is one way of keeping international focus on the situation. We do not believe in a world of frozen conflicts. We need a solution and the United Nations is one forum in which a solution could be achieved."

The UN General Assembly may not have the teeth of the Security Council (which had issued four resolutions on Nagorno-Karabakh that sought to return the land of Azerbaijan: 30 April 1993-N.822, 29 July 1993-N.853, 14 October 1993-N.874, 12 November 1993-N.884), but in its history the body has straddled the world stage with some of the most seminal diplomatic moves. Arguably this began with Resolution 177, in which the International Law Commission was directed to "formulate the principles of international law recognised in the Charter of the Nuremberg Tribunal and in the judgment of the Tribuna." which resulted in the Nuremberg Principles.

In 1962 Resolution 1761 recommended sanctions against South Africa in response to the government's policy of apartheid. Resolution 3314 in 1974 defined aggression. In

1993 Resolution 47/121 condemned ethnic cleansing of the Bosnian Muslims by the Bosnian Serbs as genocide, while, in the year 2000, Resolution 55/56 introduced a process to certify the origin of rough diamonds from sources that are conflict-free.

"The UN is important to us," says Mammadyarov. "We are talking about the occupation of an area of land which represents 20 per cent of Azerbaijan — but more than this we have one million Internally Displaced Persons and refugees."

Stating that Nagorno-Karabakh is the first, second and third subject on his agenda, every day, he adds that numbers like 20 per cent and one million constantly win over minds around the world as Azerbaijan reaches out to potential new friends and supporters on the issue.

Strengthening that posture was something that, as Ilham observes, he works on in some way every day. While an international diplomatic campaign raged abroad, there was also a battle that needed to be won at home. One million people — one in nine Azerbaijanis — are categorised as Internally Displaced Persons or refugees. They could not be forgotten.

Lin Yutang, the Chinese writer, stated that: "Hope is like a road in the country. There was never a road, but when many people walk on it, the road comes into existence." The road back to their homes and smallholdings in Nagorno-Karabakh may have seemed an increasingly distant thing at times. By now, most had spent a decade and a half first living in tent camps, and later in temporary housing. Hope has no guarantees after 15 years. Rallying the hopes of Azerbaijan's IDPs — for what the President views as an inevitable return home — is also part of his job.

"As well as ensuring that our IDPs are cared for, the President ensures that efforts are made to guarantee that national culture and civil society is strengthened, particularly near occupied territory," says Deputy Prime Minister and Chairman of State Committee for Refugees and IDPs, Ali Hasanov. "We continue to prepare for a day when this will be over."

Two examples of this played out to the backdrop of the early months of 2008, the Armenian election and diplomatic efforts ahead of the General Assembly vote.

In January 2008 the President opened a sports training complex near the tense front lines of the Nagorno-Karabakh dispute, a move symbolising Azerbaijan's intentions of regaining control of the territory, along with half the province of Agdam which is also occupied. The sports complex was located near the village of Quzanli in the zone of Agdam that remains free of occupation.

During the event, he stated that the new facility "shows that we are taking all measures for developing this region." Later the same day his motorcade headed for the ceasefire line, where he made one of his most explicit public references to a post-occupation vision, stating: "Nagorno-Karabakh may be offered a high level of autonomy, as has been done in other countries. We do not intend to think of any kind of new formulation for this because Nagorno-Karabakh is an age-old part of Azerbaijan."

Asked by reporters about the most recent efforts by the Organisation for Security and Cooperation in Europe, he said that their latest proposal was not entirely satisfactory, "but, in general, the process is going in a positive direction."

"His duties bring him into contact with the men of our armed forces, he sees them for what they are, young men in their 20s and 30s, who have wives or fiances, parents and siblings.

He does not want to put them in harm's way — absolutely not," says Novruz Mammadov, a department head in the Presidential Administration.

In April 2008, the Azerbaijan government announced another enormous increase in the country's military budget as tension continued. Figures showed that defence spending could reach almost $2 billion according to the state news agency which quoted Ilham as stating: "...for the first time in Azerbaijani history, the Ministry of Defence Industry was established. This body is responsible for ensuring the maintenance of defence technology for Azerbaijan's military, and producing various types of weapons. With this step, the Azerbaijan armed forces have become the strongest in the region."

"Increased military spending should be analysed in the context of a growing national budget. He sees war as a last resort," says Ali Hasanov. "I believe that he would rather see Armenia at the centre of a trading bloc, enriching the economies of the region and driving up the standards of people's lives."

Adds Natig Aliyev, Minister of Industry and Energy: "If you see the trajectory that Azerbaijan's economy is on, it becomes clear what he stands for. You would be hard pressed to identify a leader in this part of the world who has done more to boost economic ties between nations."

Again, during the same period that Armenia was preparing to elect its new President, arguably an ideological clone of his predecessor, evidence continued to emerge of Azerbaijan's progress. The year 2007 had ended with another slew of top notch economic data being released. On January 13, some 37 days before ordinary Armenians would return to power an administration that had overseen the disastrous economy there, Azerbaijan was stamped as the fastest growing nation in the world in terms of GDP.

GDP for 2007 rose by 24.7 per cent, approaching $30 billion, amid a global economic slump, and this was over a record 2006, which had seen a 35 per cent growth in GDP.

"The volume of the country's economy has nearly doubled in the past four years, which had no precedence in the world," says Ilham.

Diversification of the economy, the redirection of oil revenues into non-oil sectors, and foreign direct investment, resulted in a 24 per cent growth of the economy in 2008 and 9.3 per cent growth in 2009, even while the world was struggling with a financial crisis. These indicators reflect a small country facing up to some big international challenges.

There was more good news for Azerbaijan to follow. In February, the government announced that his programme had created 650,000 jobs over the preceding five years. In the hotly contested 2003 Presidential Election campaign, his opponents had scoffed when he pledged 600,000 new jobs.

That was fundamental to him. Ilham had himself been jobless, after being removed from his position at the Moscow State Institute of International Relations in 1990. From that experience, he personally knew about unemployment and understood that a job is pivotal to life.

"This is one of the things that people like about Ilham Aliyev," says Baku mechanic Siraj Kazimov. "I don't know how many jobs are created, but there are jobs, and each job had a ripple effect through society, to family and friends, in terms of spending power and economic security. A single job feeds many and affects the lives of even more."

Says Jafar Baghirov, who works in a city centre telephone retail outlet: "The minimum wage grew even for jobs like this. From my graduating class everyone found a job, and that never happened before."

According to statistics, the number of new jobs that had been created was 480,000 and 170,000 seasonal or part-time. Many had been created through the State Programme for Socio-economic Development of Regions, while the emerging private sector had weighed in. In 2010, the number of new jobs created is estimated to reach 800,000 places. Industry will experience eight per cent growth and the agriculture sector is now capable of meeting the demands of 90 per cent of the population.

"Jobs for people strengthen local production capability. In turn, this promotes development of the non-oil sector. The economy of the country is built on free market principles and we have sought to develop the private sector," says Baghirov. "The problem of unemployment will be completely eliminated in Azerbaijan."

Pursuing this agenda, what Azerbaijan did not require was regional instability.

Georgia's President Mikheil Saakashvili was inaugurated in January 2004. Despite soothing noises, Russia remained concerned he was too Westward-leaning. When Georgia expressed its desire to join NATO, part of its overall effort to assimilate into Europe, the separatist regions of Abkhazia and, to a lesser degree, South Ossetia emerged further on the agenda. Political mistakes in the early 1990s led to conflicts in these regions and separatists in Abkhazia and South Ossetia continued to assert themselves.

By now Moscow enjoyed a *de jure* official relationship with Abkhazia and South Ossetia, where Russian peacekeeping forces had been deployed since the early 1990s. The increase of pressure against Georgia came in the context of Georgia's transatlantic aspirations. Months of escalation on both sides dramatically burst into the open when conflict began on August 7. Over the next nine days, according to Human Rights Watch, all parties committed serious violations of international human rights and humanitarian law. According to Russia there were 162 civilian deaths, while Georgia stated that there were 228 civilians dead or missing. At least 158,000 civilians were displaced with the Georgian Coordinator for Humanitarian Affairs stating that number at somewhere around 230,000.

Even a somewhat limited conflict such as this underlines the human suffering that follows when politicians fail. Tony Benn, the great left-wing political figure of British politics stated that: "All war represents a failure of diplomacy." He was not wrong, and neither was Benjamin Franklin when he said: "There was never a good war or a bad peace."

Setting aside, if it is possible, those who died, the injured and the tens of thousands of others who had their lives shattered, no-one, on any level, came out of the 2008 South Ossetia War with anything other than their reputations tarnished. After the war, recognition of South Ossetia and Abkhazia as independent came from the Russian Federation and those 'heavyweights' of Euro-Asia politics, Venezuela and Nicaragua.

Beyond that, the conflicts in South Ossetia and Abkhazia set back the cause of regional stability and development for years. When the new millennium was clearly the time to focus on an East-West Energy Corridor and playing a role in the euphemistically termed new Silk Road, this was not just a step backward. It was an utter disaster for the protagonists and their neighbours.

"What foreign direct investment goes into an unstable region?" says British banker Malcolm Corrigan. "What causes domestic capital flight more than war? How much does war affect the GDP of a country and how much after the war has to be spent on dealing with the humanitarian result, reconstruction and repairing shattered infrastructure? Aside from arms manufacturers, who wins?"

It is worth noting that Nagorno-Karabakh is some 8,223 square kilometres and the land around the territory that even Armenia recognises as occupied Azerbaijani territory, along with no-man's land between the armed forces of both, represents an area equivalent to Abkhazia. If diplomacy does fail, Nagorno-Karabakh has the potential to be another disaster.

Yet the earlier United Nations General Assembly Resolution, a diplomatic victory for Azerbaijan, represented the beginning of a seminal year when the international community forged on with efforts to avert yet another war in the Caucasus. At the same time Azerbaijan found a softening in Washington.

In 1992, Congress had responded to Azerbaijan's attempts to free Nagorno-Karabakh by enacting Section 907 of the Freedom Support Act, a law prohibiting certain types of direct U.S. assistance to Azerbaijan until it lifted its blockades against Armenia and Nagorno-Karabakh. The most interesting part of the issue was that by applying section 907, the U.S. was keeping the Jackson-Vanik Amendment, (intended to allow people, refuseniks and religious minorities, mainly Jews, to emigrate from the Soviet Union) which had been approved during Cold War times. The implementation of this bill, covering a now independent Azerbaijan, a country where Jews live in peace, was effectively meaningless.

Azerbaijan had slowly chipped away at the success of the Armenian lobby and opinions changed on Capitol Hill. On February 1, 2008, Senator Richard Lugar introduced a bill to 'authorise the extension of nondiscriminatory treatment (normal trade relations) to the products of Azerbaijan.' Congressman Robert Wexler stated that Section 907 "does not meet and enhance America's national security interests." On October 24, 2001, the Senate adopted a resolution giving the President powers to waive Section 907, which he has done until the present day.

"The problem with Section 907 is that it was framed without an understanding of the truths of the situation," says Hafiz Pashayev. "Gradually, as we pointed out the deficiencies in the Armenian argument, support for Section 907 dried up and Senators and Congressmen began to view Section 907 as punishing the victim, at the behest of the aggressor."

The Bishkek Protocol of May 1994 signalled a ceasefire on the ground. Since then Azerbaijan and Armenia have been engaged in on-off talks ever since.

The OSCE Budapest Summit of 1994, the OSCE Lisbon Document of 1996 and the Goble Plan of 1999 achieved little — indeed the prospect of compromise as per the Goble Plan was so controversial in Yerevan that gunmen stormed a session of the Armenian National Assembly, killing eight officials including the Prime Minister.

Since then the diplomatic track continued unabated, but with similarly limited achievement, including Presidential meetings at the UN Millennium Summit in 2000 and in Paris in 2001, followed by a much hyped summit at Key West, Florida, in 2001, all the way through to the November 2008 Maindorf Declaration and beyond.

In reality, little in actual progress is perceived.

Some never caught on however. The sovereign status of Nagorno-Karabakh is not recognised by any state, including even Armenia. Four UN Security Council Resolutions and two UN General Assembly resolutions refer to Nagorno-Karabakh as a region of Azerbaijan.

Yet remarkably, in 2009, at a time of global financial meltdown, when the U.S. economy was in trouble, two Congressmen set aside their constituents' pressing problems with joblessness and lost homes, among the many troubles of the day, to write a joint letter. Frank Pallone and Mark Kirk sent a congratulatory letter to the region's 'President' Bako Sahakyan stating: "We are writing to congratulate the people of the Nagorno-Karabakh Republic, Artsakh and you on your 18th Anniversary of Independence. This historic day represents another important milestone in Nagorno-Karabakh's path to freedom… We look forward to the day when we can join you in celebration of the flag of an independent Artsakh proudly flying in capitals all over the world."

On June 13, 2002, Pallone was presented with the Order of Mkhitar Gosh, awarded to him by President Kocharyan of Armenia. According to the Armenian National Committee of America, Pallone was at the top of a list of 'Members of Congress who received the highest levels of campaign contributions from Armenian Americans.' Kirk's financial controversies include a donation from Tony Rezko, convicted on federal charges of attempted extortion, money laundering and fraud, and Congressman Bob Ney, who pleaded guilty to bribery. Kirk is House Representative from Illinois' 10th district, while Pallone is House Representative from New Jersey's 6th district.

Amid one of the world's deepest and most profound fiscal crises, the electorate of both districts must be proud that both took time out from dealing with their constituents' very real problems to hail the 'President' of a nation that under international law and the norms of statehood does not, in reality, exist.

Chapter Thirty-Four

Swearing In

The spirit of democracy cannot be imposed from without. It has to come from within.
— Mahatma Gandhi, Indian philosopher

In October 2008, Ilham was inaugurated for his second term as President of the Republic of Azerbaijan. He expressed his gratitude to Azerbaijani people for their confidence, to his New Azerbaijan Party and his rivals, who had offered their congratulations after the election result was announced. But there was a serious message to his address. He offered a synopsis of work completed during his first term, before going in to underline that Nagorno-Karabakh would remain his administration's top priority and that negotiations would only go ahead within the framework of Azerbaijan's territorial integrity. On a wider note, he highlighted a continuation of the policies of his predecessor and promised a raft of new policies and initiatives in the economy, the military and social development of the country.

Ilham's speech was the culmination of a lively election campaign, a seminal poll that would hone the shape of Azerbaijan for generations to come. Assessing the actual election, a U.S. Congress report published on October 27, 2008, stated.

In anticipation of the 2008 Presidential race, changes to the electoral code were approved by the legislature in June 2008. Some of the amendments had been recommended by the Venice Commission, an advisory body of the Council of Europe. However, other Venice Commission recommendations were not enacted…

In late June, Azerbaijan's Central Election Commission (CEC) announced that media campaigning would be permitted for less than one month before the election, which critics termed too short a time for candidates to present their platforms…

…Campaigning was low-key. Campaign posters could be displayed only in designated sites. Public television devoted three hours a week of free air time for the candidates, and there was scant paid political advertising…

…Despite media reports that the election had failed to interest the public, the CEC reported that more people had voted (75.1 per cent of 4.93 million registered voters) than in 2003, when the turnout was 71.2 per cent. Incumbent President Aliyev won a resounding victory, gaining nearly 89 per cent of the vote. The remaining six candidates each received about one per cent to three per cent of the vote, with Agazada coming in a distant second place with a little over 100,000 votes. Hasanguliyev and Hajiyev gained slightly more votes than when they ran in 2003.

…According to a preliminary report by election monitors from OSCE/ODIHR, the Parliamentary Assembly of the Council of Europe (PACE), and the European Parliament, the election "marked considerable progress towards meeting OSCE and Council of Europe commitments and other international standards but did not meet all… the

> *principles of a meaningful and pluralistic democratic election." The observers commended a peaceful voting process that was "well organised and efficient," but were critical of a "lack of robust competition and of vibrant political discourse facilitated by media," and the decision by some opposition parties to boycott.*

The election was observed by more than 500 international observers, mostly from the Organisation for Security and Cooperation in Europe. The OSCE reported that there was progress in the elections compared to the past, yet stated that it did not meet international standards because of the lack of competition to the incumbent.

NATO Secretary General, Jaap de Hoop Scheffer commented: "I welcome reports from the international election observers from OSCE, Council of Europe and the European Parliament indicating progress in the conduct of Azerbaijan's Presidential Elections on October 15, 2008. Azerbaijan should build on this achievement and address the remaining shortcomings that were noted. Azerbaijan is a long-standing and valuable partner of the alliance and we look forward to continuing and strengthening our dialogue and practical cooperation, and our support to reforms."

U.S. Deputy Secretary of State, John Negroponte, told journalists that over the past two years Azerbaijan had gained significant achievements in democratic reforms. The last word on the election can go to *Al Jazeera*, which interviewed Sona Azimova, a pensioner in Baku, who told the channel that she voted for Ilham because he "is the only one who helps and thinks about the people."

A total of 3,232,259 voters cast their votes for Ilham, roughly the same number of persons as the population of Sydney, Singapore, Casablanca, Berlin and Ankara.

"It is humbling. I don't think it's possible to consider so many of your countrymen putting their faith in you and not feel so," says Ilham. "It would be enormously arrogant not to understand that the Presidency is a mandate that is given by the people. You have to deliver. You have to serve."

"The morning after the election I got a call from the Presidential Administration.

I assumed the President wished to touch on what happened," says Natig Aliyev. "We talked about our policy over an upcoming contract and a few other issues, but he said nothing about what had happened the previous day. So I asked him."

Only hours after it had been confirmed that he had been re-elected, Ilham replied with a business-like: "Yes, it was good… So come back to me on the contract…" With that, the call was over. "It was time for us to move on," says Ilham. One month earlier Lehman Brothers had filed for Chapter 11 bankruptcy protection, the largest bankruptcy in American history. Immediately following the filing an already distressed financial market began a period of extreme volatility and the world suffered what many have called the "perfect storm" of economic distress factors. Azerbaijan would not suffer the deep economic stresses of the "perfect storm," but she would be affected within the global downturn, yet to this backdrop the nation's many challenges remained.

In April 2009 the *World Bank* reported:

> *Despite the fact that poverty has significantly dropped during 2003-2006 (from 39.7 to 20.8 per cent) it continues to be one of the challenges for Azerbaijan. At the same time, access to electricity*

> *and natural gas supply and safe water and sanitation have been improved, and schools and health facilities are being refurbished and equipped. While the government is making efforts to reach the entire country, improvements in living standards have been most notable in the capital city of Baku, with rural areas and especially secondary cities trailing behind.*

"I love my job," says Ilham. "Every day there are decisions to make, and policies to forge, that will change people's lives and improve Azerbaijan. There is nothing more satisfying than that."

Chapter Thirty-Five

Cloudy Summits of our Time

We have not wings we cannot soar; but, we have feet to scale and climb, by slow degrees, by more and more, the cloudy summits of our time.
— Henry Wadsworth Longfellow, American poet

On October 25, 2008, Ilham began his second term as President of Azerbaijan. Perhaps only he knew the ambitious agenda that lay before the government. But one thing he was sure of was that he now had the Political Capital to achieve it.

There once was a time when people used the phrase Political Capital to mean a nation's seat of government. In more modern parlance 'Political Capital' means the power that popularity confers on a politician and defines how he utilises this.

It is an indispensable cliché. Yet also a truism. A politician spends his Political Capital. He gains more by pursuing popular policies, achieving success with initiatives, performing favours for other politicians. But then Political Capital must be spent to be useful, for example in attempts to promote unpopular, yet often necessary policies. One modern example can be defined through the case of Barack Obama, who won the U.S. Presidency roughly a month after his Azerbaijani counterpart. Obama moved to the White House with tremendous Political Capital and chose to invest a lot of this in a bruising battle over healthcare reforms.

On October 30, 2008, *Voice of America* reported:

> *...But whatever the shortcomings of the election, President Aliyev enjoys enormous popularity in his own country, according to Paul Goble, Director of Research and Publications at the Azerbaijan Diplomatic Academy in Baku. Speaking with host Judith Latham of VOA News Now's International Press Club, Goble says, even if the election had been fully free and fair with all the major parties taking part, the Azerbaijani President would still have been re-elected with a significant majority.*
>
> *...Paul Goble says that stability has been an important factor in one of the most dangerous and unstable parts of the world. A key reason is Azerbaijan's strategic position on the pipeline carrying crude oil from the Caspian Sea through Georgia and Turkey. Goble notes that Azerbaijan sits at a unique juncture of a north-south, and an east-west, axis of influence. Therefore, he says, Azerbaijan almost has to pursue what President Aliyev has called a "balanced" foreign policy, taking into account the views of Russia, Iran, Central Asia, Turkey, Europe and the United States...*

Unarguably the biggest use of Political Capital in the first year of Ilham's second term would be a move to amend Azerbaijan's constitution to remove Presidential term limits. The issue was first raised in the Milli Majlis, where the assembly voted and overwhelmingly found the idea appealing.

In late December, Azerbaijan's Parliament passed a bill to hold a referendum on March 18 to amend the Constitution. According to Article 152, the Constitution can only be amended via referendum.

On December 24, the Constitutional Court ruled in favour of the legality of the referendum, after which the Milli Majlis voted 100 to seven to hold a referendum on March 18.

Term limits are increasingly an issue that is being debated in many parts of the world, while other nations already have no limit at all. In recent years there has been an increasing movement to removing term limits. In January 2009 voters in Bolivia approved a new constitution that gave President Evo Morales a shot at remaining in office through to 2014.

There are no term limits in Britain, where Margaret Thatcher served as Prime Minister from 1979 to 1990 and Tony Blair from 1997 till 2007. Other major nations without term limits include India, Japan, Singapore, Germany, Australia and Canada.

The President of the European Union Commission serves a renewable five-year term.

Other nations are very strict. The President of the Philippines gets one six-year term, the President of South Korea one five-year term. In France, the President may serve for two terms of up to seven years each. Article 16 of the Republic's constitution allows the President a limited form of rule by decree for a limited period of time in exceptional circumstance. This has been used only once, by Charles de Gaulle during the Algerian War.

In America, the Constitution's 22nd Amendment prohibits a President from being elected to more than two terms in office. Yet as late as 2009 the House Committee on the Judiciary considered a bill that would repeal the 22nd Amendment. In the past, Dwight Eisenhower, Bill Clinton and Ronald Reagan were all on record of being critical of the 22nd Amendment. Prior to Franklin Roosevelt, Presidents honoured the precedent established by George Washington, who — though widely popular — refused to run for a third term of office. Thomas Jefferson not only affirmed this but foresaw the 22nd Amendment.

Yet in 1807 Thomas Jefferson warned that Presidents not bound by term limits could use their popularity and power to become kings. "If some termination to the services of the chief magistrate be not fixed by the Constitution or supplied in practice," Jefferson wrote to the Legislature of Vermont, "his office, nominally for years, will in fact become for life; and history shows how easily that degenerates into an inheritance."

Two centuries after Jefferson, the subject of inheritance and the Presidency of Azerbaijan had been well-aired, particularly abroad. Yet this had receded during post-2003 years of economic growth, job creation and stability. Instead, Jefferson's definition of inheritance was now to the fore, that the Presidency belongs to a single individual.

But in Azerbaijan there appeared to be general consensus that Ilham was the man for the job. When this issue appeared on the radar there was no great outcry. The people, in general, seemed to want him to see through his programme and therefore there was no large-scale movement against the issue.

Adds Ali Hasanov, Deputy Prime Minister, Chairman of State Committee for Refugees & IDPs: "Lest we forget, that the people of Azerbaijan have suffered as much as any from political instability and intrigues, which paralysed the country prior to the return of Heydar Aliyev."

If one accepts that premise, then the 'Aliyev brand' remains potent among ordinary people. Heydar Aliyev brought stability, ended civil war, and ushered in the prospect of modernity and economic progress. Ilham delivered on the latter.

The election several months earlier indicated that the 'Aliyev brand' represented what they wanted. The government, and the President, were willing to invest Political Capital in the assumption that the people of the country would not wish to see the brand disappear.

In the event, surprisingly the referendum went without much fuss considering the importance of the subject.

Half a year after the poll, Ilham states: "Azerbaijan has so far to go, there is so much work for me to do. I have no intention of being President-for-Life. That has no appeal to me. I'm not here for power. I'm here to complete my programme."

He also discounts the Aliyev name coming to represent for Azerbaijan what the Bushs or Kennedys do to the United States, the Gandhis for India or the Bandaranaikes in Sri Lanka. When it is suggested that son Heydar Jr may one day go into politics he frowns and shakes his head. "I won't encourage that," he says. "It is a tough career. I would rather he takes a different path."

But controversy was always apparent, not helped by an opposition which spent more time stoking up opinion abroad than trying to win over the electorate in Azerbaijan. Bainbridge Colby, Woodrow Wilson's last Secretary of State, stated that: "An intelligent and conscientious opposition is a part of loyalty to country." Many in Baku considered their opposition to be shirking this responsibility.

During the pre-referendum period 17 groups opposed to scrapping term limits registered with the Central Election Commission.

One human rights activist claims that "hundreds" of other people were arrested nationwide during this period, a figure that was widely touted. Yet the Interior Ministry challenged this, asking for relatives of these hundreds to come forward, confirming two arrests, a pair of Popular Front activists in Sabiradad.

In the positive column for the referendum was the use of technology. The Central Election Commission had dabbled with webcams in polling stations during the Presidential poll, used to monitor voting, and rolled out a bigger programme for the referendum.

Opposition leaders claimed that they suspected the timing reflected government concerns that plunging oil prices and economic troubles could damage its popular support and weaken its grip, but the public at large seemed not to consider this. On March 19 the Central Election Commission reported 92 per cent of voters approved the measure, with 71 per cent turnout, overwhelmingly choosing to scrap Presidential term limits. Official turnout of a minimum of 25 per cent was required to make the referendum count, and each proposed change required a simple majority of votes cast. International reaction was generally warm.

The *Associated Press* reported:

> *President Barack Obama telephoned Azerbaijan's President on Tuesday and told Ilham Aliyev the United States is committed to a strong relationship with the oil-rich former Soviet Republic. The White House said Obama expressed support for resolution of*

Azerbaijan's dispute with neighbouring Armenia over an Armenian-dominated enclave, Nagorno-Karabakh, within Azerbaijan.

For Ilham himself, who had seemed to remain somewhat distant from the referendum personally, again it was a case of business as usual. Like in the wake of the Presidential Election, which he had stormed, by a similar margin, the lack of serious opposition at the ballot box meant that there was little surprise in the result.

"Two national ballots in five months had been a necessary distraction," says Hasanov. "The President was now determined to get on with the job as 2009 would represent a busy and decisive year."

If, as the opposition had claimed, Azerbaijan's economy was set to be rattled by the global economic downturn, then unflinching management of the economy was the order of the day. The country had been run prudently before the global economy slid into recession. This reflected in confidence. According to Moody's Investment Service in August 2009:

...At Ba1, Azerbaijan's credit rating is the highest level in the noninvestment-grade range. According to Moody's sovereign bond methodology, this reflects the combination of low GDP per capita and weak institutional strength set against "very high" government financial strength and "low" susceptibility to event risk.

The global economy will most likely contract for the first time since World War Two, and recovery will take longer than expected, said the International Monetary Fund.

"Never before in modern times has so much of the world been simultaneously hit by a confluence of economic and financial turmoil such as we are now living through," said Treasury Secretary, Timothy F. Geithner in a speech before the Economic Club of Washington.

Much of Azerbaijan's high economic growth can be attributed to large and growing oil exports, but the non-energy sector also featured double-digit growth in 2008, spurred by growth in the construction, banking and real estate sectors. However, the global economic slowdown presents some challenges for the Azerbaijani economy as oil prices have softened and local banks face a more uncertain international financial environment.

Despite these issues, the government announced that it would not be adjusting its 2009 budget. The budget received 98.9 per cent of targeted revenue in the first two months of 2009, leaving the projected surplus in place. It is not uncommon for an administration having won re-election to pull back from its commitments, citing new developments in the national, regional or international economy. The global downturn presented a ready-made excuse.

"Perhaps we should have retreated," says Ilham. "But when economists give their advice they don't have to do my job. They don't have to look people in the eye, those who don't have the income, or lifestyle, that an economist may command."

He had reported that the poverty level had declined to 13.2 per cent in 2008, down from a historic high of 49 per cent in 2003 (This would drop to 9.1 per cent at the end of 2010).

"Taken at face value, 13.2 per cent is a great achievement. We were happy," he says. "But that is just over an eighth of

the population. I will never accept that."
To that end, minimum wage payments and pensions were increased by 50 per cent in 2008, driving the average monthly wage to $335, while the monthly pensions average $120. Government statistics showed 839,890 new jobs were being created, between the fourth quarter of 2003 and the end of 2009.
Radical economic reforms in Azerbaijan were aimed both at strengthening the country's economic potential and, first and foremost, at improving living standards. It was working. The World Bank had projected that Azerbaijan would lead CIS and European countries in 2009 in GDP growth rates, pegging Azerbaijan's at 10.4 per cent, while Russia's would be three per cent, Turkey 1.7 per cent and Kazakhstan 1.9 per cent. The World Bank also projected Azerbaijan would head international GDP growth in 2010.
One initiative that was ring-fenced above all others in the President's agenda was the country's groundbreaking People's Computer Project. Microsoft and HP, the Ministry of Communication and Information Technology and Ministry of Education signed a protocol on April 10 that created the People's Computer Project. This had the aim to improve socially disadvantaged people's computer knowledge and to extend the use of information-communication technologies. The project will support development of the information society of Azerbaijan.
By the middle of the year, pilot projects were rolled out in selected areas. This was unarguably the most dramatic IT project ever undertaken in Azerbaijan. It is also the biggest and will eventually become a profoundly socio-transformational programme. The programme would provide vastly discounted notebooks and computers, with

interest free finance agreements over 12 months where necessary. Software for the project was secured on licence from Microsoft.

The project began with a first phase that was estimated would encompass 5,000 notebooks and computers. But within a few weeks it had attracted 3,000 applications just from teachers, quite aside from all the other groups that the President wished to see encompassed within the programme.

The first stage considered teachers, and would be extended to include students, health sector employees, government officials, among others…

The domestic agenda of the early part of 2009 gave way to a summer of diplomacy. Ilham attended the Eastern Partnership Summit of the European Union in May, an event bringing together heads of state and government of the EU and Eastern Partnership initiative member countries. Opened by Czech Prime Minister Mirek Topolane, Ilham stressed the programme will give impetus to developing and expanding Azerbaijan-EU relations, saying that Azerbaijan's political and economic progress and democratic reforms serve to bring the country closer to the European family.

But undoubtedly the highlight of the event was the signing of an $11.4 billion deal for the Nabucco project, a 3,300 kilometre pipeline that will eventually pump gas from Azerbaijan to Europe, via Turkey. Delays in securing start-up funding and political agreement mean that Nabucco will not be ready until 2015.

Gazprom, the state-owned Russian company, had done a deal for 50 billion cubic metres of Azerbaijan's gas from its Shah Deniz reserve that would flow into Moscow's $10 billion South Stream pipeline. But, from a European angle,

Nabucco would open fresh markets from the vast reserves that the nation possesses.

Nabucco was conceived to diversify Europe's gas supply after Russia turned off the taps during the winter of 2006 in a dispute with Ukraine, through which the gas flows. With a capacity of 31 billion cubic metres a year it would supply only five to ten per cent of EU demand, but it would break the supply monopoly.

José Manuel Barroso, the European Commission President, said: "The Nabucco project is of crucial importance for Europe's energy security and its policy of diversification of gas supplies and transport routes."

At the end of April 2009, Ilham was also in Belgium. Azerbaijan's integration into the Euro-Atlantic political, security and economic institutes began in May 1994 when Heydar Aliyev signed the NATO 'Partnership for Peace' (PfP) framework document at a formal meeting of the North Atlantic Council, while a Partnership and Cooperation Agreement (PCA) between the EU and Azerbaijan was signed in April 1996. The PCA governed political, economic and trade relations and lay the basis for social, financial, scientific, technological and cultural cooperation.

Heydar met with EU Foreign Ministers in Luxembourg in June 1999 to mark the beginning of the PCA on July 1 the same year. The first cooperation council meeting between the EU and Azerbaijan took place in October 1999.

Azerbaijan became a member of the Council of Europe in January 2001 and in June 2004 Azerbaijan was party to a European Neighbourhood Policy (ENP) agreement which set ambitious objectives for partnership with countries neighbouring the EU's borders.

On April 29, 2009, almost 15 years to the day after his father, the former President, Ilham made his first visit to the headquarters of the North Atlantic Treaty Organisation. The first NATO Secretary General, Lord Ismay, famously stated the organisation's goal was "to keep the Russians out, the Americans in, and the Germans down." But much had changed since NATO's founding on April 4, 1949, hardly more than half a century to the day before Ilham arrived in Belgium.

"NATO is important to Azerbaijan and we will continue to forge close relations with the organisation, as we would any major regional organisation," says Ilham. "It is natural for any member state within the world community to play a role in regional and international affairs and we have moved to integrate with a variety of Europe-Atlantic structures.

"I'm proud that Azerbaijani soldiers have served well within some of the modern era's most important international policing and peace-keeping efforts."

Azerbaijan had begun to play a role within the international community through its Armed Forces' participation in some of the world's hot spots. In 2008 Azerbaijan recalled its peacekeepers from Kosovo after the region's self-proclamation of independence, Azerbaijani soldiers having served there since September 1999. Azerbaijani soldiers also played a limited role within Multinational Forces in Iraq after 2003, particularly noted for guarding the key Haditha reservoir and a hydropower plant in troubled al-Anbar province, while soldiers also served within the forces that attempted to bring order to Afghanistan after 2003.

"We attach great significance to cooperation with Azerbaijan," said the then Secretary General of NATO Jaap de Hoop Schaffer during his meeting with Ilham, while adding that the 28-state group considers Azerbaijan an important partner in the region.

Besides high-profile appearances in Brussels and Prague, attention in Baku was being drawn towards the Russian city of Saint Petersburg. Russian President Dmitry Medvedev's administration was focusing on the upcoming Saint Petersburg International Economic Forum. This represented the main economic summit of Russia and the Commonwealth of Independent States, a new organisational form of integration for the CIS members. The Forum and its activity gave a powerful impulse to re-establishment of once broken economic relations and establishing of new connections.

But on this occasion the Kremlin was also planning a significant extension of its reach. The Presidents of Azerbaijan and Armenia were due in Saint Petersburg in June. Tri-partite talks were scheduled. It would take a strong embrace to draw progress in the Nagorno-Karabakh issue which, after the high hopes of Paris in 2007, had stumbled into a gloomy pattern of stalled talks and worsening relations.

In March 2008 Armenian and Azerbaijani forces exchanged fire for hours along the ceasefire line in the worst fighting for years, leading to deaths on both sides.

For Azerbaijan there were a couple of diplomatic successes. Meeting on the occasion of the 90th anniversary of the Azerbaijani Parliament, the first came when the speakers of the Parliaments of Belarus, Georgia, Kazakhstan, Pakistan, Poland, Moldova, Romania and other countries expressed their support for Azerbaijan's stance. Later in the year, addressing the Turkish Grand National Assembly, Ilham received a standing ovation when he reiterated that a solution needed to be found within the framework of Azerbaijan's territorial integrity.

In November 2008, the Presidents of Russia, Armenia and Azerbaijan signed a joint declaration on the peaceful settlement of the territorial dispute over Nagorno-Karabakh, pledged to improve the situation and affirmed the importance of OSCE mediation. The leaders agreed that "the peaceful settlement should be accompanied by legally binding international guarantees of all aspects and stages", the document read. This led to another meeting under a cloud of apparent optimism. Sitting together in Zurich talks ended with no breakthrough on a two-decade-old conflict, but agreement to meet again on the sidelines of the World Economic Forum in Davos. Commenting on United Nations' concern *The Associated Press* reported:

> *Washington and Moscow appear newly energised to push for peace across the energy-rich Caucasus after Georgia's war with Russia in August underlined the need to settle other regional conflicts through talks instead of weaponry... After Wednesday's talks in Zurich, however, Azerbaijani Presidential Spokesman Azer Gasymov said: "There were no breakthroughs, just discussion of the different difficult issues."... The Armenian President's press service called the meeting "constructive and positive" but gave no details.*
>
> *More than a decade of international mediation efforts led by the United States, Russia and France, under the Organisation for Security and Cooperation in Europe, has failed to reach a lasting peace. Sporadic clashes have continued, including one Monday night that left at least two Armenians dead in the first such violence in the past few months.*

Yet despite these meetings 2009 remained very much on the same course as the predecessor. On March 26 and 27 a series of fire-fights erupted in the Tovuz region and Balajafarli and Giziljahanli villages in Gazakh region. No casualties were reported, but the Defence Ministry in Baku reported that the Armenian Armed Forces violated the ceasefire.

In May, the two Presidents met again and according to U.S. officials made "serious progress" at the residence of the U.S. Ambassador in Prague. U.S. Secretary of State, Hillary Rodham Clinton, was said to be encouraging a resolution.

In June Minister of Foreign Affairs, Elmar Mammadyarov, met with his Armenian counterpart, Edward Nalbandian, in Paris along with OSCE Minsk group co-chairs. No major progress was noted, yet the Leningrad State University graduate Medvedev was preparing to launch a concerted effort at Saint Petersburg 2009.

On June 4, Ilham met his Armenian counterpart, in a meeting also attended by Mammadyarov and Edward Nalbandian and co-chairs of the OSCE Minsk Group, Ambassadors Matthew Bryza of the United States, Bernard Fassier of France and Yury Merzlyakov of Russia. This led to a further meeting, again in Moscow, in mid-July, but again things stalled. While Armenian Foreign Ministry spokesman Tigran Balaian called the meetings "constructive," Mammadyarov said that the meeting "brought no progress."

"It is frustrating, yes," says Ilham. "We go into every bilateral meeting with low-expectations, yet hoping that this will be the one, this will be the meeting where the Armenian side shows goodwill and that we can move forward towards a serious, comprehensive end.

"I personally will go to enormous lengths to achieve a lasting end to the illegal Nagorno-Karabakh occupation. Time after time our hopes have been dashed.

"Patience can only last for so long."

Chapter Thirty-Six

Blue Waters and Beyond

Never let the future disturb you. You will meet it,
if you have to, with the same weapons of reason
which today arm you against the present.
— Marcus Aurelius, Roman statesman

The year 2011 will see something of a shift in mankind's understanding of the Universe. Sometime later this year, a consortium led by IBM will go live with Blue Waters, one of the most powerful supercomputers in the world and with a peak performance of 10 petaflops (10 quadrillion calculations every second).

Nearly four times faster than IBM's Blue Gene/L, Blue Waters will be capable of changing the way we understand the Universe. Using this petascale supercomputer scientists will, for example, be able to predict the behaviour of complex biological systems and grasp how the cosmos evolved after the Big Bang. Blue Waters will allow the design of new materials at an atomic level, and allow us to prevent disasters like that which struck Japan on March 11, 2011, by predicting the behaviour of hurricanes and tornadoes and even helping formulate models to help us predict earthquakes before they occur.

When the President of Azerbaijan was born — in 1961 — the computer was in its infancy. In 1961 the first commercially available integrated circuits (microchips) went on the market for the first time. Texas Instruments initially used the chips in Air Force computers. They later used the chips to produce the first electronic portable calculators. Integrated circuits are used in virtually all electronic equipment today.

In half a century humankind has come a long way. Yet, as the great Albert Einstein warned, "It has become appallingly obvious that our technology has exceeded our humanity."

Prior to the emergence of nations, war consisted of small-scale raiding among tribes and settlements. With the advent of formal states, some 5,000 years ago, organised military activity also began. Innovations like gunpowder and 20th century technological advances served to increase the body count.

Author Conway W. Henderson states that: "One source claims 14,500 wars have taken place between 3500 BC and the late 20th century, costing 3.5 billion lives, leaving only 300 years of peace."

In these horrific terms we, in part, have also used that progress to regress.

In his seminal book, *Why Nations Go to War*, author John G. Stoessinger states that the rationale for starting a conflict depends on an overly optimistic assessment of the outcome of hostilities, both in terms of human casualties and financial costs, and on misperceptions of the enemy's intentions.

In 2011, the same year that mankind as a whole will see a leap forward with the Blue Waters, Azerbaijan remains a troubling microcosm of mankind's struggle with itself — a nation evolving, pursuing social and economic progress, yet one weighed down by the shadow of war.

The occupation of 20 per cent of Azerbaijan's internationally recognised land by a foreign force, and the stagnation of efforts to resolve the issue, hangs over Azerbaijan and its President.

Prominent psychologists, most notably John Bowlby, argued that humans are inherently violent and that our aggressiveness is heightened by displacement and projection where a person transfers their grievances into bias and hatred against other races, religions, nations or ideologies. In history there are many examples, in contemporary times perhaps best illustrated by Nazism and the Jews. But such clouded collective thinking is far too common in the 21st century. Armenia's pursuance of Nagorno-Karabakh being a fine example. Says Ilham:

> *Azerbaijan is committed to peace, and the main proof of my words is that we have been negotiating for almost 20 years already. The OSCE Minsk Group was created in 1992. In 1994 it was decided on a ceasefire and, since then, negotiations have been held. Unfortunately, they have been ineffective. Therefore, the first thing we hope for is that the peace talks will promote settlement, which is why we are active in the negotiating process. Of course, a settlement must be based on the norms and principles of international law, since there cannot be any other basis.*
>
> *...The resolutions of the Security Council, four resolutions, also prove this thesis, along with the resolutions and decisions of other international organisations. So if the Armenian side adopts a constructive stance and fully understands and accepts the thesis about the impossibility of the independence of Nagorno Karabakh, we will move forward...*

While the ceasefire continues, for now, and war remains entirely possible, Azerbaijan pursues the same progress that has taken mankind from the invention of the integrated circuit to Blue Waters. But whereas computers took 50 years to get to a petascale supercomputer, Azerbaijan has significantly less time to bring its people from its post-Soviet stupor and into the 21st century.

It is a generational task that must be completed in a single Presidency in order to bring the nation into the Developed World. But an exercise in which the nation is succeeding.

Over 4,000 hospitals and health clinics have been built in the past six to seven years. By the end of 2012 all villages in Azerbaijan, even in previously remote areas, will be linked to the national gas network. In 2011, a plethora of fresh economic indicators show a nation heading in the right direction. Unemployment was down to a historic low of 5.9 per cent from 9.7 per cent the year Ilham became President.

During the same 2003-2010 period, the average monthly salary rose by 322 per cent, the percentage of the population living in poverty dropped from 40.2 per cent to 9.1 per cent, while old age pensions rose by 367 per cent. Perhaps best of all, given the liquidity and banking crisis that gripped the rest of the world, one of the most telling figures is the combined savings of Azerbaijanis which grew by 1,100 per cent between 2003 and 2010.

The global financial crisis of 2008-2009 is quite probably the worst economic crisis since the Great Depression of the 1930s. When a vast liquidity shortfall in the United States banking system resulted in the collapse of several large financial institutions, repercussions were pronounced throughout the world. This crisis undermined the international economy, led to the failure of major corporations and in preventing a collapse there were substantial financial commitments incurred by governments in bailing out banks and other major pillars of the economy. Despite this there was a significant decline in economic activity. Worldwide, GDP began contracting in the third quarter of 2008 and by early 2009 was falling at an annualised pace not witnessed since the 1950s.

But while governments around the world struggled with the effects of the crisis and multi-millionaire bankers rushed for cover, it was the human cost that was most pronounced. Hundreds of millions of people were made unemployed worldwide.

Countries across the globe rushed to shore up their economies and prevent a slide into a biting recession. One of the few to succeed in that illusive task was Azerbaijan, whose estimated growth rate for 2009 and 2010 was 15 per cent, despite an IMF prediction that a recession-led 10 per cent decline in the oil sector would cause a significant narrowing in growth.

Azerbaijan's rebuffing the worst global economic crisis for eight decades did not come about by accident. The country's President says:

> *The right choice of strategy and programmes helped us to diversify the economy drastically… the 9.3 per cent economic growth in 2009 was much more important for me than the 25 to 30 per cent in previous years, since it was amidst the crisis, when oil prices fell four-fold and our economy was mostly oriented towards the energy sector.*
>
> *Therefore, this showed that our reforms promoted other economic sectors too. In the past seven years we have created more than 900,000 new jobs. The poverty*

level has been reduced from almost 50 per cent to 9 per cent. All social programmes have been carried out. Over half a million Azerbaijani citizens receive monthly social benefits from the state. Naturally, the average monthly salary is already more than $400, and this is not the limit. We have managed to do a great deal in the regions. We have been implementing the regional development programme since 2004-infrastructure, social infrastructure, roads, power stations — so that people live in the regions and do not migrate to Baku or other countries. And I must say that this process of internal migration has almost reached zero.

...We are always looking forward, probably, a few steps forward, though we have great oil and gas reserves and we earn a great deal of money. We want the stable development of Azerbaijan not to depend on the oil price or volume that we produce.

The transformation of oil into human capital became not merely a slogan, but reality in our case... It is most important that we did not stop halfway. Our huge oil revenues did not make us relax, we did not become complacent. I have repeatedly said; 'we must work as if we had neither oil nor gas, because the greatest achievements have been made by countries that don't have these resources. They were obliged to look for other spheres, they were obliged to mobilise human resources, technological progress; the talent of the people developed these countries.

The theory of Human Capital has its roots in the work of British economists Sir William Petty and Adam Smith. The work of John Locke, not to mention social theorist

Karl Marx, furthered understanding that while expenditure on education is costly, for governments and employers, it should be considered an investment.

Over 2,000 schools have opened during the last seven years, while there are 36 state-run and 16 private universities. The Azerbaijan Ministry of Education states that during the 2009/2010 scholastic year there were 1,635 pre-schools with 107,954 students, 4,546 primary schools with 1,367,888 students, 108 vocational schools with 25,604 students, 61 secondary schools with 52,765 students and 52 universities with 139,194 students. Universities employ 11,566 professors and 12,616 faculty members in Azerbaijan.

With a 2010 population estimate of 9,047,000 for Azerbaijan, these 1.7 million students represent nearly a fifth of the national population in full time education. Quite an investment in Human Capital, and this would be backed up by 2011's 'State Programme on Azerbaijani Youth', a unique scheme formulated through public consultation. In April, a Presidential Degree gave his administration just two months to come up with a comprehensive framework. In a meeting with representatives drawn from youth organisations Ilham stated: "…A lot has been done recently to tackle unemployment; one hundred thousand jobs have been created and new enterprises have started. There is, however, still unemployment; this is of concern to us and we have to be even more active in reducing the problem."

In what became arguably the biggest process of public consultation ever held in Azerbaijan, over ensuing months the Presidential Administration received over 2,000 suggestions from the general public, related organisations and NGOs. Many were eventually adopted into the project.

By July a framework was created, and the President approved a progressive social programme that will run between 2011 and 2015, offering thousands of social, educational and employment opportunities to young people across the country.

Each year since 1990 the Human Development Report has published the Human Development Index (HDI), introduced as an alternative to conventional measures of national development, such as level of income and the rate of economic growth. The HDI represents a push for a broader definition of well-being and provides a composite measure of three basic dimensions of human development: health, education and income. Azerbaijan's HDI is 0.713, which gives the country a rank of 67 out of 169 countries with comparable data.

Azerbaijan made the highest advance of any country in the world in the period 2005 to 2010, standing at 101st in 2005 and moving up to the 67th in 2010. Azerbaijan has been leading the former Soviet Union state with an average annual HDI growth rate of 1.77 in the decade to 2010. To put in a broader perspective, the corresponding figures for two global high performers, China and India, are 1.57 and 1.66 respectively.

In governmental terminology around the world the word "happiness" is surprisingly rare. In the tiny Himalayan Kingdom of Bhutan, happiness is codified and the phrase "Gross National Happiness" (GNH) is common in official documents. It is a theme that is gaining traction, with British Prime Minster David Cameron announcing that his government takes a quarterly "happiness" survey.

One drag on people's lives was corruption, something which the government has begun to tackle. In 2011 Ilham personally launched a rolling anti-corruption campaign that has already yielded positive results. The campaign has reportedly led to the dismissal of several officials.

On February 28, 2011, *AFP* reported:

> *Azerbaijan on Friday urged its citizens to use an anti-corruption website as part of a high-profile campaign to combat graft that has seen dozens of officials sacked in recent weeks. The site, rusum.az, which helps people to work out what they should be paying in taxes, customs duties and fines, and to report any official violations, was originally launched last year but is now being widely promoted by the country's anti-corruption commission.*
>
> *"Such sites create conditions for citizens to better know their rights," Inam Karimov, a chief advisor at the commission, told AFP. "It's necessary to convey the essence of these laws (governing payments and fines) to citizens in simple language," he said.*
>
> *Azerbaijani authorities have stepped up their anti-graft campaign after President Ilham Aliyev demanded action last month, when he noted that corruption and bribery were "damaging Azerbaijan's business reputation."*

Across the world there are too many nations blessed with rich natural resources and a hard-working entrepreneurial population, but cursed by officials focused solely upon self-enrichment. As Azerbaijan grew increasingly wealthy, defending the integrity of the nation grew more important. The 2011 initiative became even more vital given an announcement in late 2010 that Azerbaijan's already impressive array of natural wealth jewels had grown.

SOCAR announced the discovery of a huge gas field named Umid, in the Azerbaijani section of the Caspian Sea. This would be the second largest gas field in Azerbaijan after the massive Shah Deniz field. Umid's hydrocarbon reserves are estimated at least 200 billion cubic metres of gas and 30 million tonnes of gas condensate, although this may prove conservative, and a second exploratory well was underway. Experts said that the value of this find was around $45 billion.

But as Ilham observed: "I remember preliminary results about reserves stored in Azeri-Chirag-Guneshli field showed 511 million tonnes of oil. At that time, I was a bit surprised why 511 million tonnes? How it is possible to say so exactly?

"But, then further development showed that the reserves of Azeri-Chirag-Guneshli field were not 511 million tonnes, but over one billion tonnes. Over one billion. So one can perhaps suppose that this figure will rise to 1.5 billion or even higher. Time will tell. Nobody can know for sure."

There was more in September 2011, when another find was announced, this time in the Absheron field. Absheron had been discovered by Azerbaijani geologists in the 1960s, but sea depth and other technical issues had led to Absheron being abandoned by foreign firms. By 2011, a joint project between SOCAR and Total led to a find of some 350 billion cubic metres of gas and 45 million cubic metres of condensate. This meant that the proven gas reserves had now risen to 2.55 trillion cubic metres.

Said Ilham of this second find: "Azerbaijan was traditionally famous as an oil country. Today Azerbaijan is important for the world as a gas exporting country. We use these opportunities effectively. We have many plans."

Umid and Absheron would underscore a growing national confidence in the present and future of Azerbaijan. Yet if Umid and Absheron would be an additional source of national pride, perhaps there is no more public interpretation of modern Azerbaijan than National Flag Square. Opened during a grandiose ceremony by the President on September 1, 2010, amid a flurry of coverage on world television channels, the site boasts a 162 metre tall flagpole, confirmed by the *Guinness Book of Records* as the highest in the world. It was a project first conceptualised by Ilham himself in 2007, one which would be the focal point of a new National Flag Day on November 9 each year.

During an address at the event, Ilham stated: "The establishment of such a magnificent square in our capital Baku is a truly great event. Our flag is a source of our pride. Our flag is our flesh and our heart. The state flag of Azerbaijan is hoisted in all parts of Azerbaijan. After the restoration of Azerbaijan's territorial integrity, our national flag will be hoisted across lands now under occupation. Our national flag will be hoisted in Nagorno-Karabakh, Khankendi and Shusha.

"We must, and we are, making this day nearer through our work."

The restored integrity of Azerbaijan's borders cannot come quickly enough. But while Ilham and his government would continue to seek a solution, they would set about building a 21st century nation. He says: "The period of economic transition is already over in Azerbaijan. We must become one of the developed countries. This task has been set and we will reach it… Azerbaijan has a wonderful international image. Our foreign policy pursues one goal — to secure Azerbaijan's national interests to the maximum extent, to strengthen the Azerbaijani state enabling the people of Azerbaijan to live even better."

This was a message that carried all the way to New York. In October 2011 Azerbaijan was elected as a non-permanent member of the UN Security Council, the sole eastern European seat on the UN's most powerful body. Azerbaijan will sit on the body from January 1, 2012, until the end of 2013.

Welcoming this success and stressing that Azerbaijan would "serve the ideals, peace, security, democracy and justice to which adheres" the nation's President added that: "This is a victory for our nation... Azerbaijan is a reliable partner, a friendly country... this coincides with the 20th anniversary of our independence... It shows that over during the last two decades Azerbaijan has demonstrated itself as a strong independent state..."

Ilham Aliyev at the wheel of a speedboat. The Azerbaijan President was inspecting projects along the Baku coastline.

Ilham Aliyev, Kazakhstan President Nursultan Nazarbayev and Russian President Vladimir Putin share a lighter moment during a regional conference.

President George W. Bush welcomes his Azerbaijani counterpart to the Oval Office.

Baku by night. (above) Ilham Aliyev with a young voter.

Ilham Aliyev and Korean President Roh Moo-hyun during a visit to Seoul in 2007.

Ilham Aliyev poses with Georgian President Mikheil Saakashvili, Turkish Prime Minister Recep Tayyip Erdogan and British Petroleum CEO John Browne on July 13, 2006 to symbolically assemble the last pieces of the Baku-Tbilisi-Ceyhan pipeline.

Azerbaijan's President speaks at the World Economic Forum.

Joining Ilham Aliyev for talks during the GUAM Summit in Baku in June 2007 were Ukrainian President Viktor Yushchenko, Georgian President Mikheil Saakashvili, Polish President Lech Kaczynski and Moldovan Prime Minister Vasile Tarlev. Lithuanian President Valdas Adamkus and Polish President Lech Kaczynski were observers.

Ilham Aliyev reviews plans for a development in Baku.

The Azerbaijani capital of Baku blends traditional architectural styles with 21st century modernity.

Thousands of pro-government supporters rally in Baku on November 10, 2005, to celebrate victory for the New Azerbaijan Party.

Azerbaijan's 162 metre tall flagpole was confirmed by the Guinness Book of Records as the highest in the world, but above this stands as an expression of national pride and confidence in the future.

Ilham Aliyev with U.S. President Barack Obama at a bilateral meeting in New York.

Abbreviations

AAA	Armenian Assembly of America
AD	Anno Domini
AIOC	Azerbaijan International Operating Company
ANC	Azerbaijan National Council
ANCA	Armenian National Committee of America
ANZUS	The Australia, New Zealand, United States Security Treaty
APC	Armoured Personnel Carrier
APFP	Azerbaijan People's Front Party
API	American Petroleum Institute
AT&T	American Telephone & Telegraph
BBC	British Broadcasting Corporation
BC	Before Christ
BP	British Petroleum
BTC	Baku-Tbilisi-Ceyhan pipeline
BTK	Baku-Tbilisi-Kars railway
CBE	Commander of the British Empire
CEC	Central Election Commission
CIS	Commonwealth of Independent States
CoE	Council of Europe
CPSU	Communist Party of the Soviet Union
CV	Curriculum Vitae
DNA	Deoxyribonucleic acid
ENP	European Neighbourhood Policy
EU	European Union
FBI	Federal Bureau of Investigation
FM	Foreign Minister/Frequency Modulation
GDP	Gross Domestic Product
GNP	Gross National Product
ICT	Information and Communication Technologies
IDP	Internally Displaced Person

IFC	International Finance Corporation
IMF	International Monetary Fund
IOC	International Olympic Committee
IPU	Inter-Parliamentary Union
IT	Information Technology
ITC	International Finance Corporation
KGB	Committee for State Security (USSR)
KPMG	Klynveld Peat Marwick Goerdeler
MDGs	Millennium Development Goals
MGIMO	Moscow State Institute of International Relations
MP	Member of Parliament
MRI	Magnetic Resonance Imaging
NATO	North Atlantic Treaty Organisation
NBC	National Broadcasting Company
NGO	Non-Governmental Organisation
NKGB	People's Commissariat for State Security
NOC	National Olympic Committee
OAS	Organisation of American States
ODIHR	Office of Democratic Institutions and Human Rights
OIC	Organisation of the Islamic Conference
OPEC	Organisation of the Petroleum Exporting Countries
OSCE	Organisation for Security and Cooperation in Europe
PACE	Parliamentary Assembly of the Council of Europe
PCA	Partnership and Cooperation Agreement
PfP	Partnership for Peace
Ph.D	Doctor of Philosophy
PSA	Production Sharing Agreement
PWYP	Publish What You Pay
RSFSR	Russian Soviet Federated Socialist Republic
RWB	Reporters Without Borders
SOCAR	State Oil Company of Azerbaijan Republic
SOFAZ	State Oil Fund of Azerbaijan Republic

SWF	Sovereign Wealth Fund
TDP	United States Trade and Development Programme
TSFSR	Transcaucasian Soviet Federated Socialist Republic
UAE	United Arab Emirates
UNDP	United Nations Development Programme
UNESCO	United Nations Educational, Scientific and Cultural Organisation
U.S.A., U.S.	United States of America
USAID	United States Agency for International Development
U.S.S.R.	Union of Soviet Socialist Republics
VOA	Voice of America
WSIS	World Summit on the Information Society
WTO	World Trade Organisation

Glossary

Afshar Empire	Empire state in the southern part of Azerbaijan and Iran
Agh Goyunlu	State in the southern part of Azerbaijan in the 15th century
Ahameni Empire	Rose after the downfall of Midia in 550 BC
Antelope	Even-toed ungulate species found in the family Bovidae
Aotearoa	Maori name for New Zealand, translates to 'Land of the long white cloud'
Apartheid	System or practice that separates people according to race or caste
API gravity	Measure of how heavy petroleum liquid is compared to water
Arabist	Someone normally from outside the Arab World who specialises in the study of the Arabic language, culture and literature
Atabeg	Hereditary title of nobility of Turkic origin
Atropates	Leader from where Azerbaijan is said to have derived its name
Azadlig	Azerbaijani for freedom
Caliph	Spiritual leader claiming succession from the Prophet Muhammad
Caliphate	First system of governance established in Islam
Caspian	Inland sea

Caucasus	Region between the Black and Caspian Seas
Chancellor	Chief minister of state in certain parliamentary governments
Cyrillic	Alphabet used for the Russian language
Czar	Title used to designate certain monarchs or supreme rulers
Dacha	Russian word for seasonal, or year-round second homes
De-Stalinisation	Process of neutralising the influence of Joseph Stalin
Doxophobia	Fear of expressing one's opinion or being praised
Dynasty	Succession of persons belonging to the same family
Embezzlement	Act of dishonestly appropriating or secreting assets
Emir	Title of nobility or office, used throughout the Arab World
Epigram	Brief, clever and usually memorable statement
Feudalism	Decentralised socio-political structure
Gara Goyunlu	State in the southern part of Azerbaijan in 14th and 15th centuries
Glasnost	Policy of publicity, openness and transparency
Gobustan	Area in Azerbaijan
Guano	Natural manure composed chiefly of the excrement of sea birds

Habeas corpus	Allowing appeal against unlawful imprisonment
Homo Sovieticus	Sarcastic reference to people with a mindset created by the governments of the Eastern Bloc
Hormuz	Strategically important waterway in the Gulf
Intransigent	Person who refuses to agree or compromise
Ippon	Japanese for 'one full point'
Jizaya	Head Tax
Karma	Hinduism and Buddhism action seen as bringing upon oneself inevitable results
Khan	Title for a Ruler in Turkic and Mongolian languages
Khazar	Semi-nomadic Turkic people
Kombed	Committee of the Poor
Kon-Tiki	Raft used by Norwegian explorer Thor Heyerdahl
Madrasa	Type of educational institution, whether secular or religious
Magna Carta	Latin words meaning 'Great Charter'
Mamluks	Soldiers of slave origin who had converted to Islam
Manna	Divine or spiritual food
Mercenary	Professional soldier hired by a foreign army
Metrosexual	Heterosexual male with a strong aesthetic sense and/or inordinate interest in appearance and style

Milli Majlis	Azerbaijani national assembly (parliament)
Moniker	Nickname, stage name or pseudonym
Musket	Muzzle-loaded, smooth bore long gun
Myrrh	Reddish-brown resinous material, dried sap of a number of trees
Nakhchivan	Landlocked exclave of Azerbaijan
Oghuz Turks	Group of Turkic people
Oglu	Azerbaijani for 'son of'
Omphaloskepsis	The act of engaging in navel-gazing, in a self-absorbed state
Parliament	Meeting or assembly on public or national affairs
Patriot	Person who loves, supports, and defends his or her country and its interests with devotion
Pedagogy	Study of being a teacher
Perestroika	Russian for the programme of economic and political reform
Persia	Historical region of Iran, later official name of the state until 1935
Philology	Study of literary texts, establishment of their authenticity and their original form and the determination of meaning
Pluralistic	Theory that consists of two or more independent elements
Pragmatism	Character or conduct that emphasises practicality

Proletarian	Member of a lower social class, originally identified as those people who had no wealth other than their sons
Protocol	Customs and regulations dealing with diplomatic formality, precedence and etiquette
Qasida	Form of poetry from pre-Islamic Arabia
Ravine	Very small, narrow valley that usually has very steep sides
Reich	Reference to Germany, empire; realm; nation
Revcom	Committee of the Poor
Sadji	State in Azerbaijani territory during ancient history
Safavi	One of the most significant ruling dynasties of Southern Azerbaijan and Iran
Salaris	State in Azerbaijani territory during ancient history
Sanskrit	Historical language of Hinduism and Buddhism, classical Indian language
Satire	Strong irony or sarcasm
Sedition	Incitement of discontent or rebellion against a government
Seljuq	Vast empire stretching from the Hindu Kush to eastern Anatolia and from Central Asia to the Gulf
Shah	Persian name for a king/leader

Shamanistic	Term referencing a range of beliefs and practices regarding communication with the spiritual world
Shi'a	Second largest denomination of Islam after Sunni Islam
Sovietisation	Adoption of the Russian language or other Russian attributes
Stilyaga	Russian for a young person who adopted the unconventional manner of Western youth groups, as rockers or punk-rock fans
Stone Age	Period in the history preceding the Bronze Age
Sufi	Practitioner of an inner, mystical dimension of Islam
Tatars	Turkic ethnic group
Transcaucasia	Region comprising of Georgia, Armenia and Azerbaijan
Tsar	Title used to designate certain monarchs or supreme rulers
Turks	An ethnic group primarily living in Turkey and in the former lands of the Ottoman Empire
Ultra-nationalism	Belief that one's nation is of primary importance
Vikings	Scandinavian pirates who plundered the coasts of Europe from the eighth to tenth centuries
Zoroastrianism	Ancient religion, the principal beliefs of which are in the existence of a supreme deity

Illustration Credits

Page 79	
Top Left Photo	AzerTAC
Top Right Photo	Media Prima Studio
Bottom Photo	AzerTAC
Page 80	
Top Photo	Azerbaijan Tourism
Bottom Left Photo	Media Prima Studio
Bottom Right Photo	Shirvanshah Tourism
Page 81	
Top Photo	AzerTAC
Bottom Photo	AzerTAC
Page 82	
Top Photo	Heydar Aliyev Foundation
Bottom Photo	Heydar Aliyev Foundation
Page 210	Heydar Aliyev Foundation
Page 211	
Top Photo	AzerTAC
Bottom Left Photo	AzerTAC
Bottom Right Photo	AzerTAC
Page 212	
Top Photo	AzerTAC
Bottom Photo	AzerTAC

Page 213	
Top Photo	AzerTAC
Bottom Photo	Presidential Administration
Page 214	AzerTAC
Page 310	
Top Photo	Heydar Aliyev Foundation
Bottom Photo	AzerTAC
Page 311	
Top Photo	French Embassy, Baku
Bottom Photo	AzerTAC
Page 312	
Top Photo	Heydar Aliyev Foundation
Bottom Left Photo	AzerTAC
Bottom Right Photo	AzerTAC
Page 313	Getty Images
Page 431	
Top Photo	AzerTAC
Bottom Photo	Getty Images
Page 432	
Top Photo	AzerTAC
Bottom Left Photo	Wouter Kingma
Bottom Right Photo	AzerTAC

Page 433	
Top Photo	AzerTAC
Bottom Photo	Getty Images
Page 434	
Top Photo	Getty Images
Bottom Photo	Getty Images
Page 435	
Top Photo	AzerTAC
Bottom Photo	Media Prima Archives
Page 436	Getty Images
Page 437	
Top Left Photo	AzerTAC
Top Right Photo	Wouter Kingma
Bottom Photo	Getty Images

Bibliography

Newspapers and Periodicals

Armenia: AZG, Pan Armenian **Australia:** Sydney Morning Herald **Azerbaijan:** Azadliq, Baku Today, Caspian Business News, Yeni Musavat, 'Azerbaijan' Official Newspaper, Bakinskiy Rabochiy Official Newspaper, Zerkalo, Ekho **Egypt:** Al-Ahram Weekly, Cairo Times **France:** Le Figaro, Le Monde **Germany:** Der Spiegel **Georgia:** Georgia Today, Georgian Times **Great Britain:** The Economist, Financial Times, The Guardian, The Observer, The Daily Telegraph, The Times, The Sunday Times, International Herald Tribune **Iran:** Al-Vefagh Arabic Daily, Iran Daily News, Iran News **Iraq:** Al-Iraqi, Iraq Daily **Japan:** Tokyo Shimbun **Jordan:** Jordan Times **Kazakhstan:** Kazakhstanskaya Pravda **Russia:** Moscow Times, Komsomolskaya Pravda, Moscow News, Parlamentskaya Gazeta, Rossiyskaya Gazeta **Saudi Arabia:** Al Watan **Turkey:** Dunya Gazetesi, Hurriyet, Today's Zaman **United States:** USA Today, Wall Street Journal, New York Post, New York Times, Washington Post **Pan-regional:** Times of Central Asia

News Agencies

AzerTAC, Trend (Azerbaijan), APA (Azerbaijan), Agence France Press, Associated Press, China News Service, Deutsche Presse, Interfax News Agency, Reuters, Kazinform, Armenpress, Anadolu Agency, U.S. Newswire, ITAR-TASS, RIA Novosti, 1news.az

Web Resources

ceswww.fas.harvard.edu, armtown.com, cdr.gov.ae, ft.com, telegraph.co.uk, bbc.com, cnn.com, wikipedia.org, bakutoday.net, forbes.com, eurasianet.org, today.az, azer.com, karabakh.org, karabakh.az, sky.com, crisisgroup.org, foxnews.com, abcnews.go.com, cbsnews.com, usatoday.com, reuters.com, economist.com, washingtonpost.com, bloomberg.com, Azerbaijan.az, news.az, president.az

Compilations and Papers

Proceedings of the Azerbaijan National Academy of Sciences, Central Asia Caucasus Analyst (Johns Hopkins University), Media Insight Central Asia, Central Asia Compliance Monitor (Law and Environment Eurasia Partnership)

Books

Akiner, Shirin, **The Caspian: Politics, Energy, Security** (St. Martin's Press, 2007)

Al-Falah, Adil Abdullah, **Heydar Aliyev and National-Spiritual Values** (Baku, Gismet, 2007)

Altstadt, Audrey L., **The Azerbaijani Turks** (Hoover Institution Press, 1992)

Amineh, Mehdi Parvizi, **Towards the Control of Oil Resources in the Caspian Region** (Palgrave Macmillan, 2000)

Atabaki, Touraj, **Azerbaijan: Ethnicity and the Struggle for power in Iran** (I.B. Tauris, 2007)

Avakian, Arra S., **Armenia: Journey Through History** (The Electric Press, 2008) Avakov, R. and Atakishiev, A., **Public Education in Soviet Azerbaijan** (United Nations Educational, 1984)

Baser, Bahar, **Third Party Mediation in Nagorno Karabakh** (VDM Verlag, 2008)

Bayulgen, Oksan, **Foreign Investments and Political Regimes** (Cambridge University Press, 2004)

Boyajian, Artashes, **Failed Transition?** (VDM Verlag, 2009)

Buniyadov Z.M. **State of Azerbaijani Atabeks: 1136-1225** (Baku, 1984)

Buniyadov Z.M. **Armenian anonymous chronicle 1722-1736** (Azerbaijan S.S.R. Academy of Sciences, 1998)

Buniyadov Z.M. **Historical geography of Azerbaijan** (Baku, Elm,1987)

Buryakovsky, L., **Petroleum Geology of the South Caspian Basin** (Gulf Professional Publishing, 2001)

Cohen, Stephen F., **Soviet Fates and Lost Alternatives** (Columbia University Press, 2009)

Crandall, Maureen S., **Energy, Economics, and Politics in the Caspian Region** (Praeger Security International, 2006)

de Waal, Thomas, **Black Garden** (New York University Press, 2004)

Diba, Dr. Bahman Aghai, **The Law and Politics of the Caspian Sea** (BookSurge Publishing, 2006)

Dudwick, Nora, **Land Reform and Farm Restructuring in Transition Countries** (World Bank Publications, 2007)

Falola, Toyin, **The Politics of the Global Oil Industry** (Praeger, 2005)

Federal Research Division, **Azerbaijan** (Kessinger Publishing, 2004)

Freedom House, **Nations in Transit 2008: Democratisation from Central Europe to Eurasia** (Rowman & Littlefield Publishers, 2008)

Goltz, Thomas, **Azerbaijan Diary** (M.E. Sharpe, 1999)

Grachev, Andrei, **Gorbachev's Gamble** (Polity, 2008)

Human Rights Watch, **Azerbaijan: Seven Years of Conflict in Nagorno-Karabakh** (USA, 1994)

Ismayilov, Ibrahim, **Nagorno-Karabakh: Ethnic Conflict or Geopolitics?** (LAP Lambert Academic Publishing, 2010)

Kellner-Heinkele, Barbara, **Politics of Language in the Ex-Soviet Muslim States** (C. Hurst & Co., 2001)

Kenez, Peter, **A History of the Soviet Union from the Beginning to the End** (Cambridge University Press, 2006)

Khazanov, Anatoly M., **After the U.S.S.R.** (University of Wisconsin Press, 1996)

King, Charles, **The Ghost of Freedom** (Oxford University Press, 2008)

Kruger, Heiko, **The Nagorno-Karabakh Conflict: A Legal Analysis** (Springer, 2010)

Lerman, Zvi, **Rural Transition in Azerbaijan** (Lexington Books, 2010)

LeVine, Steve, **The Oil and the Glory** (Random House, 2007)

Mikheyev, Dmitry, **The Rise and Fall of Gorbachev** (Hudson Inst, 1992)

Miller, Frederic P., **Armenian Diaspora** (Alphascript Publishing, 2009)

Overland, Indra, **Caspian Energy Politics** (Routledge, 2009)

Pashayev, Hafiz M., **Racing Up Hill** (Global Scholarly Publications, 2006)

Ramiz Mehdiyev. **Defining the strategy of tomorrow: Course towards modernisation** (Sharq-Qarb, 2008)

Ramiz Mehdiyev. **Azerbaijan 2003-2008: thinking about time** (Sharq-Qarb, 2010)

Ramiz Mehdiyev. **Goris-2010: Season of theatre of the absurd** (Universal, 2010)

Suny, Ronald Grigor, **The Structure of Soviet History** (Oxford University Press, 2002)

Swietochowski, Tadeusz, **Russia and Azerbaijan: a Borderland In Transition** (Colombia University Press, 1995)

Swietochowski, Tadeusz, **Russian Azerbaijan, 1905-1920** (Cambridge University Press, 2004)

Teshebayeva, Dilyara, **Post-Soviet Energy Wealth** (VDM Verlag, 2008)

Thompson, Wayne C., **Russia, Eurasian States, & Eastern Europe** (Stryker-Post Publications, 1992)

Usa, Ibp, **Azerbaijan Diplomatic Handbook** (International Business Publications, 2008)

Wakeman-Linn, John, **Managing Oil Wealth** (International Monetary Fund, 2004)

Weems, Samuel A., **Armenia: Secrets of a "Christian" Terrorist State — The Armenian Great Deception Series Vol. 1** (St. John Press, 2002)

Zenkovich, Nikolai, **Heydar Aliyev: Life and Fate** (Moscow, 2007)

Zubok, Vladislav M., **A Failed Empire** (University of North Carolina Press, 2008) [illegible] Cords 2010 [illegible] of the [illegible] Universe [illegible]

[illegible]

[illegible] Lowell [illegible] Russia and [illegible] Trotsky [illegible] Foundation [illegible]

[illegible] The Russian Revolution 1904–1920s (Cambridge University Press [illegible])

[illegible] Soviet [illegible] Reality [illegible]

[illegible]

[illegible] Business Publications [illegible]

[illegible] Manifesting [illegible]

[illegible] A. [illegible] "Christian" [illegible] the American [illegible]

[illegible]

[illegible]

Index

B

C

F

H

I

J

K

L

M

N

S

U

V

W

Y

Z